An Introduction to the Philosophy of Religion

Modern Introductions to Philosophy
General Editor: D. J. O'CONNOR

PUBLISHED

R. J. ACKERMANN, *Modern Deductive Logic*

R. F. ATKINSON, *Knowledge and Explanation in History*

D. W. HAMLYN, *The Theory of Knowledge*

BERNARD HARRISON, *An Introduction to the Philosophy of Language*

W. D. HUDSON, *Modern Moral Philosophy*

KAI NIELSEN, *An Introduction to the Philosophy of Religion*

RUTH L. SAW, *Aesthetics*

J. TRUSTED, *The Logic of Scientific Inference: An Introduction*

OTHER TITLES IN PREPARATION

An Introduction to
the Philosophy of Religion

Kai Nielsen

M

First published 1982 by
THE MACMILLAN PRESS LTD
London and Basingstoke
Companies and representatives
throughout the world

ISBN 0 333 11436 1 (hc)
ISBN 0 333 11466 3 (pbk)

Printed in Hong Kong

Contents

Acknowledgements

I suspect for my thinking on this topic that I owe more to a series of undergraduate and graduate students in a number of philosophy of religion courses in several universities over the years than I owe to anyone else. Their probing has been invaluable, though at times unsettling to me. Of the individuals to whom I owe the most I should list Angel Alcala, William Bean, Rodger Beehler, William Blackstone, Lynn Herbert Boyer, Pat Brown, Adel Dahar, Joseph Epstein, Karl Frank, Joseph Gilbert, Jack Glickman, Harold Greenstein, Robert Hoffman, Grace Marian Jantzen, Tziporah Kasachkopff, George Kateb, William Kennick, Janet Keeping, Robert McKim, George Monticome, Robert Moses, James Moulder, Luis Navia, Murat Nemet-Nejat, Elisabeth Nielsen, Alfred Prettyman, Stanley Stein and R. X. Ware. They forced me to abandon more untenable positions than I care to remember. No doubt further such positions remain to be hounded out of me by the same or other philosophers. Part of that is no doubt rooted in my own incapacities, but, more importantly, my predicament is also the predicament of all philosophers. Reflection on it strengthens a fallibalistic conception of philosophical inquiry. What is to be hoped for is that in the long view the correction of our errors has a cumulative effect leading to an increasingly more adequate conception of what we are doing. The sceptical worry here is that we may just be going around in a parade of fashions. Is such a worry tough-mindedness or a failure of nerve?

Finally, Joan Frank, Rhoda Blythe and Beverly Forbes deserve thanks for their expert typing of various versions of this manuscript.

K. N.

To the memory of my parents, who, in ways they perhaps would not recognise, gave rise to the scepticism expressed here.

Introduction

There was a time when the philosophical debate between believers and religious sceptics turned principally on the question whether the existence of God could in some way or another be rationally demonstrated. Believers thought that it could and religious sceptics thought that it could not. A minor religious tradition, a tradition often referred to as fideistic, thought that this whole way of posing the question of belief and scepticism rested on a mistake. In the nineteenth century this minority tradition became a powerful strand of philosophically sophisticated religious belief with a diverse and extensive representation. We live in the shadow of this tradition; our general intellectual climate *vis-à-vis* religion is this: while some of the details of Hume's and Kant's treatment of the proofs for the existence of God are defective, it is clear enough in the light of their work that it is not reasonable to expect that we are going to get a proof or demonstration, in any plausible sense of these terms, of the existence of God. It is, no doubt, a mere logical possibility that there could be empirical evidence for the existence of a Zeus-like God – a sort of cosmic Mickey mouse – but such a God would hardly be an appropriate object of religious belief. Moreover, even if it were, to believe in the existence of such a Zeus-like God is to have a groundless belief in a God whose existence could be, but as a matter of fact isn't, well-grounded. It is important to note that reflective believers are as dismissive of such superstitious religious belief as are sceptics. Rather the God to be believed in by such believers is construed as an infinite individual transcendent to the world. This – or so it is widely believed – is the God to be believed in if Judaeo-Christian-Islamic religious belief is to be a serious option for a contemporary person living in a scientific culture. When it is said that it is no longer reasonable to believe that God's existence can be demonstrated, it is this conception of God that is being referred to. We need not claim that we have an *a priori* proof that such a demonstration is impossible. We can content ourselves with the recognition that (1) the often careful, sustained and repeated attempts at proofs in the past have failed and (2) that with arguments essentially derived from Hume and Kant (though beefed up and amended in certain respects) we have very good reasons indeed for believing that no proof of the existence of such a God will succeed in the future. Moreover, if God's existence cannot be rationally established it cannot be established at all. This is not to make a God of Reason but simply to be clear about what it is to establish something.

However, the Fideist tradition itself tells us that it is pointless, unnecessary and perhaps even religiously inappropriate to seek proofs. We should instead accept God humbly on faith. God is *Deus Absconditus*. A non-mysterious, fully intelligible God could not even be the God of Judaeo-Christianity. But in seeing clearly that God is *Deus Absconditus*, it has struck many, sceptics and fideistic believers alike, that religious belief is radically paradoxical and that the concept of God is problematic. What is at stake in much contemporary debate between belief and unbelief is whether the concept of God is so problematic that we must, if we would be non-evasive, conclude that God is so utterly incomprehensible as to make belief in God incoherent and irrational for a person who recognises what is at issue, or whether alternatively this deeply paradoxical belief makes just enough sense to make it the case that a leap of faith is not irrational. What is centrally at issue is whether or not it is the case that a belief in a transcendent God is a coherent though still thoroughly baffling belief. We can hardly have faith in God if we do not in at least some reasonable way have some understanding of *what* we are to have faith in. Faith requires at least *some* understanding.[1] The key question in present perplexities over Christian, Jewish and Islamic belief is whether non-anthropomorphic God-talk has sufficient sense to make faith a coherent option.

It is this logically prior consideration that I wrestle with in this book. Because I wish to probe this in some reasonable depth, I do not, once again, rehash the tired cluster of questions turning around the proofs for the existence of God or the problem of evil. It is about as clear as can be that such proofs will not work and it is almost as clear that no *a priori* disproof of God's existence turning on the problem of evil will work either. If God is the ultimate mystery Christians say He is, then it is possible to take His ways to us to be beyond our understanding. It isn't that the faithful need blinker themselves about the vast amount of suffering in the world. They can and should say they do not understand it. God's ways are beyond our understanding.

That there is no proving or disproving God's existence is fairly extensively realised in our contemporary intellectual culture, but cultural change is not uniform and there remains, as strange cultural artifacts, a couple of brave Quixotic souls, fantastically struggling against the stream, who try to use modal logic to give an *a priori* demonstration of the existence of God. These modal-logic-with-God philosophers are philosophical equivalents of a back-to-Newton movement in physics. It is very difficult indeed to work up much enthusiasm, unless one is simply enamoured of puzzles, for those rehashed versions of the ontological argument. But these baroque arguments have been met and I do not return once again to that barren discussion but turn to the logically prior and religiously more significant question of whether God-talk makes sufficient sense to make religious belief a viable option for a philosophically literate person living with some self-awareness in a scientific culture. I should add that I have on previous occasions examined the traditional arguments for the existence of God. If I were to return to that project some new moves would need to be gimmicked up to meet the newest arguments of an ontological type but still I would not say anything now essentially different from what I have argued on those occasions.[2]

While I write from inside the analytical tradition, I try to write here not only for other philosophers but in such a way that I come to grips with the reflective concerns of human beings, and not just with the concerns of a small and rather esoteric group of academics.[3] Religion and its significance for human life has been one of these questions and it is with a cluster of questions centring around those concerns that I wish to wrestle. I do indeed argue with a number of contemporary philosophers and sometimes the argument takes a linguistic turn. But my concern with these matters of conceptual analysis is instrumental. I care about getting clear about the concept of God and about the logical status of God-talk only to the extent that attaining that clarity will help to provide us with a handle on the question whether we should believe in God. It is this question that is at the centre of my attention.

If I were to start once again to write this book from scratch, I would in places adopt a less verificationist idiom, but, in spite of what would be a somewhat changed idiom, I think very little of substance would change. Empiricism has had a bad press in the last few years. My suspicion is that the case against it has been overstated and that it has been split off from realism in an unnecessary and undesirable way. But, even if I am mistaken in that belief, the move to a Wittgensteinian or hermeneutical approach or to a Kuhnian, Feyerabendish or Rortyian historicism will not 'save religious beliefs'. Christians claim that 'Christ is the Truth and the Way' and Jews and Moslems make claims which aim at having a similar authoritative weight. If such claims get the constructions that such philosophical accounts would have to put on them, they will no longer have the authority that believers believe they must have to make religious belief a live option. What the faithful demand of religious belief could not be met by such reconstructions or demythologisations.

Kai Nielsen
11 November 1981
Hastings-on-Hudson
NY

1

Perplexities about Religion

I

It has been said that clarity is not enough: we need truth as well. That is, we want something of importance, something of value that we can clearly and unequivocally endorse – endorse because we have not found it wanting after the toughest, most non-evasive scrutiny. This is obscure talk and the wary philosopher has a right to be suspicious. Philosophers, including philosophers of religion, it is often remarked, should be concerned with meaning. What do the words used in religious discourse *mean* and what function or functions do religious utterances have? Now, surely we should be concerned with meaning, for clarity is at least a necessary condition for any fruitful philosophical work. Without that we will be like blind men searching for a black cat in a pitch-black room. But we are – or at least should be – looking for truth as well. We are not only concerned with the meaning of religious utterances, but we also are concerned to discover something *vis-à-vis* religion that we can justifiably endorse. In fact, interest in the meaning of religious utterances is largely subservient to our interest in the truth or falsity of religion or religious beliefs.

What we are asking for is indeed perplexing, for in reflecting about the truth or credibility of religion or the truth of religious claims, we are not *simply* involved in an intellectual matter.[1] There is a purely linguistic fact that makes this evident. Utterances are not religious simply because words like 'God' are used in them. Thales is supposed to have told us 'All things are full of *theoi'* and Aristotle makes many statements containing the words '*Theos*' and '*Theoi*'. These *need* not be taken to be religious utterances. Similarly, I do not make a religious utterance when I report that there are twenty-three, or thirty-one, or thirteen Prime Movers, a necessary being, or a being who created all other beings but who was not and could not be created himself. Yet my statements are not meta-statements. I'm not talking about the talk about God. I am talking of God or the gods, but in so speaking I need not have made a religious utterance. To be unequivocally a religious utterance, (1) my utterance must in normal contexts be expressive of and have a tendency to be evocative of a very pervasive and focal attitude toward life, and (2) the objects of these attitudes must be objects of devotion and commitment.

The above features are certainly not sufficient to characterise religion or religious belief, and they are not even, strictly speaking, necessary conditions for an utterance to be religious. But utterances would not unequivocally be classified as religious utterances if they neither functioned in this way themselves nor were a part of a system of utterances which are so expressive and evocative. Most certainly they would not serve as paradigms of what it was for something to be a religious utterance.

This is why we find even Hume telling us that to *know* God is to love Him, and this is why Kierkegaard tells us that to be religious is to be engrossed in a passion. In short, this feature of religious discourse is symptomatic of the fact that religious belief is not simply a matter of intellectual persuasion or theoretical conviction, but is also a matter of moral conviction, commitment and concern. Religion is intimately connected with giving sense to the lives of those who are involved with it. The sincere utterance of certain key religious expressions constitutes a subscription to a certain life-orientation. If we do not understand this, we shall not even begin to understand religion or religious talk.

Given these facts about religious discourse, what then are we asking for when we ask for 'the truth about religion'? What does the Jew or Christian search for when he searches for God? On the one hand, we clearly seem to be asking about what is the case and, on the other, about what attitude to take toward what is the case and what we should try to make the case. We are asking, or trying to ask, some naggingly perplexing, disturbingly amorphous question about 'what there is' and at the very same time we are asking ourselves bottom-line questions about 'how to live' — about what finally and ultimately is worth seeking.

Such considerations make evident what should be obvious anyway, namely that religion and religious belief are not purely intellectual or speculative matters, and that interest in 'the truth of religion' is not a purely speculative concern. This accounts for the fact that discussions about religion tend to be anxiety-arousing. Our emotional energies are taken up in the discussion of religion; we are drawn into making passionate or heated affirmations and denials, or, like William James, we are tortured with doubt and irresolution. People feel, as the existentialists never tire of telling us, the 'absence of God' and feel transformed in His presence.

The obscurity and seeming unintelligibility of religious concepts disturb us, but the element of commitment, the involvement pro and con of emotional energies, is, though in a less direct manner, another source of obscurity. The obvious retort to make here is that it shouldn't be. We need not be slim to give slenderising advice; religion may engage the emotions, but philosophical talk about emotional matters need not be emotional. When we philosophise about religion, we should put feelings aside, bracket — if you will — our most precious commitments. But this sound, if superficial, methodological injunction does not get to the heart of the matter. What does is this: since religious utterances are not only about what is the case but also about how we should conduct our lives and what fundamental *focal attitudes* we should take toward what is the case, religious utterances perforce are not pellucid. In thinking about religion we should not forget the fact that a person who is wrestling with religion becomes involved with the whole 'riddle of human destiny'. When taken seriously, religion, as we have remarked, is the sort of activity that engages one's fundamental attitudes and commitments. This is why thinking about religion is so compelling and so baffling; and this is why our emotional energies are so aroused by questions of religion.

It is this *logical* feature about religion and religious talk that makes the search for 'the truth about religion' both perplexing and disturbing. Involved in it are such wild yet such compelling 'mind-breakers' as 'What is our destiny?' and 'What is the meaning of life?' We hardly know what we are asking when we ask such questions. Yet there are times when we feel compelled to ask them, for in seriously thinking about religion we – whether we like it or not – become entangled in such obscurities.

There are philosophers – philosophers whom I very much respect – who would say that such questions are not really proper questions or at least they are not proper philosophical questions. They should be left to literary folk, vacationing psychoanalysts and existentialists. Yet it is not by any means evident that such questions are illegitimate or improper. They are not improper on purely linguistic grounds as are 'Is the mind heavier than the body?', or 'Is heat more colourful than tone?' The above questions concerning religion are vague questions, but no 'category-mistake' or logical howler seems to be involved in asking them, and surely no one who has wrestled with them would deny that they are obscure questions; but vagueness and obscurity are one thing – conceptual impropriety or, worse still, meaninglessness or incoherence is something else again.

I suspect the main reason for saying they are illegitimate is that people who ask such 'questions' seem to have no clear idea what they would take as an answer. And if a 'putative question' can be shown to be *completely unanswerable in any way*, it is plainly no question. But when in a non-philosophical context we say a question is unanswerable we mean something very different and perfectly proper. What we mean in ordinary parlance by an 'unanswerable question' is a question which is exceedingly difficult to answer, a question which has resisted all solution, and a question with which we can make no headway; but if we *know* that what is posed as a question cannot *possibly* be answered in any way, we cease to regard it as a question. (We may take it as some sort of 'limiting question': that is, as a non-literal, figurative question, but it still ceases to be a question in any literal sense.)

Yet our question about the meaning of life is not one which has been shown to be without an answer. What is evident is that the question is not a clear one, with a well-regulated procedure for grinding out an answer. But whoever thought that it was? When someone asks 'What is the meaning of life?', we need some fuller explanation of what is intended before we can make any headway with the question. But that often can be given. People very typically are asking the rather nebulous question, 'What, if anything, can be acknowledged to be ultimately worthwhile – to be finally worthy of pursuit and attainment?' Now it may be that there is not and cannot be any answer here; it may be that this question is merely a 'limiting question' implicitly calling for some *decision* of principle, some *subscription* to a way of life or a social policy, or some resolution of attitude on the part of the person(s) to whom it is addressed. But there is also some reason to believe that it may be a genuine question and not simply a limiting question expressive and/or evocative of human attitudes. There may be criteria for what it is for something to be worthwhile that make a reasonable answer possible. I am inclined to think there are, but rather than argue the point here, I shall content myself for the present with the counterclaim that such a question has not been shown to be a senseless question, a pseudo-question, involving a 'category-mistake', or simply a 'limiting question' masking a clash in attitude not grounded in any cognitive differences in belief.[2]

In reflecting seriously about religion, we are left with a recognition that religious questions – though perhaps not questions about religious questions – *necessarily* involve us in asking questions about what is worth seeking, or about what rock-bottom commitments or ultimate allegiances, if any, we should hold. In wrestling with religious questions, an individual cannot escape the gnawing question: 'What sort of person should I try to become?'

To stop here is to leave us with what may (for some at least) be an appealing picture of religion – or at least a picture that will appeal to people in our time who have lived through 'the death of God'. Religion – it is tempting to say – is in *essence* about how to live or about 'ultimate concern.'[3] But, after some reflection, a counter-tendency is likely to assert itself. Even Tillichians back away here. To have a genuine religion (not any old commitment or ultimate concern will do), we need, they tell us, an adequate *object* of ultimate concern: we need the 'God above God' – the transcendent *Ground* of Being and meaning. Integral to religion and indeed to religious commitment itself are not only or just fundamental commitment and ultimate concern but doctrines – claims about 'ultimate reality' as well. William Alston is surely correct when he remarks that

> . . . it is the fundamental beliefs of religion, such as the
> existence of God, the demands God makes on men, and the
> immortality of man and the concepts that figure prominently
> therein: God, omnipotence, creation, miracle, revelation,
> immortality, and sin – that they [philosophers] have sought
> to formulate and clarify; and it is on the validity, justifiability,
> or truth of such beliefs . . . that they have focussed their
> critical powers.[4]

That is to say, in asking about 'the truth of religion' we are not
only asking about what ultimate commitments we should make,
but also about the reality of God, nirvana, Tao, immortality
and so on. We want to know whether God exists (whether there
is a God) and whether God governs and arranges man's ultimate destiny.

Here our previous question about *meaning* comes sneaking
back in a ubiquitous manner. It has become increasingly evident that for theologians, philosophers and plain men alike the
most fundamental perplexity about religion is about the very
meaning of these concepts or these terms. In one plain and
uncontroversial sense, they are intelligible, do have meaning;
namely, they have some kind of fairly fixed use in our language.
To say 'God took Metrecal' is deviant; to say 'God created the
heavens and the earth' is not; 'God is good' and 'Jane prayed to
God' are in place, while 'Jane God good' or 'Jane prayed God
good' is gibberish. We may find it difficult to say what the uses
or meanings of religious terms are, but that they have uses –
play different roles in what Wittgenstein called language-games
– is beyond serious dispute.

Yet more and more people – people quite capable of playing
the 'religious language-game' – are coming to feel that these
terms are *somehow* meaningless or incoherent, although only a
few people can specify why it is they believe they are meaningless or incoherent. The whole thing seems to many people to be
unintelligible – a kind of charade people play with words.

There are atheists who say that it is not true that God exists
or that it is highly improbable that there is such a being, but
there are also atheists and sceptics who find the concept of God

and allied concepts so nebulous that they do not understand what it would be like for 'There is a God' to be either true or false. 'God', 'Atman-Brahman', 'nirvana', 'Tao', 'the trans-cendent', 'soul', 'heaven' and the like are surely thought by believers to have referents, but the anthropomorphic referents are religiously (theologically) unacceptable and with the relig-iously acceptable employment of these words the sceptic can make all too little of talk of apprehending God or Atman-Brahman. Where we are beyond anthropomorphism, he is at sea concerning the criteria which must be satisfied in order for there to be a God or Tao and the like.[5] Such talk seems un-intelligible or at least deeply perplexing to him.

We surely want to see if we can in some reasonable sense prove God's existence or give some evidence for His existence. We certainly want to examine the question of whether we could provide a new grammar of assent; but before we can even profitably begin this task, we must come to have some reason-able understanding of the meaning of these words. As they stand, they seem to many not to be symbols of great, resounding mysteries, but to be scandalously obscure terms that serve to cover up the fact that nobody really understands what he is talking about when he speaks of God, nirvana, immortality and the like. And to level my talk at Jews and Christians for a moment, the suspicion grows that neither the believer nor anyone else knows what he is doing when he talks *to* God, that is, prays to God, addresses God, entreats God and the like. It isn't just his talk *about* God that is puzzling, but his direct religious discourse remains perplexing as well. Job wanted to talk to God. Well, what do we do when we talk to God? Who or what are we talking to? How do we specify the referent of 'God'? Does 'God' indeed even have a referent? But if not, what *kind* of reality are we talking about? Are we indeed talking about or to any kind of reality at all? Many people feel that they can make nothing at all of either this 'talking to' or this 'talking about'. It isn't just theology that is in conceptual trouble but a central range of *first-order religious talk and belief* as well.

It is indeed true that the proofs of God's existence can easily be put in valid logical form; but in asking whether these argu-ments are *sound* arguments (valid arguments with true premises), the question of the truth of the premises almost always turns on questions of the intelligibility of these premises. 'If there are contingent beings then there is a necessary being. There are contingent beings, therefore, there is a necessary being' is in valid logical form.[6] But the rub comes about the first premise. What is a 'necessary being'? Necessity and contingency apply only to propositions – we are told; a *logically* necessary being is a contradiction in terms and any kind of physical necessity would allow for the possibility of a purely material 'necessary being'. If we say that the kind of 'necessity' that is relevant is a 'metaphysical necessity' or 'ontological necessity', the question immediately arises concerning what is meant by such talk. Indeed the suspicion is abroad that such conceptions have no coherent meaning. Questions of *meaning* immediately arise when we examine the alleged proofs *of* or attempts to give evidence *for* the existence of God.

In honestly reflecting on religion, we ineluctably bump up against questions of *meaning*. These religious concepts, concepts that may existentially engage us, appear at least to be in some not very clear sense meaningless or incoherent. If we are to make any sense at all of religion – of Judaism, Christianity, Buddhism or Islam – we must give some plausible grounds for believing that such concepts are intelligible. Whether we like it or not, we must, if we are to think seriously about religion, engage in that attempt at conceptual clarification that is philosophical theology.

II

The above way of looking at things gives rise to a new budget of problems. In the past it has been the case, though this is less true today, that philosophy of religion easily got identified with apologetics or at least with apologetics of a (supposedly) rational sort. Religious folk gave us a philosophical defence of religious convictions and anti-religious folk gave us another kind of apologetics, namely a critique of religion and theology. They tried to show that religious beliefs were false, pointless, absurd or without rational foundation.

This activity should be clearly distinguished from the description and elucidation of religious discourse and religious doctrinal schemes. Such a philosophical analysis of religious discourse is a *second-order* activity. It is no more religious than the philosophy of science – the description and elucidation of scientific concepts – is a branch of science. It is rather talk about the uses or meanings of key religious or scientific terms and propositions. Such an activity has, or at least aspires to have, a higher-order neutrality. It is neither reverent nor irreverent; it neither directly criticises religion nor defends it; it simply describes what it takes to be the logic of religious discourses in those areas where there is conceptual perplexity about religion. In that way it is, if done properly, religiously neutral.

It remains true that philosophers, including analytic philosophers, have tried to do more. Philosophers of science out of the analytic tradition have usually been content simply to describe and perhaps to elucidate the concepts or language of science, but philosophers of religion, including analytical philosophers of religion, have gone on to appraise and evaluate religious concepts, and have made pronouncements concerning the truth or intelligibility of whole doctrinal schemes. William Alston and Anthony Flew, for example, believe that this is perfectly proper, but proper or not, it is certainly an activity that needs to be distinguished from a purely *second-order* philosophical analysis of religion: the description and elucidation of religious concepts and properties. We should also notice that this evaluative activity takes us back to what has been called apologetics.

These by now entrenched philosophical stances deserve comment. Until very recently there was little doubt on the part of many philosophers and theologians that in addition to clarifying and elucidating the concepts of religion they should also evaluate and be prepared to defend or to criticise the claims of religion. I am convinced that this rather old-fashioned belief is correct. A central rationale – though surely not the only one – for describing and elucidating doctrinal schemes is that this puts us in a position more effectively and reasonably to assess their intelligibility or validity and this indirectly aids us in making rational judgments concerning the truth of religious doctrines and claims. As reflective persons we want, if possible, to know the truth about religion, and the philosophical analysis of religious concepts is a key *instrument* in such a discovery.

This is my own point of departure; it fires my own interest in the philosophical analysis of religious discourse. Yet a careful student of Wittgenstein could plausibly argue that such a conviction – such a point of departure – rests on a confusion. What is given, what has to be accepted, he will argue, are the forms of life; and the forms of language are the forms of life.[7] Ordinary language – including *first-order* religious talk – is in place as it is. Philosophical or theological accounts of it are typically in one way or another confused, but the *first-order* discourse itself is perfectly in order as it is; it is, and must be, our final court of appeal for intelligibility when considering religion. The philosopher can only describe language; he can in no way transcend it or criticise it as some 'distorting mirror of the divine'. Philosophical questions, including philosophical questions about religion, arise from linguistic confusions – from a failure to appreciate the style of functioning of our own language; we *know how* to use this language, but we do not know how to explain how to use this language. We do not command a clear view of it. Philosophy can give us a clear view of our language. It can break those perplexities about our language which give us that incoherent but protean urge to transcend language, but it ought not and cannot replace ordinary language, for our *first-order* talk is all right as it is when it is functioning in its natural habitat. A philosophical interest in language isn't, or at least shouldn't be, scientific or systematic. Whether we realise it or not, when we are in philosophical perplexity we are falling into confusions about the workings of our language. We can operate *with it* but not *upon it*; in certain contexts our intelligence, in Wittgenstein's striking phrase, becomes bewitched by our language; we are, in reflecting on it, thoroughly misled as to the actual workings of our language. We try to dispel this bewitchment when we philosophise. We try, where we are muddled, to command a clear view of our language; we have difficulties in *saying* what we mean or in generalising about our language but our natural languages and their parasitical, technical, *first-order* extensions are in order as they are. We can and must criticise the *second-order* talk of the philosophers and the theologians – their talk about talk – but the *first-order* talk is all right as it is; it is our *given* and is beyond criticism.[8]

I think that this advice about *first-order* talk is sometimes – on certain circumscribed readings and for certain domains – well taken, but I think that it is wrong about religious talk. Certainly the philosopher has gone wrong who gives us a clever argument to prove that time is unreal, that we never know when others are in pain or how they feel, that only sense-data are real and tables and chairs are abstractions or worse still fictitious. We may not be clever enough to pick his argument apart, but, as Moore pointed out, it is more rational to rely on our common-sense beliefs here than on the philosophical arguments purporting to establish these claims. If a philosophical analysis tells us or purports to tell us that we never see tables or chairs, but only our own brains or only sense-data, this constitutes a *reductio* of that particular account. We must – if we want to be rational – recast our philosophical analysis and find out where we went wrong. In a somewhat different way, a philosopher of physics, who went around saying that established scientific theories and laws were mistaken, false or unintelligible, would simply ex-hibit his ridiculousness. He surely can criticise some of the scientist's metaphysical excursions or the scientific mythology with which they sometimes bedeck their theories, but, where the scientist's work is a legitimate part of a well-established science, the philosopher can only describe and elucidate the working concepts of actual scientific discourse or, somewhat as Feyerabend did in his early work, show how they compare to other modes of conceptualisation.

Wittgensteinians would surely stress that we can criticise the theologian's talk about the uses of religious talk or criticise the metaphysical arguments used by Occam, Aquinas, Schleier-macher or Tillich. Such natural theology is most likely – they would claim – a house of cards, but what we cannot legitimately do (as philosophers) is criticise the *first-order* religious discourse itself. That is our *given*. We must start and finally return to such a form of life. There is no rational method of criticising a way of life as a whole. Here we have the prologomena to a philo-sophical rationale for a new Fideism – a Fideism that I shall dub Wittgensteinian Fideism.

I, by contrast, want to say that it is not only the philosopher's and theologian's accounts of religious discourse that are inco-herent and in important ways unintelligible, but also the very *first-order* discourse itself. And here we have the prologomena for a new philosophical rationale for a new atheism or a new agnosticism. Such talk about talk has normative implications.

Such a critique should indeed follow a conceptual analysis of the concepts of religion. I heartily agree with Wittgensteinian Fideists that the first philosophical task is to characterise the discourse in question. Until we have given a perspicuous representation of the discourse, until we have displayed how its characteristic and troubling propositions work in their living contexts, we are in no position intelligibly to appraise or criticise religious concepts or religion. If we can understand 'God shall raise the quick and the dead' or, as it says in the *Mundaka Upanisad*, 'Brahman shines forth, farther than the far, yet close at hand', we will understand them in their natural setting where they are doing their characteristic work. Religions and religious talk are co-ordinated with the very social structures in which they find their home. Torn from this context such talk is indeed unintelligible. Religious talk like talk of electrons or photons can only make sense (if it makes sense at all) in a certain determinate context and to people familiar with a certain tradition.

So far, I would make common cause with Wittgensteinian Fideists. Yet in passing we need to notice this: even within such a context we do not have the 'agreement in judgments' about religion which we have concerning the objects of our common-sense experience or in our culture's science. Educated people do not think the whole of science is spurious or gibberish. But many people, some from the earliest recorded time but in ever increasing numbers now, have thought just that about religion. Some have not been very articulate about it, and *perhaps* everyone who has said or thought that has been in some way confused. Some, who have thought that, may have simply been rejecting a certain philosophical chatter about religion, for example, 'God is a necessary being', 'God can be known by a special religious way of knowing', 'God is ineffable', and the like. They rejected this talk – material mode talk about religious talk – and mistakenly thought that in doing so they were rejecting religion. But some have also rejected and/or found unintelligible such *first-order* statements as 'God created the heavens and the earth', 'There is a God', 'God is in Christ' and the like. Given this very lack of agreement among people of a similar religious background and of the same cultural and linguistic family, it does not seem to me that we can make this Wittgensteinian appeal without some additional justification. But the arguments here need careful sifting. I shall attempt to do that when I discuss Wittgensteinian Fideism.

III

There are for this preliminary chapter two final bits of pro-legomena that I want to consider very briefly.

First, if the issue I have raised above is at all a live issue, we cannot so confidently speak of 'being sure of God, yet tentative about theology' as does the Oxford theologian, I. T. Ramsey.[9] We should not say, as he does in *On Being Sure in Religion*:

> Let us frankly acknowledge theological uncertainties. Let us not conceal them from our congregations or our audiences; let us not perpetuate schemes that demand or imply greater certainty than we possess. Still more, let us not build, on mistaken foundations, vast systems which suffocate religion. Let us acknowledge where at various points we are doctrin-ally 'unsure' . . . recognizing that it is *not* inconsistent to claim at the same time that we are sure of God – God given to us in a disclosure to which all our discursive theology will ever in-adequately try to talk about, of which all our pictures are at best temporal projections.[10]

Ramsey is indeed right in stressing that the crucial subject of a Christian theology is God, and while we speak of God in words, use the label 'God' for God, still words cannot embody God. But words cannot embody red either, though 'red' names red and is used to describe certain things that are red. What we say *about* the concept red or about the use of the word 'red' may be confused, but there are generally accepted paradigms for, if you will, the 'disclosure of red'. That is to say, colour-blind people apart, we *all* feel sure in certain typical circumstances about red, but God, as Ramsey stresses over and over again, is the Mystery.[11] Many perfectly normal people, well drilled in relig-ious talk, perfectly capable of playing the 'religious language-game', can make nothing of God. They are bitterly baffled by religion. It is not just the discursive talk of theology that perplexes them, but they have no idea of what would count as a disclosure of God, or as an apprehension of God, or as an encounter with the Divine. They may have *feelings* of contingency, awe, dependence, concern; they may commit themselves to certain things, or trust certain things or people, but they have never had a disclosure of God. They do not even know what to expect. They have no idea what would constitute such a disclosure. In such a situation we can hardly be justified in saying, as Ramsey does, that we can be *sure* of God. What we should say is that we should be tentative – 'contextually tentative' if you like – in our theology, but tentative as well in our *first-order* claims to have knowledge of and an acquaintance with God. We cannot reasonably get away with a facile certainty in religion coupled with a humble tentativeness in theology. There is no certain disclosure which enables us with certainty to get to the reality which our 'best temporal projections' or 'best theological maps' inadequately try to talk about.

My remarks about I. T. Ramsey's methodological claim lead to my second point. A natural response to what I have just said is this: 'If you ever had had the overpowering experience of a Divine disclosure you would have known it.' Certain theologians would go on to add: 'And unless you are committed to Christ, unless you are a person of faith, you will not have such experiences or be able to understand them. Religion is not the sort of thing you can understand if you are neutral about it.'

Both of these separable but frequently fused claims deserve careful consideration. But in closing this first chapter I will only make some brief, inconclusive, and perhaps seemingly dogmatic remarks. If we try to attain the certainty of a religious disclosure at this price, we too closely assimilate God to a psychological reality. We *may* indeed be certain that we are in pain or that something we are tasting has a lemon taste, and until we have been in pain or tasted lemons, we may not be able properly to understand talk of pain or of the taste of lemons. Such a remark is plausible enough for psychological realities, but it is not plausible to make parallel claims about non-psychological realities. I know perfectly well what a Grayling is or what a Pygmy is, though I have never seen a Grayling or a Pygmy. And while God is certainly not a Pygmy or, for that matter a Giant, the faithful will not take him to be simply a psychological reality either. There is no reason to believe God's reality must be or can be disclosed the way a psychological reality can be disclosed.

Finally, it is very questionable whether only people who are within the circle of faith can understand religion. Feuerbach and Freud claimed just the opposite: only the man free from the claims of faith could really understand religion. Both views embody at best half-truths. Ninian Smart's remarks on the Fideist's claim seems to me to be apt here:

> It is true that we must have some fairly extensive experience of religion and religious activities in order to have a rough comprehension of the point of religious utterances. . . . But it follows neither that one should believe in some creed at the time of philosophizing in order to give a reasonably accurate account of what the creed amounts to nor that such a belief would necessarily help the philosopher. For often the strength of conviction will make philosophy appear trivial, or more dangerously it will tempt one into substituting apologetics for analysis.[12].

To say that either the believer or the non-believer alone really understands, often hides a quite arbitrary *persuasive* definition of 'really understands'. What, after all, is it to 'really understand' the concept of God or the concept of Atman-Brahman? Given an immersion in a culture in which these concepts are alive, given thorough drill in *first-order* religious talk, the believer and the non-believer alike are both on an equal footing in understanding the logic of religious discourse. We need neither an act of faith nor a Promethean denial to understand this discourse in the way they both clearly understand it. We need only to have been taught this God-talk in an appropriate religious context. That is to say, we need to have undergone a certain socialisation. That there is or can be any other kind of understanding of religion is just one of those problematical points that should be argued, rather than begged through a persuasive definition.

In sum, what I think we need to keep steadfastly before our minds is that religion, crucial as it is to us, is a very mystifying phenomenon. We have no way of being certain here, either theologically or religiously. Theological talk about religion is shot through with obscurities and many of the key terms of theological elucidation are of doubtful intelligibility, but so too is direct religious talk itself. Its very coherence and intelligibility is so seriously in doubt that what a scientific study of it would be or should be is far from clear. And neither apologetic defence nor natural theology can reasonably proceed until the question of the intelligibility of the key conceptions of religious discourse is squarely faced and at least to some tolerable degree resolved. [13]

2

The Intelligibility of God-Talk

I

There are certain primary religious beliefs which are basic to a whole religious *Weltanschauung*, for they are the cornerstone of the whole edifice.[1] If these beliefs are unintelligible, incoherent, irrational or false the whole-way-of-life, centring around them, is 'a house of cards'. Certain segments of it may still be seen to have a value when viewed from some other perspective, but if these primary religious beliefs are faulted, the religious *Weltanschauung* itself has been undermined. If it has been undermined and if people recognise that it has been undermined and still go around believing in it, accepting and acting in accordance with its tenets, they are then being very irrational. And while in humility we should recognise that we all suffer from propensities to irrationality and perhaps in some spheres of our life cannot help being irrational, it is a propensity we should resist, for to be irrational is to do something we ought not to do.

I greatly admire Wittgenstein and Austin, but I remain unconvinced that we can have no theses in philosophy. I shall here introduce a whopping thesis of my own, namely that, for people with a reasonable understanding of science and with a tolerably good understanding of philosophical analysis, acceptance of the Christian *Weltanschauung* is irrational because the primary religious beliefs it enshrines are, depending on how they are taken, either absurdly false or, in an important sense, incoherent. Some primary beliefs of Christianity – at least until Tillich and his understudy Bishop Robinson hove into sight –

have been that God exists, that there is for man the possibility of
a blessed after-life, that God created and sustains the world,
that God loves and protects His children and that in Him can be
found the ultimate ground of right and wrong. These are some
of the primary beliefs or articles of the Judaeo-Christian tradition, and it seems to me that they are all either false or in an
important sense incoherent. But perhaps I am deluded, puffed
up, as Bultmann would have it, by sin and pride.[2]

  Let us look into the grounds for claiming that these primary
Judaeo-Christian beliefs are either false or in an important way
incoherent. Consider the cornerstone of them all, 'God exists' or
'There is a God'. Rudolf Carnap long ago pointed out that on
the one hand 'God' is sometimes used mythologically or anthropomorphically and on the other 'God' is sometimes used
metaphysically or theologically.[3] Carnap is making an important point here, though I do not like the last two labels, for many
modern sophisticated Christians, who reject an anthropomorphic God, also reject metaphysics and natural theology.
But terminology apart, Carnap's basic point is sound enough.
Within Christianity and Judaism there is an anthropomorphic
and a non-anthropomorphic concept of God. 'God', on its
anthropomorphic or mythological use, denotes some kind of
incredibly powerful physical being. Such a use of 'God' is
indeed meaningful. Taking an essentially Carnapian line here,
Paul Edwards confidently asserts that when most people think
of Him in this anthropomorphic way they vaguely think of him
'as possessing some kind of rather large body'.[4] It is extremely
doubtful whether many Christians or Jews – even the rustic
materialists Flaubert describes – are quite that crude. But
whether any or many people so conceive God is a sociological
point; the important conceptual point is that anyone who did
believe in such an anthropomorphic Deity would be holding
an intelligible belief which is manifestly absurd and false. Here
Tillich and Robinson, with their strictures against such a Super-
naturalism, make a sound critique. But a non-anthropomorphic God – the God which seems to be the God of traditional
Christianity – does not topple so easily. Yet when we reflect on
this conception, we very soon begin to have philosophical
cramps. When 'God' is construed non-anthropomorphically
there *seems*, at least, to be no way of showing that 'There is a

God' or that 'God exists' is either true or false. Because of this philosophical difficulties arise about the very coherence of such a concept of God and about the intelligibility of the string of words 'There is a God'.

However, we should say straight off, that there are some senses of 'intelligible' according to which 'God' is perfectly intelligible even when used non-anthropomorphically. 'God exists' or 'There is a God', unlike 'Irglig exists' or 'There is a Trig', are perfectly familiar word-strings to native speakers of English, for they have been part of the corpus of English for a long time. Cognate expressions have been part of French, Swedish, German, Spanish and so on. Viewed both diachronically and synchronically they are, and have been, and no doubt will continue to be, a part of the language. In this way they are perfectly intelligible.

We should also note (and this is but a corollary of the above) that 'God' has a role in the language; 'God' has a fixed syntax. We have *some* understanding of 'God created the world' or 'A mighty fortress is my God' but none of 'A God fortress is my coat' or 'Created clauses God the'. 'God' is not used as a verb or as an adverb, conjunction or preposition. 'Jack God Jill God down the hill to fetch a pail of Jesus' or 'The Yankees God the Tigers in ten innings' are so deviant as not to be intelligible. 'God' does not take just any word-slot in the English language, thus it is evident that there is a sense of 'intelligible' in which plain God-talk is perfectly intelligible. We can make inferences from 'God created the world'. 'If God created the world', the world is not uncreated, the world just didn't happen to come into being, and the world did not exist before God. Moreover, if God created the world, God is not, as he would be in Spinoza's, Hegel's or Tillich's conceptual system, dependent on or identical with, the world or some part of the world. That these sentences and many more like them stand in such deductive relations shows quite unequivocally that we have *some understanding* of them.[5]

Yet to be intelligible in *this sense* is hardly enough to satisfy the philosopher who believes that the sentences expressing such primary religious beliefs are unintelligible or incoherent. Still, the above remarks about linguistic regularities have the merit of bringing to the fore that the philosopher who finds such discourse unintelligible has a rather special sense of 'unintelligible' in mind. And it puts the onus on the philosopher to show in what relevant sense or senses such discourse is unintelligible.

By now I have stirred up enough difficulties to be in the midst of critical philosophical questions. First we should note that the facts of usage that we have just alluded to do not provide us with an adequate criterion of significance for such religious utterances, for the very same criterion would sanction the most obvious sorts of gibberish. Words like 'entelechy', 'Spiritual Cybernetics', 'infraconsciousness' and the like also would have to be said to be intelligible. 'The Absolute is in a dialectical process of transmutation', 'Consciousness is transcendentally present in infraconsciousness', 'Nothing noughts itself' would all, on the same grounds, count as intelligible utterances. Inferences of the same sort can be drawn from them, so that their irregularity is not such as to establish their unintelligibility. (Ziff has shown in his *Semantical Analysis* that not all or even most deviant utterances are unintelligible. When some philosopher says of a strange utterance, for example, 'He cultivates weeds': 'That's odd!', the proper reply should be 'So what?') Yet if we keep to such a grammarian's criterion of intelligibility, we will be committed to accepting as intelligible utterances which are plainly recognisable intuitively to be unintelligible, for example, 'Consciousness is in a dialectical process of transmutation'.

There is a point to this reply. Yet it will at best only dispose of the claim that an utterance is intelligible if inferences can be made from it. Against my argument in the previous paragraph one can counter-argue that my examples of unintelligible utterances were not firmly a part of the corpus of English while 'God exists' or 'There is a God in heaven' plainly are. We have learned from Wittgenstein, it will be continued, that where there is an ongoing activity with its attendant linguistic forms, we can have no good grounds for claiming that utterances or any forms of speech, which are a standard part of these linguistic forms, are unintelligible. But actual *first-order* religious discourse is such an attendant discourse while my other examples are not.

There is a further related point that needs to be frankly and carefully faced. If we depart from a grammarian's criterion of intelligibility/unintelligibility, we immediately run athwart the problems John Passmore presses on Hume and the logical empiricists. Hume and the logical empiricists are in effect saying that some words have *no right* to be in the language. They indeed are an established part of the language, but they are unintelligible all the same; 'they take part in sentences and win a place in dictionaries, nevertheless they have not satisfied the minimal entrance requirement for being intelligible expressions.'[6] Passmore pertinently asks: what *right* has a philosopher, or for that matter anyone else, to set up an entrance examination for meaningful or intelligible expressions and demand certain minimal entrance requirements? Will it not always be the case, Passmore continues to query, that here the philosopher is being thoroughly arbitrary in refusing the title 'intelligible' to any term that does not meet what are in effect his stipulated requirements? Others can make their stipulations too. He has given us no reason for accepting his and he does not even make it clear that he is stipulating. Such a positivistic approach is arbitrary.

A challenge like Passmore's is a formidable one and, if my claims concerning religion are to be sustained, I must meet it. Such general attitudes as Passmore's concerning the intelligibility of God-talk have had in recent years some powerful statements. Before taking to my own keenly disputed ground, I should carefully examine whether it is really necessary for me to do so. Perhaps God-talk in all important senses is perfectly intelligible and indeed not at all incoherent. It may be simply a philosophical prejudice to think otherwise. It behooves me to look into these claims.

II

A very strong case is made for taking an attitude like Passmore's in Paul Ziff's essay 'About "God"'.[7] It has been subjected to very searching criticisms particularly by Hick, Clarke, Hoffman and Edwards, and Ziff has been staunchly defended by Glickman.[8] By sifting out some of the issues here, we can get to the heart of some of the central issues concerning the intelligibility of 'God exists' and the coherence of God-talk.

Ziff thinks 'God exists', as now conceived by the plain man, is perfectly intelligible but, he adds, we now have very good grounds for asserting that such a God does not exist. That is to say, we have very strong grounds for asserting that there is no such being as Ziff describes in his essay and labels 'God'. But, he allows, there are now many different conceptions of God and there can be many new ones. That the old questions about God's existence should always have been answered negatively proves nothing about tomorrow. About tomorrow's questions one can only remain blank.

Like Edwards, Hoffman and others, I find much to take exception to in Ziff's last remarks. Given Ziff's conception of a plain man's concept of God, there are indeed good reasons for claiming that such a God does not exist. But Ziff's reason for such a claim, namely that a belief in God's omnipotence is not compatible with physics, is not a sufficiently adequate reason for asserting the non-existence of God. Believers could, and many would, reply that God, being God, could always perform a miracle. To make his case here convincing, Ziff, perhaps by using an argument like Hume's or Nowell-Smith's, would have to give good grounds for claiming that miracles are either in some way impossible or that they never have occurred or that they could ever occur is highly improbable.[9] That Ziff does not do. I think he could defend such a claim, but simply to make reference to physics in the way he does is superficial and unconvincing and rightly brings forth criticisms on this score by such different philosophers as Hoffman and Edwards, on the one hand, and Father Clarke on the other.[10]

I do not wish or need here to defend, or even further to consider, this side of Ziff's argument. What is relevant for my purposes are Ziff's arguments for the *intelligibility* of 'God exists'. But before starting Ziff's actual analysis, I would like to quote a warning he gives about analyses like mine. Its force, I should add, holds independently of the validity of Ziff's own attempt to show that 'God exists' is intelligible. It is a bold and rather arrogant utterance, but it needs to be pondered and I would suggest that as you follow my argument you keep it in mind and ask yourself if the shoe doesn't fit Nielsen's foot and perhaps Flew's, Hoffman's and Edward's too? Ziff's warning is this:

It is an extraordinary fact that in rightly opposing obscur-
antism contemporary philosophers have often become ob-
scurantists: that it is in a good cause is hardly an excuse. To
put the point bluntly, the utterances that contemporary
philosophers, e.g. logical positivists, so-called 'ordinary
language philosophers', and others say are devoid of significance are not devoid of significance. The utterances they say
are incomprehensible are not incomprehensible. It is too bad
that they are not right for then there would be nothing to be
alarmed about. But the danger of philosophical rubbish is
that it is comprehensible and incomprehensibly contagious.
Metaphysicians and theologians are generally no harder to
understand than poets or novelists. There is as much philosophical rubbish in Dostoevsky and Kierkegaard as there is in
Hegel and Heidegger. The difference between a work of
metaphysics and *Finnegans Wake* is that what is said in the
former is likely to be false when interesting and platitudinous
when true, whereas such questions are not likely to arise in
connection with the latter.[11]

This warning firmly in mind, now let us consider Ziff's arguments concerning the intelligibility of 'God exists'. Ziff first
argues that 'God', as it is used in sentences and utterances in
religious discourse, is a noun of a distinctive sort; to be more
specific still, it is a proper noun, that is, a proper name. Yet it is
not a name like yours and mine, but like 'Caesar' or 'Pegasus'.
The reason that it is not a name like yours and mine is that
'God', according to Ziff, can only be introduced into a particular discourse by 'intralinguistic means'. There is no way of
simply ostensively teaching what 'God' refers to. Thus there is
no extralinguistic means of introducing 'God' into the discourse. One cannot point to God, but one can point to Hans or
Hildegard and so introduce 'Hans' or 'Hildegard' into the
discourse. 'God', however, must be introduced into the discourse by intralinguistic means. This is done by associating the
name with certain expressions in the language. Since these
expressions will have certain conditions associated with them,
derivatively the name also will have certain conditions associated with it.
    One might already challenge Ziff on two counts. First, many

plain people and some theologians speak of an apprehension of God, of a direct awareness of God, of a beatific vision and the like. They might even argue that in the last analysis this would be the only way we could understand what the word 'God' really means. I think there are plenty of counters to this claim, counters of the sort C. B. Martin has gone over so carefully.[12] Still it is not self-evidently clear that we cannot introduce the term 'God' extralinguistically.

On Ziff's behalf it should be replied that there is no reason to think that Ziff thought it was. It is reasonable to conclude that he recognised that one cannot argue on all fronts at once and that Ziff chose not to do battle here. Moreover, where 'God' is used non-anthropomorphically, what it would be like to teach the term 'God' ostensively, in the way one would teach someone the referent of a proper name, is, to put it conservatively, not at all clear. More generally, what it would be like in any way ostensively to define or to teach 'God' is thoroughly mystifying.

The second way one could challenge Ziff here is to take the tack that someone like Geach, Kenney or Durrant would surely take and challenge Ziff's claim that 'God' is a name. 'God', Geach would argue, is not a name but is really a definite description. God is 'the maker of the world', 'the ruler of the Universe'. Yet this seems to me to be neither decisive nor, for that matter, very important, for after all Ziff does argue that 'God', unlike 'Hans', can only be introduced into the language 'by means of descriptions'. To understand 'God' is to understand these descriptions, to fail to understand the relevant descriptions is to fail to understand 'God'. Perhaps it is best to say, as Father Clarke does, that in the case of the very unique word 'God' the two functions are indissolubly combined. 'God' functions primarily as a description,

> But since one of the notes of the description is that it can be verified by only one referent ('God' means 'the one infinite Creator of all things'), this particular descriptive term can also be, and traditionally has been, used as a direct form of address or as a proper name.[13]

Clarke's claim here seems reasonable to me, but perhaps it is too quick and too superficial. But I mention these issues, only to put them aside, for whether 'God' is a proper name or a definite description, it remains the case, on Ziff's analysis, that 'God' can only be understood if certain descriptions can be understood.

I shall henceforth, for convenience only, talk about 'God' as if 'God' were a name. The set of conditions we associate with the name determines our conception of the referent of the name. We can introduce 'Wittgenstein' intralinguistically by specifying certain conditions, 'The author of The Blue and Brown Books', 'the unwitting founder of the two most influential types of analytic philosophy', 'the philosopher most admired by Norman Malcolm' and so on. To understand what one is talking about when one uses a name, one must be able at least in principle to specify the relevant set of conditions associated with the name; if the alleged word is a genuine name, actually has such a role in the language, it must be possible to specify such a relevant set of conditions associated with the name.[14]

To find out, Ziff contends, if anything is actually named by the name – whether the name actually has a referent – we must determine whether anything or anyone satisfies the conditions of the set. But to establish that 'God exists' is intelligible, we need only show, according to Ziff, that the conditions associated with the name are intelligible and that the set of conditions is consistent. This, for Ziff, is necessary and sufficient to establish the intelligibility of 'God exists'. Unlike a large and influential group of philosophers, he does not think the question whether anything or anyone could satisfy the set of conditions has anything to do with whether either 'God exists' or 'God' is intelligible.

However, we cannot let this pass so easily for Hoffman's criticisms of Ziff on this point forcefully bring out very clearly the controversial status of Ziff's claim. (What is involved will be brought to the fore in a few paragraphs.)

To answer our question concerning the intelligibility of 'God', we must first determine what are the conditions associated with 'God'. Here Ziff tells us we must consider the plain man's concept of God and not confuse it with 'the excubant theologian's febrile concept'. (Given the obscurities of Tillich and Bultmann one can well understand why Ziff approaches the subject matter in this way.) But at different times and different places there are different plain men with different conceptions of God, and different men, even when members of particular denominations, may have different conceptions of God at different periods in their lives. To make his subject matter manageable, Ziff settles on a particular conception of God, though, if his analysis is to have a tolerable degree of relevance, it will have to be a conception that is held by a considerable number of plain Jews and plain Christians.

As we follow through Ziff's analysis, it is fairly evident that this is, in the main at least, true of his conception of God.

Ziff points out that 'God' has associated with it both problematic and unproblematic conditions. That the unproblematic conditions are satisfied or satisfiable, is, according to Ziff, fairly obvious. The unproblematic ones are 'being a being, a force, a person, a father, a son, a creator, spatiotemporal, crucified, just, good, merciful, powerful, wise, and so forth'.[15] The problematic conditions are 'being omnipotent, omniscient, eternal, creator of the world, a non-spatiotemporal being, a spirit, the cause of itself, and so forth'. Ziff thinks that if anyone were to maintain that such a traditional conception of God is unintelligible, he would argue that these problematic conditions are unintelligible.

To say that these conditions are unintelligible is to say we cannot understand them. But in reflecting on this, we must not forget that understanding and hence intelligibility *admit of degrees*. We have, Ziff argues, some understanding of these conditions, and hence, though 'God exists' may be mysterious, as it most certainly should be, it still need not be completely unintelligible.

Ziff argues for this point in a way similar to the way in which I have already shown that 'God' has a fixed syntax. We understand all of the following:

(1)   If God is omnipotent there is nothing he cannot do owing to lack of power.
(2)   If something is the cause of itself then we cannot succeed in finding another cause for it.
(3)   If something is the Creator of the world then prior to its act of creation the world did not exist.

Ziff argues that the fact that we can make such inferences

indicates that we have some understanding of the conditions involved.[16]

Ziff realises that many philosophers, particularly those who take some form of the verifiability principle seriously, might still not be satisfied. They would argue that these conditions are, in spite of such inference patterns, unintelligible, because 'it is evidently difficult to establish whether or not any of them are, in fact, satisfied.'[17] But Ziff does not think this is a good reason for saying the conditions are unintelligible, for 'understanding a condition is one thing; knowing how to establish that it is satisfied is another.'[18] I say to my wife, 'I'll stick my tongue out at Reagan on condition that you will do it.' I can understand the condition and what will satisfy it. But consider 'I agree to take a swim in the East River on the condition that the last man ever to live, were he alive now, would approve of it.' Ziff remarks of such a sentence 'There is still no difficulty in understanding the condition and yet I have no idea how actually to establish that such a condition is satisfied.'[19] What this should teach us, Ziff argues, is that we should not, in talking about what makes a sentence intelligible, stress verification. Positivists, Ziff believes, have lead us down the garden path here.

To accept Ziff's point here and to reject what is more or less a verificationist approach, affects in a radical way our conception of what it is proper to say about large issues. While, for example, Ziff admits that to speak of 'a spirit' or of '*creation ex nihilo*' is indeed difficult, he does not think it is impossible. In fact he thinks these old conundrums can be solved. They do not exhibit the unintelligibility or incoherence of God-talk.

At this point in his argument Ziff is certainly, to put it conservatively, making it very easy for himself, while evading, by the simple expedient of dogmatic declamation, what many would take to be crucial problems about God-talk. How are these old problems to be solved? Are they genuine problems at all? Or are they muddles felt as problems? Why is it that there is no serious question concerning the intelligibility of these conceptions? We need here something more than oracular *ex cathedra* remarks from Ziff. We need something more than the striking of a posture. Ziff simple declaims, for our trusting acceptance, that difficulties concerning spirit and creation *ex nihilo* only show that the concept of God is a difficult one. They do not point toward its *unintelligibility* or incoherence. Well, *perhaps* Ziff is right here, but since he makes no argument for his rather extraordinary claim, he gives us no reason for thinking he is right. What conditions are we to associate with being a spirit, a non-spatiotemporal entity, a creator *ex nihilo?* What principles of individuation can we utilise here? How do we identify such beings? Perhaps such questions have answers, that is, perhaps they are genuine questions. Alternatively, it may be the case that they are wrongly put. But we need to show either that they have answers or that such questions are wrongly put in this context, or that it is a mistake to think they are conceptual confusions misleadingly put in the form of questions. We need very much to have some reasonable response here and not to be put off with the remark that these are old questions.

Similarly there is the problem of the consistency or compatibility of the conditions associated with 'God'. How can something be a being and at the same time be non-spatiotemporal? Worse still, how can something be a spatiotemporal being and a non-spatiotemporal being, a son and the cause of itself, a person and an unlimited being? These surely look not merely like paradoxes, but like flat contradictions. One cannot say without being thoroughly evasive (as Ziff is on this issue) that 'Such problems . . . are readily dealt with in obvious ways: contradiction can always be avoided by an appropriate and judicious feat of logistic legerdemain; conditions can always be weakened, modified, and so made compatible. This game has been played for over a thousand years.'[20]

Against such a boast, it needs to be pointed out that many theologians have come to feel that the conflicts here are such that all the predictions involved in the statement of such conditions should be understood in some non-literal way. Taken as they ordinarily would be taken, we have a tissue of contradictions and absurdities. Of course we can always modify or weaken our conditions, we can always stretch our terms, but then we are no longer talking about the same God or using the terms with the same meaning. (Recall here that if Ziff is right, we have and can have no extralinguistic understanding of 'God' and thus we cannot use that as a check on whether we are still talking about the same God or the same reality.) To alter the meaning of these terms does not help at all to make intelligible the plain man's concept of God that Ziff was supposed to be talking about. Ziff's talk of 'logistic legerdemain' is but a fancy name for changing the subject. To reason in the way Ziff does is not to show that the set of conditions are mutually consistent; it is simply to rationalise and be evasive. Perhaps these conditions can be shown to be mutually consistent, but on face value they appear to be inconsistent and Ziff has not begun to show that they are consistent. Since they most certainly appear to be mutually inconsistent, we have reason (though surely not a conclusive reason), quite apart from any commitment to verificationism, for believing that such a plain man's concept of God is unintelligible or incoherent. (Of course to be unintelligible in this way, it must be intelligible in the trivial way that any self-contradictory expression or proposition is intelligible.)

So far Ziff's case for the intelligibility of 'God exists' does not look very good. Yet I think the impression I have given may be misleading. Certainly Ziff needs, if his argument is to be philosophically air-tight, to make out a case for the exceptional claims he makes and not just to bluster his way past difficulties. But it should also be remembered that his short essay is a very methodological one. He is, I believe, in effect trying to suggest that most analytic philosophers have gone at the analysis of God-talk in the wrong way. He is trying to suggest a new approach to the subject and in such a programmatic essay he could hardly be expected to consider all the problems. It should be further noted in this vein that Ziff's sins are sins of omission. They weaken but do not constitute a death-blow to his defence of the intelligibility of a plain man's account of 'God exists'. But Ziff's own *argued* claims have been subjected to trenchant criticisms which, if correct, would utterly invalidate his argument. I shall now turn to them.

III

For anyone deeply influenced by empiricism there is a very natural counter to make against Ziff. This is exemplified in some of Robert Hoffman's arguments against Ziff's account.[21] Hoffman makes what in effect is a verificationist argument against Ziff and I too would like to press some form of this argument. But it seems to me that Jack Glickman is perfectly

correct in contending that Hoffman simply assumes this criterion of meaningfulness or intelligibility and thus does not
meet Ziff's challenge, for Ziff does not assume such a criterion
and, as we have seen, he gives us some reason to be wary of it.
That is, Hoffman begs the central question with Ziff.

Hoffman responds by acknowledging that he is committed to
some version of empiricism or the verifiability theory of meaningfulness while denying that he has begged any issue with Ziff.
He thinks he has not done so because he does not simply assert
some formulation of the verifiability principle but points out
that it is not enough (*pace* Ziff) to exhibit the intelligibility of a
condition simply to relate it intralinguistically to other expressions by displaying a pattern of definitive and analytic relationships between the putative statement being examined and
another expression or cluster of expressions. For utterances
allegedly asserting some condition to have 'factual intelligibility', one must show in addition, Hoffman contends, what
would at least in principle have to obtain if what that condition
signifies were satisfied. But such an account of 'factual intelligibility' just assumes, in the way Ziff is challenging, the verifiability criterion of factual intelligibility. Hoffman stresses the importance of distinguishing 'what it makes sense to say' from
'what is grammatically secure', but he just assumes the verifiability criterion is the criterion for what it makes sense to say,
assuming that a statement must be devoid of factual content
and thus be factually meaningless if it is not at least in principle
verifiable (confirmable or disconfirmable).

What is involved here needs some spelling out. In reading the
exchange between Ziff, Hoffman and Glickman it becomes
apparent that the central issue is the matter of accepting one
rather than another of two very fundamental criteria of intelligibility. (I do not deny there could be other alternatives.) It is
also true that Hoffman's account clearly falls foul of Passmore's
strictures about a philosopher setting up special entrance requirements for what counts as a meaningful or intelligible
expression. Yet there is merit in having these conflicting underlying assumptions clearly brought to the fore.

Hoffman argues that Ziff has not shown that it is mistaken to
believe that questions concerning the intelligibility of 'God' are
logically tied to questions concerning what would at least *in*

principle satisfy the conditions for the use of 'God'. One of Ziff's problematic conditions is that of being omnipotent. But some would argue, as Ziff is perfectly aware, that 'being omnipotent' is not itself an intelligible expression. In this, Ziff believes, they are deluded, for even if we do not know what would establish the truth or falsity of 'being omnipotent', still we understand that condition. Ziff writes, 'that a certain being did not perform a certain task could not in itself establish that the being was not omnipotent, no matter what the task was. Again, that the being performed the task would not establish its omnipotence, and again that no matter what the task was.'[22] To this Hoffman quite understandably responds:

> But surely unless we can establish, though not necessarily conclusively, whether or not the being is omnipotent by ascertaining whether or not it performs or fails to perform certain acts, considered severally or jointly, we cannot establish it at all. For if the allegedly non-analytic assertions (A) that a certain being is omnipotent and (B) that the being is not omnipotent, are equally compatible with the performance or non-performance of any act(s) by that being, then the assertions are *meaningless, for* they are *compatible with any state of affairs whatever.*[23]

Such an assertion clearly commits Hoffman to some version of empiricism or the verifiability theory of meaning. If we give a charitable interpretation to his remarks, we should take him as giving us to understand that if a putative factual assertion and its denial are equally compatible with all logically conceivable states of affairs, then they are both without factual content. That is to say, if it is logically impossible to confirm or disconfirm them to the slightest degree then they are devoid of factual intelligibility. Yet since they allegedly are factual statements they must then in this crucial way be meaningless, that is, devoid of factual content.

But, as Glickman points out, Hoffman gives us no reason at all to accept this very philosophical and controversial litmus-paper test (criterion) for a meaningful assertion or a meaningful factual statement. Ziff would not accept it, so Hoffman has not refuted Ziff but merely begged the question with Ziff.[24] To complete his argument against Ziff here Hoffman would have to give adequate grounds for his claim that Ziff *should* accept such a controversial criterion of meaning or criterion of factual intelligibility.

It will not do to respond, as Hoffman does, by asserting that Ziff is merely giving a grammarian's criterion of intelligibility, for Hoffman has not shown (1) that Ziff would accept such a distinction or that he need accept it, and (2) even if we are justified in speaking of 'factual intelligibility', that verifiability is essential for 'factual intelligibility'. He has just assumed those things – assumptions which Ziff either challenges or does not make – and so he has begged the question with Ziff.

I agree with Hoffman that there is the distinction he refers to between being syntactically secure and talking sense. An utterance could perhaps be syntactically in order and still be incoherent, for example, 'The tune was rectangular'. It may be, that where stating facts is at issue, talking sense is to be identified with making utterances which are at least in principle verifiable. I shall argue that this is the case, but Ziff and many others, not implausibly, believe that it is not the case and give some reasons for thinking that it is not the case. Hoffman simply makes a contentious distinction between 'factual intelligibility' and 'grammatical intelligibility' and then assumes a verificationist account of 'factual intelligibility'. Ziff makes neither of these assumptions and indeed challenges the latter, so the crucial issue between them is begged.

Hoffman also argues that Ziff in effect confuses verifiability (confirmability/disconfirmability) in principle with verifiability (confirmability/disconfirmabiity) in practice or in fact. Ziff rightly argues that he can understand certain conditions, for example, 'what the last man ever to live, were he alive now, would approve,' without having any idea of how actually to establish when such a condition is satisfied. But, Hoffman argues, it is not whether we actually know how to satisfy a given condition that is crucial to the question of intelligibility, but whether it is in principle empirically satisfiable, that is, whether it is *logically possible* to state (to describe) what one would have to observe or fail to observe for the conditions to be satisfied. If a condition is unsatisfiable in *this sense*, then, Hoffman claims, it is unintelligible.

Glickman in turn points out that Hoffman (1) does not explain what he means by 'satisfiable in principle' and (2) 'he leaves us to guess . . . why he believes satisfiability in principle is a necessary condition of intelligibility.'[25] It does not seem to me, given the context of the dispute, that what is intended by 'satisfiable in principle' should be such a big mystery. Presumably condition x is satisfiable in principle if it is logically possible to state what would, to any degree at all, count as evidence for or against x.[26] But this brings us back to some empiricist condition for meaningfulness (or for factual intelligibility or cognitive intelligibility). Since this is so, Glickman's second point mentioned above effectively reduces to that consideration. Glickman indeed exaggerates his point when he says Hoffman's 'whole argument rests on this assumption', but certainly the central segments of it do. And Glickman is perfectly justified in saying that Hoffman does nothing at all to justify that assumption. Though to say this is, of course, not to say that some such an assumption is not *justifiable*. But certainly in view of the chequered history of the verifiability criterion of meaning, it needs a very considerable and careful justification.

In this chapter I shall not try to give a full-scale justification for making this assumption, where it is considered, as it should be, as a criterion of factual significance, though I shall show (1) how considerations involving it can hardly be avoided in carefully reflecting on God-talk, and (2) I shall give some considerations which should make it evident that its employment in such contexts need not be the imposition of an empiricist dogma. I am going to do this in an indirect manner. I shall first consider some other arguments against Ziff – arguments which in my opinion do draw blood. I shall then proceed to show how some of them can at least be partly countered. The unfolding of the argument here will lead us to see both how an argument of Ziff's type cannot be decisive for questions about whether God-talk is coherent, and how considerations arising from this discussion naturally push us back to a reconsideration of the plausibility of using the verifiability principle in such contexts.

IV

Such very different philosophers as John Hick and Paul

Edwards deploy some arguments against Ziff that, at the very least, raise serious questions concerning the viability of his analysis.

I shall first consider one of Hick's arguments. Ziff distinguishes between problematic conditions and unproblematic conditions. Hick argues that Ziff's unproblematic conditions, *when associated with the word 'God'*, are just as problematic as his problematic conditions.[27] What Ziff's argument actually shows is that 'Father', 'person', 'force', 'good', 'loving,' 'just', are in certain contexts expressive of unproblematic conditions because these terms have an established or primary use in secular contexts. Hick argues that it is critical to stress 'secular contexts', for it is here where they have their ordinary everyday use. But 'they have been adopted by religion and given a secondary use.' However, with the terms expressive of Ziff's problematic conditions, Hick continues, the situation is quite different since ' . . . "Spirit", "omnipotent", "omniscient" have no familiar established use in the language of everyday life.'[28] While they indeed occasionally occur in secular discourse, they do not have an established use there; rather they were 'originally formed for theological purposes'. It is there that they are at home; it is there that they have their primary use. Hick stresses that the really crucial thing to see is that both what Ziff calls the 'unproblematic conditions' as well as the admittedly problematic ones become problematic when applied to God.

> Certainly we know what we mean when we say of a fellow human being that he has a loving disposition. But what does 'loving' mean when it is transferred to a Being who is defined, *inter alia*, as having no body, so that he cannot be thought of as performing any actions? What is disembodied love, and how can we ever ascertain that it exists?[29]

When used in secular discourses, 'loving' has a firm foundation but when used in certain key religious discourses, it is quite unclear what, if anything, is meant. Some native speakers do not understand, or at least *feel* they do not understand, its use in a religious context and many religious believers think that its use is somehow stretched or analogical or symbolic or linked with experiences that can be interpreted in conflicting ways.

We cannot, Hick argues, take the term, in such contexts, as expressive of unproblematic conditions.

Ziff might reply that he only intended by his unexplicated term of art 'unproblematic conditions' to signify that 'loving' and terms like it, by contrast with 'omnipotent' and terms like it, are terms that sometimes have a settled application and that in such contexts they typically do not give rise to conceptual confusion. But Hick is surely right in pointing out that in the linguistic environment of *first-order* God-talk all of these terms have a usage which does provoke dispute and conceptual confusion. Whether it is correct to say, as Hick does, that their 'original use' was secular is much more disputable, for after all, who knows and how could we even tell, what was their original use? It is not even evident that their use in religious contexts is secondary. 'Triangle' in 'marriage triangle' is secondary to the primary use of 'triangle' in geometry. We readily grasp the meaning of the former by making an immediate connection with our understanding of the latter. In that way the former is parasitical on the latter. This *may* be true of 'loving' in secular contexts and religious contexts; but we should not simply assume that this is so; we need an argument to establish that it is. It is also disputable, though some philosophers blithely assume this, that ordinary use is only secular use. Whether this is so or not certainly seems to depend on *whose* ordinary language it is and when and where the sentences are (were) uttered. In certain environments the religious use might occur just as frequently and seem just as natural.

Yet these criticisms of Hick's critique of Ziff, even if perfectly correct, are piddling criticisms, dialectical diversions, that do not touch the nerve of Hick's argument, which is (to put it in my own way) that for native and/or fluent speakers of all ideological convictions there is a massive agreement about how correctly to apply 'loving' in secular contexts but that in a Christian or Jewish religious context 'loving' is a dispute-engendering term. Some feel they can make nothing of its religious use at all. Thus in such contexts it is a problematic condition in the sense that people do not agree that they understand its employment there.

Paul Edwards, in effect, develops and qualifies Hick's argument by pointing out that if 'God' is construed anthropomorphically, 'loving' is used with some intelligibility, for given such an anthropomorphic employment of 'God', we have some-where in the background a picture of God as in some mysterious way having a body. This makes it possible to conceptualise Him as acting in the world and to think of Him as loving. But, I should add, religious reflection cannot tolerate such a picture. For a long time Jews and Christians have regarded it as gross blasphemy to think of God 'as possessing some kind of rather large body'.[30] This is reflected in the very *first-order* God-talk itself. It could only be a joke to ask how tall God is, how much He weighs or where He comes to an end. A whole range of conditions associated with something said to possess some kind of gigantic body are not associated with 'God' as the plain man uses that term. God, in Jewish and Christian discourse, could not be any kind of material object, no matter how huge, for this would limit Him and subject Him to the conditions of change and corruption; only a completely disembodied Creator could be an object *worthy* of worship.[31] (This is what Wittgenstein would call a grammatical remark.)

It may well be that when the engine isn't idling, when people are praying or worshipping, their childhood pictorial images of God as a material being unwittingly reassert themselves and in that way 'loving' comes to have an application when applied to God. But to reflective religious consciousness, He is 'Pure Spirit', and 'disembodied mind', but then, given their use of 'God' as 'Pure Spirit', we cannot understand what it would be for such a being to act and thus to be loving, merciful or just, for these predicates apply to things that *a person does*. But we have no understanding of 'a person' without 'a body' and it is only persons that in the last analysis can act or do things. We have no understanding of 'disembodied action' or 'bodiless doing' and thus no understanding of 'a loving but bodiless being'.

Moreover, we must ask, as Edwards does, 'What would it be like to be, say, just, without a body? To be just, a person has to *act* justly – he has to behave in certain ways . . . [this] is a simple empirical truth about what we mean by "just"'.[32] No sense has been given to what it would be like to act or behave in the required way without a body. Being good and being loving are on Ziff's account supposedly unproblematic conditions, but it is evident from the above that they are problematic when applied to a 'disembodied being' or 'Pure Spirit'. In fact 'problematic' seems too weak a word, for we have no more understanding of what is meant here than we have when we say 'a Plymouth talks faster than a Ford'; 'a Plymouth talks' has no use in the language.[33]

To Edwards's point, it might be countered, that he, like Hoffman, is implicitly relying on the verifiability principle. 'God's actions', 'God's love', are not like 'a Plymouth talks' or 'Stanfield sleeps faster than Lewis'. They are established bits of ordinary usage; they have a use in the language. When Edwards asks us, so the objection would run, what it would be like to be just or loving without a body, he is *not* pointing to a misuse of terms as in 'sleeps faster' but he is in effect calling to our attention that we do not know what we would have to observe or fail to observe for it to be true or false, or even probably true or false that x was disembodied and x acted lovingly or justly. But Ziff would not accept the verifiability criterion as a test for intelligibility. Again the crucial question has been begged.

It is certainly natural to ask at this point: when, with a concrete issue like this, one reflects on what nonsense one talks without assuming this principle, doesn't it become evident that one with suitable restrictions ought to accept it? As an argument, this of course is question-begging and thus no decent argument at all, for to establish that this is 'nonsense' is just what is at issue. But surely many people – and I am among them – can make nothing of 'disembodied action'. Religious people, or at least those who reflect, are themselves perplexed about it. To those who think they can understand it, it is well to ask them, in a concrete way, for the truth-conditions of their claims. If they can give none, we have good grounds for being sceptical that they, their protestations to the contrary notwithstanding, understand what they are saying.[34].

This consideration, which I admit is still ultimately fundamentally question-begging, gains in an indirect way added force when we recall that 'God's acts' and 'God's love' could have a use through an ancient concept of God in which God is thought to have a body. (Recall Moses' encounters with God on Mount Sinai.) This use is still lurking, though officially re-jected, in the background of our present use (a kind of cultural lag in language). When religious believers are not reflecting but simply using God-talk, it comes to be their active use. 'God', as a name, as Ziff himself nicely put it, 'is a fixed point in a turning world. But as the world turns, our conception of that which is named by a name may change.'[35] Yet the associations, the usages that developed around the earlier conceptions, may linger on when they have long since ceased to be apposite and thus we can come to have the illusion of understanding when in reality we have no understanding. This, if correct, does not show that 'God's acts', 'God's love', are unintelligible: it only explains how, if we have good grounds for thinking that they are unintelligible, it could remain true that so many, in spite of their perplexities concerning them, continue to believe they are intelligible. But this account surely shows that being just and being loving are, in such linguistic environments, problematic conditions whose very intelligibility is in serious doubt.

Ziff anticipates these difficulties, but what he says about the above problem is inadequate. Edwards is quite justified in remarking:

Ziff does not show himself the least bit aware of the seriousness of this problem. He merely assures us that 'the condition of being a non-spatiotemporal being can be viewed as a result of an abstraction from the condition of being a spatiotemporal being.' This dark saying he elaborates by pointing to the 'ease of such abstraction' which is 'testified to by the fact that plain people sometimes say they find it difficult to keep body and soul together' merely an irresponsible play on words, since there is not the least reason to suppose that anybody who has the occasion to complain that 'he cannot keep his body and soul together' is in any way trying to assert the existence of an entity that does not occupy space or is in any sense nontemporal.[36]

Edwards also raises pertinent points about Ziff's problematic conditions. Ziff argues, as we have seen, that we have some understanding of them, for example, 'I know that if something is the creator of the world, then prior to its act of creation the world did not exist.' We could not make such inferences without some understanding of the conditions involved. To this Edwards replies:

> Surely this argument is fallacious. There are any number of sentences which in the opinion of practically everybody, atheist or believer, positivist or metaphysician, are meaningless, but which can at the same time be used as premises of valid deductions. From 'the Absolute is lazy' it follows that the Absolute is not industrious; from 'Box sleeps more rapidly than Cox' it follows that Cox sleeps more slowly than Box; from 'everything has increased tenfold in size since yesterday', it follows that my right hand is ten times as large as it was yesterday (which in this context is also meaningless); etc., etc. From 'there is a being that created the universe out of nothing', it certainly follows that 'there was a time when the universe did not exist'. But this would have a tendency to show that the former sentence is intelligible only if it is granted that its consequence is intelligible, which is one of the main points of issue.[37]

The difficulty, Edwards argues, lies in Ziff's slippery phrase 'some understanding'. We, unlike a person who has no knowledge of English, have some understanding of 'The Absolute is lazy', but, Edwards adds, 'this means no more than that I am familiar with certain rules of substitution governing the relative employment of the words "lazy" and "industrious".'[38] In this sense I understand 'The universe has a Creator', but, Edwards rightly replies, to point to such an understanding is to point to something that 'is trivial and irrelevant. Nobody who has seriously discussed the question as to whether we understand "problematic" theological sentences has used "understand" and related terms like "intelligible" or "meaningful" in this sense.'[39·]

We have now come around full circle. Edwards surely is making an important point here, but Ziff has an important Moorean counter, namely he admitted and stressed that the concept of God, even his plain man's concept of God, was a difficult one; and he also stressed that 'understanding admits of degrees'.[40] He was only concerned to show that we have *some* understanding of 'God' and 'God exists' and Edwards concedes he has done that. Thus Ziff surely has shown that it is not correct to assert that 'God exists' is utterly unintelligible. Ziff could further claim that he has in effect brought to the surface the fact that when philosophers claim that 'God' and 'God exists' or 'There is a God' are unintelligible or meaningless they have something very special in mind: they have a special and idiosyncratic criterion of intelligibility or meaning in mind; and here Passmore's nagging question again becomes pertinent: why accept this philosophical entrance requirement?

I think, however, that reflection on Edwards's arguments against Ziff will give us part of the reason why it is at least tempting to set up and accept such philosophical entrance requirements. 'God is our loving Father', 'God's acts are just', 'God is the creator of the world and Father of all mankind', are *first-order* religious utterances – live bits of God-talk. Yet, where God is not thought to have a body, we can make nothing of such sentences. That is, we have no idea of whether they are used to make true or false statements. If this in turn forces us back to anthropomorphism, we must remember that a God with a body would be a religiously inadequate conception of God from the point of view of what has become of the Judaeo-Christian tradition.

Even reflective religious men are frequently perplexed by such religious utterances: that is, they are puzzled by 'God is our loving Father' and not just by the theological analyses of such utterances. Many of them come to be overwhelmed, as were Kierkegaard and Pascal, by doubt. It isn't that the man in the circle of faith knows what he means, though he may not know the proper *analysis* of what he means, while the secularist does not understand such utterances. Both can make the inferences Ziff alludes to; both know how to *use* God-talk; yet both may find its very *first-order* use thoroughly perplexing. We are supposed to understand what it is to talk of something beyond the universe. Yet many a believer and non-believer alike come to feel, without being able to say exactly why, that such word-strings are without cognitive significance. We are here, as Wittgenstein once put it, thrusting against the boundaries of our language. The sceptic draws attention both to the fact that such discourse utilises terms like 'persons' and 'acts' which are common to more mundane contexts, and to the fact that in the religious contexts they function in a different way and that their very use in such religious contexts is thoroughly perplexing to believer and unbeliever alike. In Ziff's terminology 'being an act' and 'being a person' are in this linguistic environment problematic. No-one, not even the knight of faith, seems to know what he is asserting when he employs them to make what he alleges to be statements. Thus in a very natural way – independently of some disputable philosophical criterion of meaning – questions concerning their intelligibility naturally arise – questions that will not be stilled by noting and taking to heart the facts of usage noted by Ziff.

Philosophers observe that Christians are, in virtue of being Christians, committed to such putative statements as 'We have a loving Father who created us all and who looks over us as an omnipotent, omniscient and just judge', 'In the Last Judgement God will judge the acts of man.' These are putative statements, allegedly bits of fact-stating discourse; the philosopher then reflects on what sort of criterion we in fact normally employ for deciding whether a statement really is a factual statement; he notes that those statements which have an *unquestioned* status as factual statements or factual assertions are all at least confirmable or disconfirmable in principle. But when he examines religious utterances of the type I have just quoted, he notes that they are not, as they are now typically used, confirmable or disconfirmable even in principle. They parade as factual statements, but actually do not function in this very crucial sense, like statements that would, with no question at all, pass muster as statements of fact.[41]

Noting these linguistic facts, a philosopher can suggest, as a criterion for factual intelligibility, confirmability/disconfirmability in principle. This is not an arbitrary suggestion and it would, if adopted, not be an arbitrary entrance requirement, for it brings out the procedures which are actually employed in deciding whether a statement is indeed factual. It makes explicit an implicit practice. Moreover, there is a rational point to setting up such a requirement, given the truth of what I have just asserted. The point is this: if we have such a requirement, it can be used in deciding on borderline and disputed cases. Where certain utterances are allegedly bits of fact-stating discourse yet function in a radically different way than our paradigms of fact-stating discourse, we have good grounds for questioning their factual intelligibility. My criterion makes explicit just what it is that makes a bit of discourse fact-stating discourse.

Using such a criterion, the religious utterances we have just discussed can be seen to be devoid of factual intelligibility, where 'God' is *not* thought to have a body. Similar things should be said for the other central claims of non-anthropomorphic Theism. By now it is evident that I, like Hoffman and Edwards, have operated with a fundamentally empiricist requirement in talking of the intelligibility of such religious discourse. But I have tried to give some justification for using such a criterion. I have tried to show how it states in capsule form and generalises a method that is repeatedly used in practice by reflective men when they try to decide whether a given use of language makes a factual claim, that is, makes a claim about what there is.

Indeed there are those who think this criterion is in one way or another too stringent. Some will argue that it fits some clear cases of unequivocally factual statements but *not* others of a quite mundane and paradigmatic sort; others will assert that these key religious utterances should not be construed as putative statements of fact; still others will argue that such a criterion is alien to religious discourse itself and thus cannot possibly be justified. It is to these questions that I must turn in later chapters, but by now it should be evident that Ziff's considerations, as interesting and important as they are, do not close the issue concerning the intelligibility of God-talk.

3

The Challenge of Wittgenstein

I

There are many who think that the kind of challenge I raised against Ziff is radically mistaken. To raise questions of confirmation/disconfirmation in the context of talking about the meaning of religious utterances is to show a rather complete lack of comprehension of their actual role in our lives. It, so the argument would run, is to treat them too much like hypotheses and to model God-talk too much on scientific discourse. A sensitive understanding of God-talk in its living contexts will show that it has a logic of its own which is in its own proper order. Dogmas and doctrines should not be regarded as opinions or hypotheses. They have an entirely different logic – a radically different role in human discourse. All a philosopher can properly do is to characterise it, to display perspicuously the actual function(s) of religious utterances so as to relieve our perplexities about it. He, *qua* philosopher, can in no way legitimately criticise this whole mode of discourse or claim that it is unintelligible or incoherent, though he can, and often should, criticise what theologians or philosophers say about it. What we in effect learn from Moore and directly learn from Wittgenstein is that in any mode of discourse the *first-order* discourse is all right as it is, it is only the second-order discourse – the talk about the talk – that frequently is in conceptual disarray. The philosopher's job is to cure this *malaise*; but the *first-order* discourse itself is simply his uncriticisable given. That pre-Wittgensteinian philosophers thought they could criticise it and that some post-

Wittgensteinian Neanderthals still think they can only attests to their confusion.

We are back to the central problems raised in the first chapter. It is this attitude toward religion and religious discourse that I call Wittgensteinian Fideism. It is here that I feel the most profound challenge to what I want to say about religion, for, if Wittgensteinian Fideism is right, I am most surely mistaken in some of the fundamental claims I make concerning religion. Yet it is just here that I feel the greatest ambivalence, for as I read Wittgenstein himself or Malcolm, Cavell, Winch or Ambrose I feel profoundly drawn toward such a manner of philosophising. I feel in general, though often not with respect to details, 'Yes, this is the right way to do it. Yes, here we will get a genuine advance in philosophy.' None the less, this approach seems to me profoundly misguided when applied to religion (say after the manner of Phillips or Dilman) and Winch's claims about Azande magical practices, brilliant as they are in execution, seem to me a *reductio* of such an approach.[1] Yet am I failing to note the mote in my own eye? Am I unwittingly turning into an ideologue here? Are my own attitudes, my own emotional commitments, blinding me to a patent truth? I shall in this chapter and in the following two chapters examine Wittgensteinian Fideism from the inside. I shall begin by discussing Wittgenstein's *Lectures on Religious Belief* from his *Lectures and Conversations on Aesthetics, Psychology and Religious Belief*.[2]

II

The first thing to be noted about what I have called Wittgenstein's *Lectures on Religious Belief* is that they were not written by Wittgenstein himself. They are notes taken by Yorick Smythies at lectures given by Wittgenstein in 1938. Moreover, Smythies does not vouch for their accuracy in every detail, for they are lecture-notes and not dictations from Wittgenstein. But they are the most extended account available of Wittgenstein's remarks on religion. Here I shall supplement them by reference both to Wittgenstein's enigmatic remarks on religion in his lecture on ethics given in Cambridge 'sometime between September 1929 and December 1930' and by reference to G. E. Moore's paragraph on Wittgenstein's remarks about 'God' from his notes on Wittgenstein's lectures from 1930–3.[3] The latter corresponds very closely to Wittgenstein's remarks in his 1938 lectures. His 'A Lecture on Ethics', however, still shows much more of the effect of the *Tractatus* than do the 1938 lectures or the remarks Moore has recorded.

Smythies' notes have the illusiveness yet the penetration and the capacity to challenge which we have come to expect from Wittgenstein. (It is not for nothing that Iris Murdoch has spoken of Wittgenstein's 'exasperating hints'.) Wittgenstein's remarks here, assuming (as I shall assume) that we can take them as his, are just that. They are not extended, carefully wrought arguments, but brilliant *aperçus* that drive one to reflection and suggest a new way of viewing the matter, but hardly ever convince by the sheer force of argument.

My interest in Wittgenstein's remarks are essentially two:

(1)   Do his own claims fit in the peg 'Wittgensteinian Fideism', and

(2)   Is what he says about religion true and does it help us in our quest to grasp the truth about religion?

I shall argue that the general tenor of Wittgenstein's remarks cut in the direction of Wittgensteinian Fideism, though a few, depending on how they are interpreted, cut in my direction; and I shall further argue that suggestive as Wittgenstein's remarks are, they are too fragmentary and apocalyptic in tone to be much more than exasperating hints.

I should like to begin by quoting what I take to be a very central remark at the beginning of Part II of his *Lectures on Religious Belief.*

The word 'God' is amongst the earliest learnt – pictures and catechisms, etc. But not with the same consequences as with pictures of aunts. I wasn't shown (that which the picture pictured).

The word is used like a word representing a person. God sees, rewards, etc.

'Being shown all these things, did you understand what this word meant?' I'd say: 'Yes and No. I did learn what it didn't mean. I made myself understand. I could answer questions, understand questions when they were put in different ways – and in that sense could be said to understand.'[4]

It is evident that here Wittgenstein is talking about a plain man's concept of God similar to the one Ziff talks about. It is also evident that the understanding Wittgenstein acknowledges of 'God' is the kind of understanding Ziff talks about, namely that, as a fluent speaker of two languages used in Christendom, he has a grasp of the linguistic regularities of 'God' and '*Gott*' and related terms. In that way he understands them – he made himself understand them. But it is significant that unlike Ziff, Wittgenstein also says 'No' about understanding such terms. This indicates that in an important sense he thinks he does not understand the concept of God. If my arguments against Ziff are correct, the kind of understanding Wittgenstein acknowledges of the concept of God is not adequate to establish or support a claim that, mysterious as it is, it is a coherent concept.

But why does Wittgenstein say that in a way he does *not* understand 'God'? Moreover, what is involved in understanding 'God' and generally in understanding religious belief that is not involved in more ordinary beliefs and with other terms? Wittgenstein, unlike Ziff, stresses that something very different is involved here.

In a passage immediately after the one I have just quoted, Wittgenstein makes some remarks that indicate how idiosyncratic he takes religious discourse to be. Pushed in a certain direction these claims could lead to the contention that we have in God-talk a *sui generis* mode of discourse that can only be understood and appraised in its own terms.

If the question arises as to the existence of a god or God, it plays an entirely different role to that of the existence of any person or object I ever heard of. One said, had to say, that one *believed* in the existence, and if one did not believe, this was regarded as something bad. Normally if I did not believe in the existence of something no one would think there was anything wrong in this.[5]

In the closing pages of his lectures Wittgenstein again returns to his theme that religious talk is *sui generis*.[6] To say 'There is a God in heaven', 'God created me and looks after me', 'We might see one another after death', is not, Wittgenstein insists, simply to express our attitudes and to try to evoke like attitudes in others.

Such a non-cognitivist approach does not do justice to the subtlety of the discourse. To say to a friend, on a parting that looks permanent, 'We might see one another after death' is not the same as saying 'I'm very fond of you'. But, Wittgenstein directly adds, 'it may not be the same as saying anything else. It says what it says. Why should you be able to substitute anything else?'[7]

The *sui generis* pitch apart, Wittgenstein, after the passage we quoted in *in extenso* above, goes on to point out, as he also pointed out in the first part of his lecture, that 'believe' in religious contexts has an extraordinary use. If a man says 'I believe in the Last Judgement', 'believe' in such a context does the work of 'faith' and not of 'suppose', 'have an opinion', 'opine' or 'have evidence that'. There is and can be nothing tentative about it, as there is in the ordinary case, yet it is not used here 'as we generally use the word "know"'.[8]

Wittgenstein makes a further claim – and similar claims are stressed by Wittgensteinian Fideists – when he asserts that 'Whatever believing in God may be, it can't be believing in something we can test or find means of testing.'[9] Wittgenstein parries the argument that this last remark of his is nonsense because people as a matter of fact do cite as evidence religious experiences or say that they believe on evidence; he rightly counters this by pointing out that, if someone *says* he believes on evidence that isn't enough to carry conviction, for his belief about his belief or use of language may be mistaken. He needs to be able to show that he so uses 'God exists' that something actually could count as unsatisfactory or insufficient evidence for it. Consider, by way of analogy, other cases. Suppose a lot of people stand in a ring, all hand in hand, and suppose *everyone* says he has seen one of his dead relatives on the other side of the ring. Suppose a sceptic asks everyone in the ring 'Whom did you hold by the hand?' and suppose *everyone* says that he held some living person by the hand and can state who it was. Now even if, after this fact is brought to the light, they all continue to *say* they saw a dead relative on the other side of the ring and *say* they have good evidence for believing they saw a dead relative, we would rightly not take their say-so in such a circumstance. After all, everyone also maintained in the hearing of everyone else that they held a living person by the hand in the ring. Similar things

would be said for 'I saw my dead cousin' or 'Dead undergraduate speaks' or 'Dean sleeps faster than Nixon'. Even if
someone maintains that they had an extraordinary experience
which confirms such an alleged statement, it is altogether
absurd to admit that they do have any evidence for it. To speak
of their alleged evidence as being insufficient, even grossly
insufficient, would be as absurd as saying one had made a
blunder in addition if one said '2 + 21 is 13'. But when someone
utters something like 'You'll see your dead friend again', Wittgenstein would *not* say that such a person is being superstitious,
he would just say 'Such an utterance does not mean much to me
at all. It's not a way that I would talk.' Similarly if someone
utters 'I believe I shall see my dead friend again' or 'I believe in
the Father and the Son and the Holy Ghost', one is using
'believe' in an extraordinary way – a way which indicates that
one's emotional reaction to the claim is crucial, but in which
questions of evidence have no living role at all.

   It is also crucial to note that when someone says 'I believe in
the Last Judgement' and another opposes him by replying 'I
don't', it need not at all be the case that the person who says 'I
don't' believes the opposite of the Last-Judgement man, namely that there won't be such a thing. It is not like one man
asserting 'I believe it will rain today' and another countering
with 'I don't'. If I'm the one saying 'I don't' to the Last-
Judgement man, I will – given my reasons for rejecting his belief
– be on what Wittgenstein calls an 'entirely different plane'. I
would, according to Wittgenstein, mean something altogether
different than does the man who gives voice to such a religious
belief.[10] Yet, paradoxically enough, 'the difference might not
show up at all in any explanation of the meaning.'[11] For the
religious man, it might be an unshakable belief, that is, an
unshakable conviction; but this would show itself not in what he
offers as evidence but in how it regulates his life. His belief may
be well-established in *that* distinctive way while, supposing he
has the temperament of a Kierkegaard, he may regard it as so
poorly established as an evidential claim as to be a scandal to
the intellect. The man who believes in the Last Judgement, on
the one hand, and a man like Wittgenstein or Russell, on the
other, may 'think differently, in a way', say different things to
themselves, 'have different pictures'. Be that as it may, Witt-

genstein maintains, it is wrong to say that they believe in opposite things and that they contradict each other.

> If you ask me whether or not I believe in a Judgement Day, in
> the sense in which religious people have believed in it, I
> wouldn't say: 'no. I don't believe there will be such a thing.'
> It would seem to me utterly crazy to say this.
>
> And then I give an explanation: 'I don't believe in
> . . . ', but then the religious person never believes what I
> describe.
>
> I can't say. I can't contradict that person.
>
> In one sense, I understand all he says – the English words
> 'God', 'separate', etc. I understand. I could say: 'I don't
> believe in this', and this would be true, meaning I haven't got
> these thoughts or anything that hangs together with them.
> But not that I could contradict the thing.
>
> You might say: 'Well, if you can't contradict him, that
> means you don't understand him. If you did understand him,
> then you might.' That again is Greek to me. My normal
> technique of language leaves me. I don't know whether to say
> they understand one another or not.[12]

Such controversies, Wittgenstein goes on to say, 'look quite
different from normal controversies'. Reasoning has a different
role here; such controversies are always quite inconclusive, and
there is no point in talking about evidence here. It appears at
least that Wittgenstein is denying that when people believe or
disbelieve in the Last Judgement or in God that they believe or
disbelieve in empirical propositions, for which evidence is in
principle relevant.[13] That is, such religious utterances are not
on Wittgenstein's account used to make empirical statements.
Wittgenstein tells us that if the belief in some sort of Judgement
Day was simply a prediction, 'belief in this happening wouldn't
be at all a religious belief.'[14] A believer might be perfectly aware
that the evidence against a belief in the Last Judgement is
overwhelming but believe in it all the same. Belief here plays
more the role of a directive concept. To come to have such a
belief comes down to having a conviction and to making a
decision concerning how to direct one's life.

This is why we speak of 'dogma' and 'faith' in such contexts rather than of 'hypothesis' or 'high probability' or 'knowing'. When it is said, for example, that Christianity rests on a historic basis, this is very misleading, for 'it doesn't rest on a historic basis in the sense that the ordinary belief in historic facts could serve as a foundation.'[15] Such religious beliefs 'are not treated as historical, empirical, propositions'.[16]

Should we, Wittgenstein asks, call religious people unreasonable? After all they base their belief on 'evidence which taken in one way seems exceedingly flimsy'.[17] Wittgenstein wants very much to avoid the rebuke that 'unreasonable' implies. He remarks in his 'Lecture on Ethics' that he takes his hat off to such people and that he would not for his life ridicule them.[18] But he also has said that 'they are certainly not reasonable, that's obvious.'[19] But this is so, because they don't, where they know what they are doing, 'treat this [that is a belief in something like the Last Judgement] as a matter of reasonability'.[20] Wittgenstein, like Kierkegaard, believes that those theologians and philosophers who try to make religious belief a matter of being reasonable are being ludicrous. 'Not only is it not reasonable, but it doesn't pretend to be.'[21]

At this point Wittengstein sounds a *leitmotif* of Wittgensteinian Fideism. He rhetorically asks: 'Why shouldn't one form of life culminate in an utterance of belief in a Last Judgement?' and he clearly implies that it perfectly well could.[22] Such a belief as a part of such a life would be perfectly in order. He, Wittgenstein, does not play this language-game and does not understand it very well. *In a sense* he does not understand it at all, for he could not say 'Yes' or 'No' or 'Perhaps' or 'I'm not sure' to the statement that such an event will come to pass.[23] All the same, in an important sense he does understand what such talk means – he has been able to read the accounts. It is not like his not being able to understand a language – a language foreign to him that he hears in the street or sees written in a book or newspaper. Moreover, he does not want to say there is anything wrong or incoherent about such a form of language embedded in such a form of life. Rather he wants to say that an atheist or a man who reasons very differently is in another system; his statements make very different connections. No direct conflict is possible. Of any of these systems, religious or non-religious, we cannot justifiably assert of the central beliefs embedded in their forms of life that they are either mistaken or blunders or incoherent. These are the kinds of remarks that we will find such Wittgensteinian Fideists as Winch, Phillips and Malcolm building on. They are classic expressions of that tradition. But Wittgenstein, characteristically enough, leaves us with this jarring remark:

> You could also say that where we are reasonable, they are not reasonable – meaning they don't use *reason* here.
> If they do something very like one of our blunders, I would say, I don't know. It depends on further surroundings of it.
> It is difficult to say, in cases in which it has all the appearances of trying to be reasonable.[24]

This remark is jarring because, while Wittgensteinian Fideists attempt to show that there is reasoning and reasonability in religion and over religious matters, though it is of a distinctive kind, Wittgenstein, quite differently, gives us to understand in that passage (or at least seems to) that they don't reason at all. Yet his talk about 'the appearance of trying to be reasonable' sits badly with this as well. We have here the kind of enigmatic remarks which I quote Murdoch as calling, not without reason, 'exasperating hints'.

Moore's remarks about Wittgenstein – his notes on Wittgenstein's 1930–3 lectures – indicate that Wittgenstein, like Ziff, stressed that 'God' is used in many grammatically different senses. And it is because of this that many controversies about God were really pseudo-controversies, which could be settled by one of the disputants pointing out that 'I'm not using the word in such a sense that you can say . . . .'[25] Moreover, where the issue is belief versus unbelief, the typical case is that of discovering they do not contradict each other. In fact in this sphere they cannot contradict each other – their use of religious language is too different. If some 'people use "god" to mean something like a human being, then "God has four arms" and "God has two arms" will both have sense . . . .'[26] Moreover, they will contradict each other – both statements cannot be true. But others, presumably most of us, use 'God' so that 'God has arms' is nonsense. When *such* people dispute with a man for whom 'God has two arms' is true or false, it is not the case that one can be said to say something false and the other something true, though at least one of them indeed claims to be saying something true-or-false. But *vis-à-vis* each other the two are in such different systems, play such different language-games, that it can only rightly be said that their beliefs are not comparable.

Taking into account the other things we have already noted about Wittgenstein, it is fair to say that he suggested another *leitmotif* of Wittgensteinian Fideism: There are many different forms of life with their characteristic forms of language. 'God' and cognate expressions are used differently in them and in some forms of life they are not used at all. Where the forms of life are radically different, there is no possible philosophical or rational standpoint in virtue of which we could appraise them or justifiably judge one to be correct or true or to be more reasonable than another. Here, if we are aware of what we are doing, we can only speak in the *first person* and give voice to our commitments.[27]

III

These remarks seem to make Wittgenstein into at least an ambivalent Wittgensteinian Fideist. He does, however, make remarks about pictures, God and similes worthy of note which have not been characteristic of much of Wittgensteinian Fideism. But they too culminate in a stress that could be used to support such a Fideism.

Take 'God created the world'. Wittgenstein asks us to reflect on Michelangelo making pictures of God creating the world: 'In general there is nothing which explains the meanings of words as well as a picture . . . .'[28] And *vis-à-vis* God creating the world, it is reasonable to expect that Michelangelo did as well as anyone would be likely to do in this respect. Here we have a picture of God creating Adam. But this must be taken in a very different way than a picture of Henry Moore making a bust, or a picture of a carpenter making a house. We must use Michelangelo's picture in a very different manner in order for it to be an instrument in teaching or learning the way Jews and Christians characteristically use 'God'. Someone who catches on to this talk doesn't call the man in the queer blanket 'God'. This is not a portrait of God in the way a given portrait might be a portrait of Stalin or Johnson. If we try to say, as some have, that we can *only* express what we mean by 'God' by means of pictures we are, Wittgenstein points out, in trouble. I might show someone a picture of a certain fish he has never seen and thus teach him what I mean (and what is meant) by 'a grayling'. Yet there is a technique which the person I am teaching must have mastered in order to be able to understand me – a technique of comparison between picture and fish. Moreover, to utilise such a technique here, graylings or fish very like graylings must have been available to *someone* at some time and we must know what it would be like for them to be available again. There must exist situations in which both picture and fish are or could be available to us to make the comparison. But with God we are told there are *only* the pictures; God is *never* available to us so that we could compare Him with our pictures. But then how can they either be or fail to be pictures of *God?* We cannot say that *x* is a picture of —————— where we cannot say what it pictures! Wittgenstein, however, does not draw what seems to me the inescapable conclusion, that is, that 'picture' is used incoherently in such religious contexts, but again takes the *sui-generis* line of a Wittengensteinian Fideist: 'It is quite clear that the role of pictures of Biblical subjects and the role of the picture of God creating Adam are totally different ones.'[29]

In his somewhat earlier, rather more positivist-sounding, lecture on ethics, Wittgenstein says similar things with similar Fideistic consequences about God-talk and similes. He tells us that a 'certain characteristic misuse of our language runs through all . . . religious expressions. All these expressions *seem*, *prima facie*, to be just similes.'[30] He adds that 'when we speak of God and that he sees everything and when we kneel and pray to him all our terms and actions seem to be parts of a great and elaborate allegory which represents him as a human being of great power whose grace we try to win, etc., etc.'[31] All religious terms seem to be used as similes or allegorically. But to say there is and can be no non-allegorical or non-literal reading of 'God' or 'God created the world' or 'In the Last Judgement your sins will be weighed' gets us into difficulties comparable to saying we can only understand what we talk about when we speak of God by means of pictures. Wittgenstein remarks in this earlier lecture that 'a simile must be the simile for something. And if I can describe a fact by means of a simile I must also be able to drop the simile and to describe the facts without it.'[32] But again religious discourse is idiosyncratic. What at first seem to be similes actually no more function as similes than what we have called 'pictures of God' actually function as pictures of God. Consider 'God created the world' or 'God shall raise the quick and the dead'. Here, as soon as we try to drop what appear to be the similes, the metaphorical and allegorical remarks, and simply state the facts which stand behind these putative non-literal remarks, 'we find that there are no such facts. And so, what at first appeared to be a simile now seems to be mere nonsense.'[33]

Yet Wittgenstein says that certain experiences that go with religious claims seem 'to have in some sense an intrinsic absolute value'.[34] Yet he also, at least in 1929–30, wants, or wanted, to say that it is nonsense to say this. Furthermore, he wants, or at least at one time wanted, to claim that these 'nonsensical expressions were not nonsensical because I had not yet found the correct expressions, but that their nonsensicality was their very essence. For all I wanted to do with them was just *to go beyond* the world and that is to say beyond significant language.'[35] In talking about religion we are thrusting against the limits of our language. Man has a deep urge to do so, but this is an urge doomed to frustration. There can be no knowledge of God; there can be no grasp of the ultimate meaning of life. Such a search is 'perfectly, absolutely hopeless'. Such thrusting against language, unavoidably involved in religious discourse, Wittgenstein concludes in this earlier lecture, is 'a tendency of the human mind which I personally cannot help respecting deeply and would not for my life ridicule it'.[36] Nevertheless, it remains the case that it is only a tendency of the human mind; it is not something which can give us knowledge or truth or even falsity, for humanly significant as this God-talk is, it is without literal sense. Yet these nonsensical remarks of religion, Wittgenstein told Waismann, are something which lie 'close to my heart'.[37]

We should recognise that there is a difference between Wittgenstein's 1938 lecture on religious belief and his 1929–30 lecture. The 1938 lecture is already moving – though ambivalently – in the direction of his *Philosophical Investigations*. In the lectures on religious belief, the role of pictures and pictorial talk seems to be such that Wittgenstein has in effect abandoned the claim that for a non-literal utterance to be intelligible it must be at least in principle alternatively expressible in some literal way. That is to say, on this view, which he appears to have abandoned, it must be at least possible to give some partial literal paraphrase which will show what the non-literal utterance says (what informational or what conceptual content it has). Though, from what he says in the lecture on religious belief, it is not at all evident how he thinks he has surmounted the difficulties raised in his lectures on ethics about such allegedly non-paraphrasable, non-literal utterances. There is no suggestion at all that such non-literal utterances are thought to express propositions, that is, claims which could be true or false.

The general problem carried over from his lecture on ethics is that while religious utterances appear to be *figurative*, there are very good reasons for believing that they actually do not even succeed in being figurative, for if they really were figurative they would also, at least in principle, be expressible in a non-figurative way. In his conversations with Waismann in 1930, Wittgenstein sounds almost like a Zen Master when he tells us that speech isn't even essential to religion and thus it is not crucial to religion whether religious utterances can be used to make, on the one hand, true or false statements or, on the other, nonsensical utterances. What is crucial here are the human attitudes and behaviour integral to religion.[38]

The remarks in the lecture on ethics about religious discourse being a misuse of language and about their being nonsense certainly fit neither with the general approach to language we find in the *Philosophical Investigations*, nor with Wittgensteinian Fideism. Rather, as Rhees points out, they still go back too much to the view of the *Tractatus*. In his 'Lecture on Ethics', Wittgenstein is still thinking of language as primarily descriptive and he is still operating with the belief that there is a single standard of intelligibility which is independent of any particular form of life or language-game. In fine, Wittgenstein is still of the opinion in this 1929–30 lecture that there is such a criterion of intelligibility underlying all languages and providing them with their fundamental criterion of intelligibility. This criterion of intelligibility, expressible by logic, is our key to what can be thought and said. However, we have seen that in his lecture on religious belief he had already, though not with any very considerable clarity, proceeded beyond this view.

Later Wittgenstein came to repudiate the views expressed in his lecture on ethics and Wittgensteinian Fideists also repudiate them. Moreover, there is no private meaning that religious language could have that would not be an integral part of the form of life in which such talk is embedded. And it could not be true, on Wittgenstein's later views, that the essence of religion could have nothing to do with speech. The very actions that are characteristically religious are so tied to the forms of language, which are embedded in or perhaps are constitutive of the forms of life, that there could be no understanding of religion at all, no religious behaviour even, without a grasp of religious language. The attempt in any way to pry them apart is senseless. We cannot, as the arch-Wittgensteinian Fideist, D. Z. Phillips, put it, 'have religion without religious discourse'.[39]

Still much of what Wittgenstein says about pictures, similes and nonsensicality can be, and would be, interpreted by a Wittgensteinian Fideist, and I believe by the later Wittgenstein himself, as obliquely attesting to the *sui-generis* character of religious discourse. God-talk must not be assimilated to any other kind of talk but must be understood in terms of its own logic. It is as complete as any other form of language or form of life or system of human communication. In saying this we are giving to understand, as Rush Rhees well puts it, 'that you fall into confusion if you try to provide a more ample and more perfect system for what may be said in it'.[40] To try to correct the person who plays this language-game, to try to say he is playing the wrong language-game or an incoherent language-game too much under the influence of a certain picture or set of pictures, would be, as Wittgenstein put it, 'philosophically arrogant'; rather all one should do *qua* philosopher is to characterise and clearly display the conventions that the language user, be he atheist or believer, wished to draw.[41] Again we are back to Wittgenstein's famous remark that philosophy leaves everything as it is.

The upshot of this indicates that Wittgenstein in certain key respects came to have many of the commitments of Wittgensteinian Fideists. (The crucial respects in which he differs from Wittgensteinian Fideists is that he nowhere indicates that he thinks religious claims can be either true or false and he thinks that it is a mistake to think of religious beliefs as being reasonable.) Do such Fideist claims give us a true insight into religion, do they help us to come to know the truth about religion or, what is a logically prior question, to know what we are asking for when we ask for 'the truth about religion'? I have already suggested that in certain respects they do: they teach us to attend to the *first-order* discourse in its live contexts; they warn us against trying to translate God-talk into some other kind of talk or against looking for some 'transcendental logic' that is the real logical form of God-talk. But I think there is also much to question and to criticise in Wittgenstein's account. In particular his claims about the autonomy and uncriticisability of the forms of life need to be examined. We should also look with a cold eye at the very notion of 'a form of life'. Does it become in Wittgenstein's hands and in the hands of his· followers an ill-defined term of art that leads us into the very kinds of conceptual confusion and philosophical evasion that Wittgenstein would have us avoid? Similar considerations apply to 'language-game'. What are we talking about here? And why should we accept the claim of conceptual sufficiency for all the forms of language? Indeed we must take as given the forms of language, but why exactly must we believe that such forms of language with their forms of life are beyond philosophical criticism? Why can't a given language-game be incoherent or absurd or simply the carry-over of superstitious beliefs?

These very questions of mine may embody mistakes and questionable assumptions of my own; at the very least, they tend to make things sound simpler than they are. Certainly a Wittgensteinian would, and indeed should, at the very least claim that. Wittgenstein, as I noted initially, does not in these lectures carefully argue for or clearly develop these Fideistic claims as some of his followers did. Since this is so, I shall postpone critical examination of central strands of Wittgensteinian Fideism until in the next two chapters I have stated the case for Wittgensteinian Fideism as powerfully as I can. But I will, in section IV of this chapter, critically inspect some of Wittgenstein's claims that are not developed by Wittgensteinian Fideists.

IV

Wittgenstein stressed that the statements that there is a God, that God created man in his image and likeness, and that there will be a Last Judgement are not empirically testable. Christianity claims to be a historical religion resting on a momentous historical fact – the Incarnation – but the central doctrinal statements of Christianity are not empirical propositions assessable in the way empirical statements about the past are assessable. If they were there could be a direct conflict between atheist and believer, but since they are not we must simply acknowledge that atheist and believer play different language-games.

This contention is criticisable on several grounds. It is not true that all believers always treat such beliefs as untestable. Consider the remarks of the twelfth-century poet Walther von der Vogelweide about the *Dies Irae*.

> Sleepers, awake! that day draws near
> on whose approach all Christendom and
> Jew and heathen must in terror wait.
> the signs are clear
> whereby we can detect its coming,
> even as the Word foretold.
> the sun no longer shows its light,
> perfidy spreads its seeds at night
> on all the roads:
> father is by his child betrayed
> and brother lies to brother;
> robed sanctity is fraudulent
> that should make straight heaven's highway;
> power mounts unchecked; justice before the court
> of justice dwindles.
> take heed! too long we've lain in slumber while
> God's judgements wait.

He not only says that experiences confirm when the Last Judgement is imminent, he shows what the confirmatory experiences are by describing situations – empirically identifiable situations – that would confirm it for him and others with similar beliefs.

In short he gives us evidence for or against asserting that there will be a Last Judgement and when it will occur. And his claim for his time is hardly an atypical claim.

Wittgenstein could indeed object that Walther von der Vogelweide's *saying* he has evidence for claiming that the Last Judgement is imminent does not establish that he has such evidence. Perhaps he is like the people in the circle who claim that they have seen a dead relative? But Vogelweide surely seems to have described conditions under which it would be correct to speak of the impending occurrence of the Last Judgement. The burden of proof is on Wittgenstein to show that we have no idea of what would count as evidence for such a belief.

Wittgenstein should have made the point John Wisdom has stressed that for more and more contemporary men religious beliefs like the Last Judgement are no longer treated as experiental or experimental issues. Better still, Wittgenstein should have said that they are only ambivalently treated as non-experiental issues. In certain situations (most notably in situations of a non-theoretical sort) they seem unwittingly to be treated as experiental issues. Walther von der Vogelweide's attitude remains in the background. And where they are not testable, there are problems about them which are not acknowledged by Wittgenstein. (This may seem like a dark saying but note how I develop and clarify it in my chapter 'On Fixing the Reference Range of "God" '.) Do not forget that Wittgenstein remains thoroughly perplexed by God-talk. He recognises that religious utterances are not just the expressions of fundamental convictions but that they are also *somehow* supposedly claims about what there is. But Wittgenstein is perplexed about what this comes to. The key religious utterances we have in mind try – though Wittgenstein asserts they must fail – to 'go beyond the world'; they are supposedly assertions yet they are not empirical propositions asserting that things stand thus and so and not otherwise. But how then can they be assertive of what there is – how could they possibly be true or false? And if they cannot be true or false how can they be assertions: how can they assert what there is?

Surely to deny 'God made the world' is an assertion about 'how things are', is to 'sublime God-talk', to give a perplexing discourse a *new* use and not, as Wittgenstein would have us do, to elucidate the use it has. It may indeed be true with some believers that their use of 'God' has undergone such a sublimation and this discourse has now become their *first-order* discourse. Think here of those believers who are taken up with Kierkegaard, Weil and Buber. But if their claims are totally non-experiental then how can, on their use or on any non-anthropomorphic use, 'God made the world' or 'The Last day of Judgement will come' or 'There is a God in heaven' be assertions – statements of fact? How can they be factual assertions unless they are at least in principle testable? There are indeed many questions here. Perhaps, after all, there are 'untestable statements of fact', but, at the very least, this is perplexing. Wittgenstein, making the claims he did, should have come to face these issues.

In his remarks about the reasonableness of religious belief, Wittgenstein sounds more like a Kierkegaardian than a Wittgensteinian Fideist. (Recall that von Wright points out that Wittgenstein was deeply influenced by Kierkegaard and Dostoevsky.) As I have already remarked, Wittgenstein in characterising religious belief wished to avoid the rebuke implicit in 'unreasonable'. Wittgenstein recognised and stressed that 'God' has a use in the language, that God-talk for many people is bound up with their sense of the meaning (significance) of life and that religious beliefs are to the believer of great emotional and ethical significance. But beyond that he could make nothing of such talk. He did not try to construe it in a non-cognitive way, but he still thought that religious beliefs were not reasonable – in the sense of being rationally intelligible – and he heaped great scorn on those who tried to prove the reasonableness of Christianity. (Father Corbishley's *Religion is Reasonable* would, as did the writings of Father O'Hara, certainly seem to Wittgenstein an absurdity.) Religion is not to be established by argument or to be shown by philosophical or any other kind of rationalisation to be rationally justified or even reasonable; it is simply to be lived or not lived; and whether one lives it or not is presumably dependent on what cultural circle one happens to be in or what one happens to commit oneself to. But these commitments, though they may be personally decisive, could on his own account only be arbitrary. That is to say, on his account there is and can be objectively speaking no ground for making one such commitment rather than another, though later Wittgenstein came to reject the identification of the groundless with the arbitrary.

Even if we grant Wittgenstein his point that Christian and Jew, Buddhist and Moslem, Theist and Atheist, do not directly contradict each other and are talking on different planes, it does not follow that they are all equally right or that no significant argument between them is possible. Euclidian and Lobatchevskian geometry do not conflict either, but there can be argument about which is better to use for aerial navigation. There is plenty of room for argument in such a case about what framework to adopt even if there are no logical contradictions between statements in such different frameworks.

The above account of Wittgenstein's is only plausible if the central claims of Wittgensteinian Fideism are well taken. That is to say: only if we can show that 'reason', 'reality' and 'evidence' are systematically ambiguous and form-of-life dependent, and only if we can establish that any form of life is beyond the scope of philosophical or rational criticism, can we have a rationale for such an account. Otherwise a counter that Wittgenstein would detest is quite apposite: it is a truism to say that we ought not to believe what is not reasonable. Religious belief is not reasonable. Therefore we ought to reject religious belief and people should stop being religious, for example, stop being Jews, Christians, Moslems and the like.

I said in the preceding paragraph that Wittgenstein's approach here depends in an important way on the tenability of Wittgensteinian Fideism and so it does, but in a way it is also natural for a Wittgensteinian to make a Jamesian–Kierkegaardian–Pascalian appeal too. Perhaps the most accurate thing to say is that both appeals to be convincing depend on each other. What I have in mind is this: when it is pointed out that religious belief is not reasonable there remains the Kierkegaardian–Pascalian defence which would show that in the case of religious belief it is reasonable *all told* to believe something which from a purely intellectual point of view it is not reasonable to believe in. The claim is, as we can most clearly see in Kierkegaard's *Sickness Unto Death*, that for a probing human being, a life without religious belief is senseless, quite without significance. Unless one can become a 'knight of faith', one cannot, if one is unblessed with being perceptive, avoid total despair and 'Sickness Unto Death'. Given this situation, the claim is that it is in the largest sense reasonable *vis-à-vis* religion to believe that which is not reasonable: one has the best of reasons for crucifying one's intellect *vis-à-vis* religious belief if only one can.

This familiar fideistic claim needs challenging. Why assume that without a belief in God life is intolerable? Many people in cultures other than our own have no conception of God or an 'afterlife' and yet these cultures have been as integrated as ours and within our culture there have been plenty of sceptics and atheists around for a long time who have not suffered Sickness Unto Death and who often have been very sensitive and perceptive human beings. Some, like Sartre, suffer from a need to believe in God, but they are by no means all in such a predicament. Wittgenstein spoke for himself, and speaking for myself, giving voice to my own feelings, I can say that I honestly feel not the slightest need for religious belief and I am not alone in that feeling. I have no doubt that many people do indeed suffer from the Pascalian syndrome and, given their set of attitudes, would be miserable without a belief in God. But this reveals something about how *they* were brought up and nothing about the very condition of man. There is no good anthropological or psychological evidence to believe that man must despair or remain basically unsatisfied until he can come to believe in God. We are not all hounded by the hound of heaven.

Finally, I want to draw attention to something rather special in Wittengenstein's remarks about religion. First note that Wittgenstein, neither as a human being nor as a philosopher, engaged in God-talk himself, though as a philosopher he quite appropriately talks about the talk about God. Only at the very end of his lecture on ethics, which he mingles confusedly with religion, does he speak for himself, give voice to his convictions. Though here he feels we are 'beyond all argument'. But here, in accordance with what I said above, we can query this claim, for 'irrational convictions', 'unjustified convictions', 'extravagant convictions', 'well-founded convictions', 'rational convictions' and even 'true convictions', whatever may be their proper analysis, are neither misuses of language nor pleonastic. Moreover, can Wittgenstein justify having the convictions he has concerning religion? Recall that while he does not engage in God-talk he moralises about religion and religious people. If he really believes, as at one time at least he did, that in speaking of God we are trying to go 'beyond the world' and that such talk is unintelligible, why should he have such a respect for those who are religious and for those who give into this tendency of the human mind? Why not take a Nietzschean or Russellian atti- tude toward religion? Why take off your hat to someone who persists in believing (more accurately, in claiming to believe) what, if Wittgenstein is right in his *above* claim, is demonstrably unintelligible? Why encourage people in this? Certainly one might respect religious believers for their integrity and, in some instances, for their battle to help men to overcome an excessive narcissism. But there are other ways of overcoming it, other ways of giving sense to human life. Why encourage a kind of ideology that rests on something that is incoherent ('beyond significant language')? Why, it might be thought, encourage man in his infantilism?

Presumably Wittgenstein would think that such a Humean–Russellian-type response is a superficial, rationalistic one. (Note his remark here about Schlick's ethics.[42]) Perhaps he would claim that of Nietzsche's or Feuerbach's responses as well. But why? What justification could he give for claiming that his own attitude was the deeper one? From his own theoretical remarks, one would think that whatever conviction one gave voice to over such matters would be arbitrary.

Why believe that a man with Pascal's or James's attitudes has a deeper, profounder grasp or vision of life than a man with Feuerbach's or Freud's? It looks as if Wittgenstein's own com- mitment here is on his own showing an arbitrary one. Yet presumably Wittgenstein did not think it was arbitrary. In some way he thought his attitudes were the right ones. But why are they the right ones – or are they the right ones?

Perhaps there is, and in the very nature of the case can be, no non-question-begging answers here. Perhaps no justification can be given for saying Wittgenstein's attitude was or was not deeper than Feuerbach's or Feuerbach's deeper than Wittgen- stein's? But then, if we are to keep our integrity, we should not insinuate anything about depth here.

Faced with such considerations Wittgenstein might have

said, as Phillips does, that whether they are or not is *not* a *philosophical* matter. Such an issue could never be settled by philosophy. But to say, 'It is not a philosophical matter' would be to engage in a *persuasive* definition of 'philosophy' and this, in turn, would require justification. To say that philosophy could not settle such questions or that no *rational* measures could settle them, would itself require philosophical justification; a philosophical justification which would have to come to rest on a full-blown acceptance and justification of the central theses of Wittgensteinian Fideism. It is to such claims that I shall now turn. But let me leave this reminder. Even if we are led – through a *persuasive* definition of 'philosophy' – to accept a characterisation of philosophy that would lead us to the conclusion that philosophical reasoning cannot resolve such issues, it still remains the case that human ratiocination most certainly appears to be relevant to our beliefs here. Whether or not we call such reasoning or argumentation 'philosophical' is a comparatively trivial issue.[43]

4

Wittgensteinian Fideism: I

I

What I call 'Wittgensteinian Fideism' emerges from certain remarks made by Winch, Rhees, Hughes, Geach, Malcolm, Holmer, Dilman, Holland, Cavell, Cameron, Coburn, Mounce and D. Z. Phillips.[1] Some of their contentions will serve as targets for my argumentation, for as much as I admire Wittgenstein, it seems to me that the fideistic conclusions drawn by these philosophers from his thought are often absurd. This leads me back to an inspection of their arguments and the premises in these arguments.

These philosophers argue that religious concepts can only be understood if we have an insider's grasp of the form of life of which they are an integral part.[2] As Malcolm puts it, the very genesis of the concept of God grows out of a certain 'storm in the soul'. Only within a certain form of life could we have the idea of an 'unbearably heavy conscience' from which arises the Judaeo-Christian concept of God and of a 'forgiveness that is beyond all measure'. If, as Malcolm maintains, one does not have a grasp of that form of life from 'the inside not just from the outside' and if, as an insider, one does not have 'at least some inclination to *partake* in that religious form of life', the very concept of God will seem 'an arbitrary and absurd construction'. There cannot be a deep understanding of the concept of God without 'an understanding of the phenomena of human life that gave rise to it'.[3]

Much of what Malcolm says here is unquestionably true. For

years anthropologists have stressed, and rightly, that one cannot gain a deep understanding of the distinctive features of a tribe's culture without a participant's understanding of the way of life of that culture. Concepts cannot be adequately understood apart from a grasp of their function in the stream of life. If a man has no experience of religion, has never learned God-talk where 'the engine isn't idling', he will not have much of an understanding of religion. But having such an understanding of religion is perfectly compatible with asserting, as did the Swedish philosopher Axel Hägerström, that the concept of God is 'nothing but a creation of our own confused thought' growing out of our need to escape 'from the anxiety and wearisomeness of life'.[4] And this comes from a philosopher who, as C. D. Broad's biographical remarks make evident, was once thoroughly immersed in the religious stream of life.

Malcolm's above contention is only one of the Wittgensteinian claims that I shall examine. The following cluster of dark sayings have, when they are accepted, a tendency to generate what I call Wittgensteinian Fideism.

(1)   The forms of language are the forms of life.

(2)   What is *given* are the forms of life.

(3)   Ordinary language is all right as it is in the contexts of its standard employment and for an understanding of those contexts.

(4)   A philosopher's task is not to evaluate or criticise language or the forms of life, but to describe them where necessary and to the extent necessary to break philosophical perplexity concerning their operation.

(5)   The different modes of discourse which are distinctive forms of life all have a logic of their own.

(6)   Forms of life taken as a whole are not subject to criticism; each is in order as it is, for each has its own criteria and each sets its own norms of intelligibility, reality and rationality.

(7)   These general, dispute-engendering concepts, that is, intelligibility, reality and rationality, are systematically ambiguous; their exact meaning can only be determined in the context of a determinate way of life.

(8)   There is no Archimedean point in terms of which a philo-

sopher (or for that matter anyone else) can relevantly criticise a whole form of life or a way of life. He cannot even criticise a whole mode of discourse, for each mode of discourse as each form of life has its own specific criteria of rationality/irrationality, intelligibility/unintelligibility, and reality/unreality.[5]

A Wittgensteinian Fideist who accepted such contentions could readily argue that religion is a unique and very ancient form of life with its own distinctive criteria. It can only be understood or criticised, and then only in a piecemeal way, from within this mode by someone who has a participant's understanding of this mode of discourse. To argue, as I do and as C. B. Martin has, that the very *first-order* discourse of this form of life is incoherent or irrational can be nothing but a confusion, for it is this very form of life, this very form of discourse itself, which sets its own criteria of coherence, intelligibility or rationality. Philosophy cannot relevantly criticise religion; it can only display for us the workings, the style of functioning, of religious discourse.

I agree with such Wittgensteinians that to understand religious discourse one must have a participant's understanding of it. But this does not entail that one is actually a participant, that one *accepts* or *believes* in the religion in question. (Here Max Weber showed a more acute understanding of the conditions requisite for understanding religious discourse than do the Wittgensteinian Fideists.) But I do *not* agree that the *first-order* discourse of religion is – indeed must be – in order as it is, and I do not agree that philosophy cannot relevantly criticise religions or forms of life.

II

In discussing C. B. Martin's *Religious Belief*, G. E. Hughes has defended in an incisive way the claim that as a whole rock-bottom, religious utterances or propositions are in order as they are.[6] He does not claim that they are *all* in order but only that generally speaking they are.

Hughes starts by asking what are our criteria for conceptual confusion when we claim that *en bloc first-order* religious propositions are in conceptual disarray. He remarks, 'I should guess that it is possible to show any category of statements or expressions to be conceptually confused if one is allowed to insist that they must conform to the logic of some other category or categories of statements or expressions if they are to be said to make sense.[7] Max Black and a host of others have made it evident that if we try to treat inductive reasonings as if they were deductive ones, we would make nonsense of them. Similarly, if we try to construe moral statements as if they were empirical statements, and moral reasoning as if it were scientific reasoning, we would make nonsense out of morality. We have learned to treat these concepts and modes of reasoning as being *sui-generis*; inductive reasonings and moral reasoning have, in the sense Ryle uses 'logic', a logic of their own. Our job as philosophers is to come to understand and display that logic, not to distort it by trying to reduce it to the logic of some other preferred type of discourse or to try to interpret it in terms of some ideal language such as that found in *Principia Mathematica*. We should, Hughes argues, in doing the philosophy of religion adopt 'an alternative programme for meta-theology . . . that . . . consists in allowing the actual use of religious terms and statements to determine their logic, rather than trying to force an alien logic upon them.'[8] Hughes remarks that if we adopt this programme rather than the one Martin adopts (a programme similar to the one I have adopted) our philosophical arguments about religion can be seen in quite different light. Arguments which show how religious statements generate contradictions when they are construed on the model of other types of statements 'can now be construed as showing some of the peculiarities of their own logic'.[9]

Hughes illustrates his argument with an example from Chapter Four of Martin's *Religious Belief*. Martin argues there (pp. 40–1) that 'God' may be used in either of two ways: as a proper name referring to a particular being (a name such as 'Charles' or 'Sven') or as a descriptive term. Martin tries to show that using it in both ways at once leads to a contradiction. Hughes then remarks that Martin 'makes out a massive and powerful case for this contradictoriness *provided that the alternatives are as he states them*'.[10] That is to say, Martin's remarks are well taken about 'proper names and descriptive phrases *as applied to particular things*.[11] But these acute remarks are beside the point, Hughes contends, for God is not thought of as a 'particular thing' within orthodox Jewish and Christian thought. The 'patterns of what makes sense and what does not, in the case of names and descriptions of particular things, does not fit the pattern of usage of the word "God" on the lips of believers.'[12] Here Hughes's stress is very like the one we saw Wittgenstein making. It is, he maintains, about as sensible to speak of God as a particular being, as it is to speak of the number 18 or perfect moral virtue as a particular being.

Hughes maintains that, on the approach Martin advocates and I advocate, 'the fact that the pattern of usage of a term such as "God" does not accord with that of other non-theological terms with which it is taken to be analogous, is made a basis for the charge that that use of the term is logically incoherent.'[13] But on Hughes's programme – a good programme for a Wittgensteinian Fideist – the 'same non-accordance is regarded as showing that the terms are not as analogous as they have at first appeared, and the actual usage of religious terms within religious language is taken as normative for the logical type and the kind of meaning they have.'[14] Hughes goes on to remark that 'which of these programmes is preferable is perhaps the most important question for meta-theology (even, *mutatis mutandis*, for all meta-theorising)'.[15]

Hughes defends his crucial Wittgensteinian methodological preference on the grounds that religious language is a long-established *fait accompli*, and something which does a job which no other segment of language can do. It is because of this that he is tempted to think that religious statements are in order just as they are, that is, in their own kind of order, and, as a whole, in a coherent order.[16] This is a significant claim the ramifications of which I will later consider in detail, but for the moment I shall content myself with a brief sociological remark. We should counterpose against the fact that religious language is a *fait accompli* another fact, namely that at all times and at all places, even among the most primitive tribes, there have been sceptics and scoffers, people who, though perfectly familiar with the religious language-game played in their culture, would not play the religious language-game, not because they could not, but because, even though they had an insider's understanding of it, they found, or thought they found, it incoherent. But our *first-order* operations with what some *philosophers* call 'material object talk' and our actual operations with arithmetic are not in this state of controversy. (Meta-mathematics may be in a shambles, but not arithmetic or algebra.) In this respect religion is very different. There are people who can play the language-game, even people who *want* very much to go on playing the language-game of religion, but they morally and intellectually speaking cannot continue this activity because their intellects, not their natural sympathies, make assent to Jewish or Christian doctrine impossible. Moreover, their doubts are often much older than their acquaintance with theology or philosophy and they were only reinforced by their acquaintance with these disciplines. There are people – and among the educated a continually growing number of people – who find, or at least think they find, the religious language-game they have been taught as children either nonsense or at best, in Santayana's celebrated phrase, 'moral poetry'. We should remember here the powerful case that Weber makes for the inevitability of *Entzauberung* (the demystification of the world) in the social evolution of societies. Such considerations seem to me to count heavily, though *surely* not decisively, against thinking that at rock-bottom such talk must have a coherent order.

Hughes's other consideration, that is, that religious language does a job which no other segment of language can do, is more troubling. The truth of this very claim could be challenged, but this is not something I wish to do at this juncture. Rather I want simply to point out that in a culture such as ours, religious discourse is coming to fail to do its distinctive tasks because many people do not find it coherent. Perhaps they are profoundly deceived; perhaps it is after all a perfectly coherent mode of discourse, but, given their beliefs, to point out to them that such a language-game is played is not enough. They perfectly well know how to use this discourse; they know that it is an ancient and venerated part of their culture; they know that it has a distinctive role in their culture. Knowing so well how to play the language-game, their very perplexity is over the at least apparent incoherence of just this familiar discourse. They are not in Moore's position: it is not as if they are simply puzzled by what Bradley and other philosophers said about time but it is as if they were perplexed about time themselves. After all a man could be puzzled about the correct analysis of 'time' without being puzzled about time. People in religious perplexity often are puzzled first and primarily about the very *first-order* God-talk itself and only secondarily about the theologian's or philosopher's chatter about this chatter. Moreover, if one looks over the range of practices that have counted as religions (if one looks at Confucianism and Therevada Buddhism for example) one finds functioning in cultures, and very ancient cultures at that, religions that in terms of our religions (not just in terms of our theologies) are atheistic or agnostic. Given this, it is perfectly possible that certain *ersatz* religions, for example, Spinoza's, Fromm's and perhaps even Comte's 'atheistical Catholicism', could, given certain cultural conditions, become religions. But given these facts and these possibilities, the fact – if it is a fact – that religious discourse does a job no other segment of discourse can do, does little to show that Christian or Islamic or Jewish *first-order* God-talk or any God-talk at all is in a coherent order just as it is.

Hughes could reply that the part of religious talk that is in order just as it is, is what is really alive in religion; it is such discourse which is essential to religion, constitutive of 'True Religion', that is, that which is shared by all these religions and by *ersatz* religions as well. But if this reply is made we are likely to end up (1) with a very unWittgensteinian essentialist bogeyman, and (2) with treating religion or 'True Religion' as little more than 'morality touched with emotion', that is, Santayana's 'moral poetry'. Given that the Christian Creed as well as the Christian code is crucial to Christianity, as understood by the orthodox, such a conclusion would be most unwelcome, and would, in effect, be a capitulation to the meta-theologian who claimed that Christian discourse, as it stands, is incoherent and not a vindication of the meta-theological claim that the bulk of Christian language is perfectly in place if only metaphysicians and theologians would not tinker with it.

I do not claim that anything I have said against Hughes settles anything very fundamental. So far, I have only tried to show that there is something to be settled and that we cannot take this short Wittgensteinian way with the concepts of religion. The central considerations here are (1) is the *first-order*

God-talk of Judaism, Christianity or Islam actually, for the most part anyway, in order as it is, or is it in some way fundamentally incoherent, and (2) how could we decide this issue? These issues need a careful conceptual investigation.

III

Someone might continue to insist that religion is indeed a *fait accompli*. The trouble is that we have not understood how this is so; we do not even have a tolerably clear command of the most fundamental uses of religious discourse. Hughes has missed it and both theologians and anti-theologians have blurred our vision about the workings of our language in religious contexts. However, if we come to understand the unique functions of religious discourse, we will feel the full weight of Hughes's claim. At best arguments like Martin's, Hepburn's and presumably mine show what religion cannot do, that is, give us 'cosmological information'. But they fail to catch what it does do and so fail to show that as a whole or generally *first-order* religious discourse is in disorder.

Robert Coburn, it might be contended, fills this lacuna or at least takes an important first step toward filling it in his 'A Neglected Use of Theological Language' by characterising the distinctive set of functions of religious discourse.[17] In doing this he could provide an important support for Wittgensteinian Fideism just where Hughes fails.[18]

It is Coburn's contention that there is a distinctive but neglected feature of religious discourse which would, if duly noted, serve to characterise the *sui-generis* nature of the discourse, help to break perplexity about religion and show that religious discourse is in order as it is. To see that this is so is to see that religious discourse has its own distinctive kind of order – an order that traditional accounts, both sceptical and non-sceptical, have failed to account for, though traditional non-sceptical accounts tend in effect to defer to this use in an unwitting and reified manner.

I shall argue that Coburn's account catches at best only a necessary condition for religious discourse. I shall further contend that Coburn gives us an analysis which is in effect a reductive analysis that leaves out of account certain distinctive features of religious discourse and that it is just these features which Coburn neglects which generate distrust about the coherence of *first-order* God-talk. Thus such an analysis does not effectively support Wittgensteinian Fideism.

In trying to explicate one central use of religious discourse, Coburn calls to our attention a distinctive type of question for which religious utterances normally provide an 'answer'.[19] Following Stephen Toulmin, he calls this type of question a *limiting question*. To be limiting questions, utterances or inscriptions must have the grammatical structure of questions, but they can ask neither straightforward theoretical questions, for example, 'What are the laws of thermodynamics?' nor practical questions, for example, 'Should I vote for the New Democrats?' Limiting questions are never literal questions. Instead they express 'some "inner" passion or action', for example, 'Why did she have to die of cancer just now when finally they had got together after all those years?', uttered when one knows perfectly well why she died of cancer.

Consider some responses to 'What is the ultimate significance of life?' or 'What is the explanation of the fact that there is a world at all?' There are contexts in which these questions are asked where there is no straightforward answer or where no literal answer is possible, but where the person who engages in such linguistic performances is not conceptually confused about the meanings of the terms involved.[20] Such utterances arise out of despair or anger or grief – out of 'turmoil of soul' – or what occasions them may be the engaging in a 'spiritual' activity 'such as marvelling or worshipping or blaspheming'. Here we catch religious discourse in one of its typical employments; and here religious limiting questions find their natural home.

These questions, Coburn contends, fall into three main types arising in response to three types of problems: 'moral problems, problems of morale, and problems concerning the ultimate significance or "meaning" of things'.[21] By 'moral problems', Coburn has in mind typical philosophical normative ethical problems; by 'problems of morale', he means those problems 'which arise out of our inability to reconcile ourselves to the various ills that flesh is heir to – sickness, failure, missed opportunities, and the final, ineluctable frustration of death – death of friends and family and ultimately of our own death.'[22] The last category of limiting question is the kind of question raised by questioners such as Tolstoy's Pierre who are trying to find an intelligible pattern in experience which gives life a coherence or enduring worth.

More generally, religious limiting questions belong to that 'class of limiting questions the asking of which constitutes behavior which is part of the (or a) criterion of having a problem of one or more of the above three kinds.'[23] The discourse used in response to such questions is, according to Coburn, religious discourse. To understand that religious discourse is employed in response to such questions is to understand its use in the stream-of-life. Religious statements provide logically complete answers to religious limiting questions.

This notion of a logically complete answer may require some explanation. 'I enjoy Mozart' is a logically complete answer to 'Why are you listening to that record?' and 'Why do you listen to the music you enjoy?' is an inappropriate question in this context. Similarly in a religious context 'Why did they all have to die on their birthdays?' is completely answered by 'The ways of the Almighty and All-Wise God are righteous, though beyond our understanding'. To say 'So what? Why does this "explain" or make acceptable their deaths?' indicates that either one does not understand or that one does not *accept* certain key religious statements, for *within the religious form of life* there is no room for such a question.

'Why does anything exist?', 'Why is the world the way it is?', 'Why is it my duty to keep promises?', and 'Why is life so hard and cruel?' are religious limiting questions. They are, as Kierkegaard would say, from the emotions, they involve our deepest and most intimate concerns. It is crucial to note here that religious utterances have a key role to play in providing logically complete answers to such emotionally harassing limiting questions. Such religious utterances, as Wittgenstein in effect pointed out as well, are directive of our behaviour.

Noting and taking to heart these elements in our discourse helps make plain some things that would otherwise be paradoxical: why it is that to know God is either to love Him, fear Him or hate Him, why it is impossible to believe in God without responding to Him in some affective way, why it is impossible to have faith in God without having a worshipful attitude toward

Him and without responding to Him in contrition and thankful praise. That religious statements are answers to limiting questions also accounts for the fact that the believer is continually threatened with loss of faith, for example, 'Oh Lord, I believe, help Thou my unbelief'. Beliefs from the emotions will have that quality and they will give rise to limiting questions. In short to recognise that religious statements are answers to limiting questions is to recognise why it is they could – logically could – not fail to be inextricably linked with the passions. In this way religious questions differ from purely cosmological questions.

An understanding that religious questions are limiting questions also explains why in the theological tradition there has been 'the persistent tendency to understand God as an essentially mysterious entity, as a being of such a nature that all our words, not simply in fact, but necessarily fail adequately to describe or characterise Him, except, of course, insofar as they are used to say what He is not.'[24] To reason in the way these theologians have, is, Coburn claims, to commit a kind of *descriptivist fallacy*. That is to say, these theologians are making an error (not strictly speaking a 'fallacy') comparable to Moore's talking of non-natural qualities. In short there is a kind of reification.

The commission of this error by theologians obscures the fact that religious claims, as answers to limiting questions, are attitude-expressing. If we try to treat religious discourse as being descriptive in the same way our talk of bodily movements or animal behaviour is descriptive, we will fail to catch the distinctive attitude expressing and evoking function of religious discourse. The confused theological claim that 'God' refers to an essentially mysterious non-temporal, non-spatial transcendent entity or force arose out of a failure to take proper note of this non-descriptive function of discourse coupled with a dim but confused recognition that some added element is integral to religious talk. It is this recognition that religious talk has some distinctive element not retained by ordinary empirical statements 'about how things are', that makes the theologian, who fails to grasp the non-descriptive function of his discourse, reify his religious conceptions and try to say what is in reality incoherent, namely that language can refer totally beyond all possible experience – that it can refer 'out of the world' altogether.

But these are but the reified shadows cast by a failure to recognise that religious statements are answers to limiting questions.

Coburn's analysis makes an important point above the non-descriptive, non-cognitive functions of religious discourse, but his account will hardly do as an adequate explication of religious or theological discourse. It does not, I shall argue, catch the distinguishing traits, if any, of religious discourse and it does not even show that such discourse is *sui generis*. Coburn indeed calls attention to a genuine element in religious discourse to which attention should be called, but stressing this element as exclusively as he does obscures the fact of something equally essential, namely the crucial putatively assertional content in certain key religious utterances. Moreover, his characterisation of 'religion' is much too broad.

It is perfectly correct to point out that for those who are committed to this form of life and who are reasoning in its confines, certain limiting questions cannot be asked within that mode of life. But an acknowledgement of the existence and role of this neglected feature of religious discourse will not put to rest puzzles about the *mysterium tremendum* or the 'ineffability' of God. Jews and Christians conceive of God as transcendent to the world. His reality is thus perforce of a very distinctive sort: God is indeed *not* conceived as an entity alongside of other entities; He is infinite yet particular and utterly unique; He is transcendent, yet He is everywhere. It is this very strange metaphysical characterisation of God built into our very *first-order* God-talk which 'explains' the fact that certain theological statements provide logically complete answers to religious limiting questions. It is this fact about what 'God' supposedly refers to and not the fact that theological statements provide logically complete answers to religious limiting questions, that provides us with an understanding of why God is taken to be 'an essentially mysterious entity'. There is and can be no adequate purely empirical characterisation of 'God' because of this very metaphysical and very puzzling conception of God. It is this which makes both God and God-talk *sui generis*. The mysteriousness of God, the essential elusiveness of God-talk, is not accounted for at all by Coburn. At best he shows that there is a mistake in the theologian's account of why God is taken to be mysterious.

'God' is indeed irreplaceable by non-theological or non-religious descriptions. Talk of 'God' is very unlike talk of 'Stones', 'Jones' or 'photons'. But to account for the differences between 'God' and 'John' or 'Fido' and to bring out the most characteristic uses of religious utterances, it is not sufficient simply to move away from a purely descriptivist understanding of the uses of theological sentences to a claim that religious utterances are also attitude-expressing, attitude-moulding and action-guiding. 'God' has come to have these non-descriptivist functions because 'God' supposedly denotes a transcendent supremely wise and powerful being or reality. Moreover, if believers gave up this belief *about* what they mean, 'God' would in time cease to have that use. Yet it is exactly such talk about the denotation of 'God' that remains so utterly perplexing. Such discourse most certainly does not seem to be in order just as it is. And the very non-descriptive features of 'God' are dependent for their continued force on its *alleged* descriptive meaning. But where 'God' is used non-anthropomorphically it is most difficult, if not impossible, to say what descriptive meaning it does have. The suspicion arises and persists that it may not have any. It may only be *putatively* descriptive – an allegedly descriptive or designative word which actually fails to describe or designate.

Coburn's analysis of 'religion', 'being religious' and of 'religious limiting questions' suffers surprisingly enough a defect not unlike Tillich's. Certainly, problems posed by conflicting moral outlooks, problems concerning attitudes toward death or failure, and problems about finding an intelligible pattern in experience which will enable us to see our lives as a whole and as something possessing enduring worth are typically connected with religious answers and religious questions. But the connection is a contingent one and not a necessary one. Marx, Freud, Santayana, Dewey and Sartre wrestled with such problems and did not give religious answers. 'A religious *Weltan-schauung*' is not a pleonasm and 'an a-religious or anti-religious moral outlook or attitude toward death' is perhaps mistaken, but it is not a contradiction. Indeed 'being religious' connotes 'having a certain commitment', 'a certain inwardness', 'taking the deep things of life seriously', but these latter terms do not connote 'being religious'. Coburn tells us that we understand 'being religious' by reference to such things as the disposition to live agapistically, to exhibit hope in times of tragedy, to take the deep things of life seriously, to engage in worshipful practices of a formal and/or an informal sort, and periodically to entertain or have in mind various of the pictures, sayings, parables, doctrines, etc., of some religious tradition.[25]

But Comte and Santayana neatly fulfilled all these criteria while remaining atheists. To be religious it is not enough to entertain or have in mind certain religious doctrines, we must in addition believe they are *true*. And a Russell or a Dewey or a Feuerbach can, as well as a religious man, be disposed to 'live agapistically and exhibit hope in times of tragedy'. We must not, if we have respect for clarity, convert them into religious believers by stipulative redefinition.[26] Such attitudes, actions or commitments are not *sufficient* to mark off the sphere of the religious and thus are not sufficient to mark off a religious limiting question. There is religious *doctrine* as well, and it is here where the language-game we play with religion begins to get puzzling and perhaps incoherent.

Coburn wishes to mark off a religious use of language by way of an analysis of religious limiting questions which will free our understanding of at least some parts of religion from these doctrinal perplexities. But like the repressed they return to plague him for he is not able to specify adequately what counts as 'a *religious* limiting question'. Thus without taking into account religious doctrines and cosmological claims Coburn cannot get started on his analysis and without them he cannot finish it either, for he cannot explain in a sufficiently complex way why non-theological or non-religious descriptions never adequately characterise 'God'. Wittgenstein, as we saw, also recognised this non-descriptive function of religious discourse, but he never thought it could account for everything that religious utterances purportedly express.

Religions, as systems of salvation, do, as Coburn stresses, bring into play focal attitudes. There is no understanding of religion without understanding that. But these systems of salvation also have doctrinal schemes. Scandal to the intellect or not, they all – even Therevada Buddhism – have certain concepts which are transcendental, that is, concepts whose non-normative aspects are not completely explicable in naturalistic terms. Coburn, as his other essays make apparent, is highly sceptical about the coherence of such religious or theological discourse.[27] The use of religious discourse he attempts to explicate in 'A Neglected Use of Theological Language' tries to avoid such pitfalls, but we cannot adequately characterise theological or religious discourse without reference to such problematical conceptions and thus implicitly raising the very non-Wittgensteinian question: is such *first-order* God-talk itself in conceptual disarray? Thus Coburn's account cannot justifiably be used to support Wittgensteinian Fideism.

IV

So far we have not been able to make Wittgensteinian Fideism very compelling. However, I think the issues Hughes raises, but does little to develop, are pursued in a brilliant and even more challenging manner by Peter Winch.[28] Winch does not directly attack the problem of the intelligibility of God-talk. Rather, in examining what it is to understand radically different concepts from our own, Winch brings to the fore considerations which are central to an understanding and appraisal of Wittgensteinian Fideism.

In coming to grips with what it is to understand a primitive society, Winch examines the Azande conception of magic and subjects Evans-Pritchard's methodological remarks concerning it to a careful critical scrutiny. Evans-Pritchard indeed insists that in order to understand the Azande conceptions we must understand them in terms of how they are taken by the Azande themselves and in terms of their own social structure, that is, forms of life. But he ceases to make common cause with Wittgenstein and Winch when he argues that none the less the Azande are plainly labouring under an illusion. There is no magic and there are no witches. We know that we, with our scientific culture, are right about these matters and the Azande are wrong. Our scientific account of these matters is in accord with objective reality while the Azande magical beliefs are not.

This certainly seems like a scarcely disputable bit of common sense, but Winch is not satisfied with such an answer. While trying to avoid what he calls a Protagorean relativism 'with all the paradoxes that involves', Winch maintains that, though Evans-Pritchard is right in stressing that 'we should not lose sight of the fact that men's ideas and beliefs must be checkable by reference to something independent – some reality', he is 'wrong, and crucially wrong, in his attempt to characterise the scientific in terms of that which is in accord with objective reality'.[29] Evans-Pritchard's mistake is in thinking that, while the Azande have a different conception of reality than we do, our scientific conception agrees with what reality actually is like while theirs does not.[30]

Winch, moving from counter-assertion to argument, contends that 'the check of the independently real is not peculiar to science'.[31] It is a mistake to think, as Evans-Pritchard and Pareto do, that scientific discourse provides us with 'a paradigm against which to measure the intellectual respectability of other modes of discourse'.[32] Winch uses an example from religious discourse to drive home his point. God, when he speaks to Job out of the whirlwind, takes Job to task for having lost sight of the reality of God. Winch remarks that we would badly misunderstand that passage if we thought that Job had made some kind of theoretical mistake, which he might have corrected by further observation and experiment. Yet, Winch argues, God's reality is independent of human whim or of what any man cares to think about it.

In this context Winch makes a very revealing remark – a remark that could readily be used to put a Wittgensteinian Fideism into orbit. What God's reality amounts to, Winch says, 'can only be seen from the religious tradition in which the concept of God is used'.[33] Such a religious context is very unlike a scientific context in which we can speak of theoretical entities. Yet only within the religious use of language does 'the conception of God's reality have its place'.[34] As the concept of what is real or what is unreal vis-à-vis magic is only given within and only intelligible within the Azande form of life in which the Azande magical practices are embedded, so the concept of God's reality is only given within and only intelligible within the religious form of life in which such a conception of God is embedded. In both there is an ongoing form of life that guarantees intelligibility and reality to the concepts in question. God and Azande magic are not *simply* my ideas or Jewish or Azande

ideas. Here we have baldly stated a major motif in Wittgensteinian Fideism.

'What is real?' or 'What is reality?', like 'What is there?', do
not have a clear sense. When asked in a completely general way
these 'questions' are without a determinate sense. We can only
raise the problem of the reality of something within a form of
life. There is no extralinguistic or context-independent conception of reality in accordance with which we might assess or
evaluate forms of life.

> Reality is not what gives language sense. What is real and
> what is unreal shows itself in the sense that language has.
> Further, both the distinction between the real and the unreal
> and the concept of agreement with reality themselves belong
> to our language.[35]

Yet these distinctions, though surely not the words used to
make them, would, Winch argues, have to be a part of any
language. Without such distinctions we could not have a system
of communication and thus we could not have a language. But
how the distinction between the real and the unreal is to be
drawn is determined by the actual linguistic usage of some
particular language. Evans-Pritchard and the man who would
reject the whole mode of God-talk as unintelligible or incoherent are both unwittingly saying something that does not make
sense, for their own conceptions of reality are *not* determined by
the actual usage of 'reality' and they are mistakenly assuming
that their very specialised use of 'reality' is something they can
use as a yardstick with which to appraise any and every form of
life. But they have given us no reasons for adopting this procedure or making this assumption.

If we have been brought up in a certain tradition and understand scientific discourse, we can, while working in that discourse, ask whether a certain scientific hypothesis agrees with
reality. We can, given an understanding of science, test this
claim; but when Evans-Pritchard makes the putative statement
that 'Criteria applied in scientific experimentation constitute a
true link between our ideas and an independent reality', he has
not asserted a scientific hypothesis or even made an empirical
statement. His putative assertion is not open to confirmation or

disconfirmation; and if 'true link' and 'independent reality' are explained by reference to the scientific universe of discourse, we would beg the question of whether scientific experimentation, rather than magic or religion, constitutes a true link between our ideas and an independent reality. Winch points out that there seems to be no established use of discourse by means of which the expressions 'true link' and 'independent reality' in Evans-Pritchard's assertion can be explained. At any rate – and to put Winch's contention in a minimal way – Evans-Pritchard does not give these expressions a use or show us that they have a use. Thus when we try to say that the idea of God makes no true link with an 'independent reality' we are using 'true link' and 'independent reality' in a meaningless or at least a wholly indeterminate way.

This argument is reinforced by a further claim made by Winch in his *The Idea of a Social Science*. There Winch sets forth a central plank in any Wittgensteinian Fideism. Logic, as a formal theory of order, must, given that it is an interpreted logic (an interpreted calculus), systematically display the forms of order found in the modes of social life. What can and cannot be said, what follows from what, is dictated by the norms of intelligibility embedded in the modes of social life. These finally determine the criteria of logical appraisal. Since this is so, 'one cannot apply criteria of logic to modes of social life as such.'[36] Science is one such mode and religion another; 'each has criteria of intelligibility peculiar to itself.' Within science or religion an action can be logical or illogical. It would, for example, be illogical for a scientist working in a certain area to refuse to take account of the results of a properly conducted experiment; and it would also be illogical for a man who believed in God to try to pit his strength against God. But, Winch argues, it makes no sense at all to assert that science or religion is logical or illogical, any more than it would make sense to speak of music as either well-coloured or ill-coloured or of stones as either married or divorced.

Winch's view here has rightly been taken to involve a claim to conceptual self-sufficiency for all of the forms of life. It has also been thought that it involves a kind of compartmentalisation of the modes of discourse or forms of life. Winch is indeed saying that we cannot criticise science or ethics by criteria appropriate to religion and vice versa. Like Wittgenstein and Hughes, Winch is claiming that each mode of discourse must be understood in its own terms and that relevant criticism of that mode of discourse cannot be made from outside of that discourse, but can take place only from within it, when some specific difficulty actually arises in science or in religion.

There is much here that is very perceptive, but there is much that needs close scrutiny as well. I will assume here what in reality is quite open to question, namely that Winch is correct about the Azande. I will further assume that, given the radically different conceptual structure embedded in their language, and given the role magic and witchcraft play in their lives, we can have no good grounds for saying, as Evans-Pritchard does, that our concept of reality is the correct one and theirs is not. But even making this very questionable assumption, it does not at all follow that in our tribe religion and science are related as Azande magic is related to our scientific beliefs. There is no 'religious language' or 'scientific language'. There is rather the international notation of mathematics and logic; and English, French, Spanish and the like. In short, 'religious discourse' and 'scientific discourse' are part of the same overall conceptual structure. Moreover, in that conceptual structure there is a large amount of discourse, which is neither religious nor scientific, that is constantly being utilised by both the religious man and the scientist when they make religious or scientific claims. In short, they share a number of key categories. This situation differs from the Azande situation in a very significant sense, for in the former situation, we do not have in the same literal sense two *different* conceptual structures exemplifying two different ways of life. C. P. Snow to the contrary notwithstanding, we do not have two cultures here but only one.

Sometimes it is indeed tempting to think there really are two cultures. When I read a certain kind of religious literature – as in a recent reading of Simone Weil's *Waiting for God* – I have the *feeling* that I belong to another tribe: that what she can understand and take as certain I have no understanding of at all, beyond a Ziffian sense of her linguistic regularities. Leslie Fiedler tells us that Miss Weil 'speaks of the problems of belief in the vocabulary of the unbeliever', but that is not how I read her.[37] I find her unabashedly talking about religious matters in a way that I find nearly as incredible as some of the things the Azande say. She blithely accepts what I find unintelligible. Yet this initial impression is in a way misleading, for, as I read on, I discover that she is sensitive to *some* of the conceptual perplexities that perplex me. I find her saying 'There is a God. There is no God. Where is the problem? I am quite sure that there is a God in the sense that I am sure my love is no illusion. I am quite sure there is no God, in the sense that I am sure there is nothing which resembles what I can conceive when I say that word . . . .' When I ponder this, I realise that as much as we might differ, we are after all in the same universe of discourse. Miss Weil is not to me like the Azande with his witchcraft substance. We both learned 'the language' of Christian belief; only I think it is illusion-producing while she thinks that certain crucial segments of it are our stammering way of talking about ultimate reality. A very deep gulf separates us; we are not even like Settembrini and Naptha (in T. Mann, *The Magic Mountain*). But all the same, there remains a sense in which we do understand each other and in which we share a massive background of beliefs and assumptions. Given that, it is not so apparent that we do *not* have common grounds for arguing about which concepts of reality are correct or mistaken here.

Winch, as we have seen, argues against Pareto's and Evans-Pritchard's claim that scientific concepts alone can characterise objective reality. He is correct in his contention that their claim is an incoherent one. 'Scientific concepts alone make a true link with objective reality' is neither analytic nor empirical. No use has been given to 'true link' or 'objective reality'. When a plain man looks at a harvest moon and says that it is orange, or says that the sun rises in the east and sets in the west, or that his vineyard posts are solid, he is not making scientific statements, but he is not making *subjective* statements either. His statements can be perfectly objective; they can be about how things are, and they can be objectively testable (publicly verifiable) without being scientific or without conflicting with science. But when it is claimed – as presumably people who seriously utter certain religious propositions claim – that the *facts* asserted by these religious propositions are such and such, their claims must be open to some possible confirmation or disconfirmation: their claims must be publicly testable. They are making some assertion or trying to make some assertion about how things-are-in-the-world. But a claim like 'God created the heavens and the earth', when 'God' is used non-anthropomorphically, is not testable. That is to say, it is a claim that purports to assert a fact, yet it is devoid of truth-conditions. People who use such relig-ious talk – partake of such a form of life – cannot determine how, even in principle, they would establish or disestablish such religious claims, but they still believe that they are factual assertions: that is to say, that they have truth-conditions. They believe that it is a fact that there is a God, that it is a fact that He created the world, that it is a fact that He protects all those He creates. Yet, how could we say what it would be like for God to create the world, if it is impossible in principle to say what would have to transpire for it to be false or probably false that God created the world? Or, to put this verificationist point in a weaker and more adequate way, if we cannot even say what *in principle* would count as *evidence* against the putative statement that God created the world, then 'God created the world' is devoid of factual content.

This verificationist argument can, perhaps, be successfully rebutted, but it is far less vulnerable than the claim that only scientific ideas correspond with reality. That is to say, given the concept of objective reality that plain men, including plain religious men, utilise in everyday life, a statement asserts a fact, actually has factual content, only if it is at least confirmable or disconfirmable in principle. To count as a factual statement, it must assert a certain determinate reality (a pleonasm); that is, its descriptive content includes one set of empirically deter-minable conditions and excludes others.[38] People who argue for this would, or at least should, claim that these last remarks are what Wittgenstein would call grammatical remarks, that is, they hold in virtue of the linguistic regularities governing the crucial terms in question. But key religious utterances, though they purport to be factual statements, do not succeed in making what actually counts as a genuine factual statement. That is, as Strawson puts it, they are not actually part of that type of discourse we call a fact-stating type of discourse. Thus they lack the kind of coherence they must have to make genuinely factual claims.

I shall not here, though I have elsewhere, assess such a

controversial claim.[39] Here I want only to note that even if it turns out to be mistaken, it is a far more powerful counter-thrust against Winchian claims to the conceptual self-sufficiency and the coherence of God-talk, than is the simplistic claim that only scientific ideas are in accord with objective reality. Such a verificationist claim – a claim utilised by Ayer and Flew – stands here as an unmet challenge to Wittgenstein-ian Fideism.

Someone who wanted to use Winch to defend Wittgenstein-ian Fideism might reply that a key religious claim such as 'God created the heavens and the earth' does indeed have something to do with understanding the world. We could not have a deep understanding of our world if we did not understand *that*, but it must be realised that the understanding in question is not the narrowly factual or empirical one I have just been talking about. Supernatural facts are a *sui generis* kind of fact; we might even say that it is a fact of a very distinctive kind that God is 'the *source* of all empirical facts'. Supernatural facts are not, as Austin would put it, 'a special kind of something in the world'; and they cannot be modelled on the garden-variety concept of a fact. My argument, my critic might say, only shows that such religious statements are not factual in the way commonsensical, scientific and empirical statements are factual. It does not show religious statements are incoherent or pseudo-factual. More-over, it in effect confirms the Wittgensteinian claim that relig-ious discourse is one kind of discourse with its own distinctive logic while science and common sense are forms of life that constitute other quite distinct modes of discourse with their own unique criteria.

My reply is that the phrase 'logic of discourse' is a dangerous metaphor and that these discourses are not in actual life nearly so compartmentalised as the above argument would have it. The religious sceptic, the man perplexed by God-talk, is not like a person in our culture perplexed by Azande beliefs in witch-craft substance. He is not an outsider who does not know the form of life but an insider who does. So God spoke to Job out of the whirlwind. So how did he do it? Nobody, or at least nobody who matters, believes any more in a sky-God up there, who might have done it in a very loud voice. But what did happen? How are we to understand 'God spoke to Job'? Maybe it was all

Job's tortured imagination? Yet how do we even understand what it is that he was supposed to have imagined? And how are we to understand 'I am who am'? A person may be puzzled about the *nature* of time, but when her alarm clock rings at 5:30 a.m. and a little later the weather comes on over the radio at 6:00 and her clock shows 6:00 too, she does not, unless she is excessively neurotic, doubt what time it is. She is painfully aware what time it is. But perfectly sane people in a tribe where God-talk is an established practice, part of an ancient and venerated form of life, can and do come to wonder to whom or to what they are praying, or what is being talked about when it is said that 'God spoke to Job'. God is a person, but we can't identify Him; God acts in the world but has no body. Words here are put together in a strange way. What could it possibly mean to speak of 'action' or 'a person' here? These terms cut across activities; they are at home in religious and non-religious contexts. It is also true that some logical rules (the law of contradiction, excluded middle and the like) most certainly seem to cut across forms of life. The forms of life are not as compartmentalised as Winch seems to imply, and as a Wittgensteinian Fideism seems at least to require. Insiders can and do come to doubt the very coherence of this religious mode of life and its *first-order* talk.

They indeed do, it will be countered, but in doing that they are philosophically confused. Careful attention to the concept of reality and to the systematic ambiguity of norms of intelligibility, will show why. Moreover, though 'action' and 'person' are not compartmentalised it still remains true that their meanings are typologically variant from context to context. It is just here, it will be claimed, that Wittgenstein's insights are most enlightening. This takes us to what I regard as the heart of the matter, and here we need to consider some very fundamental arguments of Winch's.

Winch makes one central point which seems to me unassailable: to understand religious conceptions we need a religious tradition; without a participant's understanding of that form of life, there can be no understanding of religion. To understand it we must know how to operate with, to reason in accordance with, the rules of conceptual propriety distinctive of that form of life. Without a knowledge by *wont* of the norms of conceptual propriety associated with God-talk, we can have no grasp of the concept of God, and thus, without such knowledge by *wont*, there can be no quest for God or even a rejection of God. If 'we are to speak of difficulties and incoherencies appearing and being detected in the way certain practices have hitherto been carried on in a society, surely this can only be understood in connection with problems arising in the carrying on of the activity'.[40]

Surely we must start here. There could not even be a *problem* about God if we could not. But to start at this point is one thing, to end there is another. The need to start from 'inside' need not preclude the recognition of clefts, inconsistencies, and elements of incoherence in the very practice (form of life). Once magic and belief in fairies were ongoing practices in our stream of life. By now, by people working from the inside, the entire practice, the entire form of life, has come to be rejected as incoherent.

We have seen, however, that Winch, after the fashion of a Wittgensteinian Fideist, argues that we cannot intelligibly assert the incoherence, illogicality, irrationality or unintelligibility of a form of life itself. (That he remarked, on a reprinting of 'Understanding a Primitive Society', that he did not intend to claim 'that a way of living can never be characterised as in any sense "irrational" ', does not gainsay this, for (1) his actual argument clearly implies it, (2) 'any sense' leaves room for almost anything, and (3) that there can be no such a characterisation is how almost everyone [friend and foe alike] read him.) Winch argues that the forms of life are all conceptually self-sufficient; operating with them, we can say that something does or does not make sense, is logical or illogical, for example, that was an illogical chess-move. But we cannot say of the whole activity itself that it is illogical, irrational, unintelligible or incoherent, for example, chess is illogical.

The tide of metaphysics is running high here. Our everyday discourse, which is so important for a Wittgensteinian, will not support such a Winchian claim. 'An ongoing but irrational form of life' most certainly does *not appear* to be a contradiction. 'Foot-bending was for a long time an established institution but it was really cruel and irrational' may be false but it is not nonsense. 'Primogeniture had a definite rationale' and 'Magical practices are essential for the Azande' are not grammatical remarks, but this means that their denials are significant and this in turn means that we can make judgments about the rationality of forms of life. Similarly, we can say, without *conceptual* impropriety, that gambling is illogical. We might even say that French is illogical because of its haphazard use of gender, or that the irregularities of English grammar make it illogical. All of these statements may be false, they may even be absurdly false, but they certainly do not appear to be self-contradictory or senseless. It is not at all evident that language has gone on a holiday here. But to establish Winch's thesis he must show that, appearances notwithstanding, they are all either senseless or metaphorical.

It can be replied: how do you meet

(1) Winch's specific argument that 'the criteria of logic . . . arise out of, and are only intelligible in the context of, ways of living or modes of social life as such',[41] and

(2) his further contention that 'formal requirements tell us nothing about what in particular is to count as consistency, just as the rules of the propositional calculus limit, but do not themselves determine what are to be proper values of p, q, etc.'[42]

I cannot consistently assert p and not-p but what range of values the variable p takes is not uniquely determined by purely formal considerations. If I know that to say x is a bachelor entails x is not married, I know, by purely formal considerations, that I cannot assert x is a married bachelor. But what counts as 'a bachelor' or 'a married man' can only be determined by reference to the actual usage embedded in the form of life of which they are a part.

Unless we are prepared to accept the compartmentalisation thesis, dear to Wittgensteinian Fideists, the acceptance of the above claim about logic need not commit one to the paradoxical thesis that modes of social life cannot be appraised as logical or illogical, rational or irrational. Religion, morality and science may indeed each have 'criteria of intelligiblity peculiar to itself'. This means that the criteria of application for 'God', 'Divine Person', 'perfect good', and the like are set by the *first-order* religious discourse itself. However, it also remains true that

(1)   discourse concerning God goes on in Italian, German, English, Spanish and the like, and

(2)   that there is no separate religious language.

Given these two facts and given the overall universe of discourse of which religious discourse is a part, it may still be found that religious discourse, like discourse about fairies, is incoherent, for example, 'God is three and one', 'God is a person one *encounters* in prayer but God is utterly *transcendent*'. It is indeed true that seemingly contradictory statements may turn out not to be contradictory. When fully stated and understood, in terms of their distinctive contextual use, what *appears* to be contradictory or paradoxical may be seen to be straightforward and non-contradictory. Religious discourse is not something isolated, sufficient unto itself; 'sacred discourse' shares categories with, utilises the concepts of, and contains the syntactical structure of, 'profane discourse'. Moreover, where there is what at least appears to be a contradiction, or where words are put together in a way fluent speakers *cannot* understand, a case must be made out for the contention that the contradiction is *only apparent*. What appears to be unintelligible must be shown to have a use in the discourse or it must be given a use. That is to say, the words must be given an employment or be shown to have an employment so that fluent speakers can grasp what is being said.

Many central religious utterances at least appear to be contradictory or incoherent. That a *case* needs to be made out and perhaps even can be made out to show that they are not really contradictory or incoherent, shows that such a question can be raised about religious discourse. Given this fact and given the centrality of some of these religious statements, it becomes apparent that Winch's argument does not succeed in establishing that it is impossible to appraise whole ways of life as rational or irrational, intelligible or unintelligible. Furthermore, that we can ask questions about 'God is three and one' and 'A *transcendent* God is encountered in prayer' that involve appealing to criteria from the discourse as a whole and not just from religious talk, indicates that Winch's argument does not show that we can compartmentalise religious talk. In short, the Winchian arguments that we have examined do not show that we cannot raise questions about the rationality of a form of life or that religious discourse is so *sui generis* that its criteria of intelligibility are entirely contained within itself.

We are not yet at the bottom of the barrel. The question 'What is real?' has no determinate sense. What is real and what is unreal is a very context-dependent notion. What in a specific context counts as 'real' or 'reality' as in 'a real bass', 'a real champion', 'an unreal distinction', 'the realities of political life', 'a sense of reality', 'the reality of death' or 'the reality of God', can only be determined with reference to the particular matter we are talking about. We have no antecedent understanding of reality such that we could determine whether language agreed with reality, whether a specific language agreed with reality or whether a given form of discourse agreed with reality. With the exception of the *very last* bit, I agree with Winch about such matters, but alas it is this very last bit that is essential for a Wittgensteinian Fideism.

However, with this last Wittgensteinian claim, there are very real difficulties similar to ones we have already discussed. 'Reality' may be systematically ambiguous, but what constitutes evidence, or tests for the truth or reliability of specific claims, is not completely idiosyncratic to the context or activity we are talking about. Activities are not that insulated. As I have already noted, once there was an ongoing form of life in which fairies and witches were taken to be real entities, but gradually, as we reflected on the criteria we actually use for ascertaining whether various entities, including persons, are or are not part of the spatiotemporal world of experience, we (that is most contemporary westerners) came gradually to give up believing in fairies and witches. With the relentless evolution of systems of belief in the direction of what Weber called *Entzauberung*, such conceptions for more and more people became unbelievable. That a language-game was played, that a form of life existed, did not preclude our asking about the coherence of the concepts involved and about the reality of what they conceptualised.

Without a participant's understanding of religious discourse, we could not raise the question of the reality of God, but with it, this is perfectly possible and perfectly intelligible.

Indeed we sometimes judge the reality of one thing in terms of something utterly inappropriate, for example, moral distinctions are unreal because moral utterances do not make factual assertions. Here we do commit a howler. But, as my above examples show, we do not always need, in criticising a form of life, to make such blunders. 'Nixon ought to be impeached' can be seen, by an examination of the relevant forms of life, not to describe a certain happening. It is not a bit of fact-stating discourse asserting some actual occurrence, but rather it tells us to make something occur. 'Witches are out on Halloween' is a putative factual statement. It supposedly does assert that a certain identifiable state-of-affairs obtains. It supposedly is like saying 'The Klan is out on Halloween.' But the factual intelligibility of the former is not evident, for it is not clear what counts as a witch. To say 'witch' refers to a unique kind of reality only intelligible within a distinctive form of life, is an incredible piece of evasion. To reason in such a manner is to show that one is committed to a certain metaphysical theory come what may. But, if one wants to be realistic and non-evasive, one will surely say that it gradually became apparent, *vis-à-vis* forms of life in which talk of witches was embedded, that in light of the meanings of 'fact' and 'evidence' in the overall discourse of which witch-talk was a part, that witch-talk was useless, superstitious and indeed absurd. Though there was a form of life in which the existence of witches was asserted, such a way of life is and was irrational. And even if for some baroque reason I am mistaken in saying that it is or was irrational to believe in witches, the fact that such a question can be intelligently raised about one form of life plainly demonstrates that Winch's *a-priori* arguments against such an appraisal of a form of life as a whole will not wash.

Perhaps God-talk is not as absurd and irrational as witch-talk; perhaps there is an intelligible concept of the reality of God, and perhaps there is a God, but the fact that there is a form of life in which God-talk is embedded does not preclude our asking such questions or our giving, quite intelligibly, though perhaps mistakenly, the same negative answer as we gave to witch-talk.

V

There are, however, other considerations that lead to an acceptance of Wittgensteinian Fideism. It is to some of these that I shall now turn. In the next chapter I shall examine a different and very fundamental Wittgensteinian response to arguments such as mine. But in rounding off this chapter, I will turn to some specific arguments of Norman Malcolm's which would, if correct, give force to such a Fideism.

Malcolm attacks the typical philosophical assumption 'that it must be *possible* for a person to have grounds for believing in the existence of God' and that 'with this belief as with any other we must make a distinction between causes of the belief and grounds or evidence for its truth.'[43] Malcolm contends that this is an unrealistic assumption because 'the supposed *belief* that God exists (is) . . . a problematic concept, whereas belief in God is not problematic.'[44]

Belief in God is only partly analogous to belief in one's friend or doctor. The latter belief 'primarily connotes trust or faith in him'. 'Belief-in', when applied to God, has a wider meaning: it applies to a wider range of affective attitudes, for it takes as its *object* not only trust 'but also awe, dread, dismay, resentment and perhaps even hatred'.[45] If a man's chief attitude to God is one of fear, he still believes in God, though he does not place his trust in God and he does not have faith in God. But in so far as I am afraid of my friend I hardly believe in him. 'Belief in God will involve some affective state of attitude, having God as its object, and those could vary from reverential love to rebellious rejection.'[46]

Malcolm must now face the standard claim that if 'a person believes in God surely he believes that God exists'. Malcolm must surmount it, for it is his opinion that a belief *that* God exists is *problematic* while a belief *in* God is not problematic. But *if* a belief *in* God commits one to a belief *that* God exists, and if there could be no belief in God without the assumption that God exists and the logically linked belief that God exists, then, if that latter assumption or belief that God exists is problematic, so is a belief *in* God. But isn't I. M. Crombie clearly and unassailably right when he asserts that '*believing in* is logically subsequent to *believing that*? I cannot believe in Dr Jones if I do not first believe that there is such a person.'[47] If I believe in the regenerative powers of the waters at Baden-Baden then I believe that such waters exist in Baden-Baden. If I believe in the wisdom of

Trudeau's policies, I believe that Trudeau has some policies.

Malcolm tries to go around this seemingly unassailable argument in what seems to me to be a very peculiar and quite unconvincing manner. First he tells us that he finds the statement 'If a person believes in God then surely he believes that God exists' far from clear. He thinks that what is behind it is that some think that 'you could believe *that* God exists without believing in God.'[48] Malcolm then, like a good Wittgensteinian, reduces this to absurdity. He points out that anyone who understands *dieses Sprachspiel* we play with 'God' could not say 'I believe that God exists but His existence is a matter of indifference to me.' A completely non-affective belief that God exists is in reality not a belief that *God* exists, for it makes no sense to say that one conceives of God as one's loving and absolute sovereign creator and judge and that one believes that this God exists, but all the same one is not at *all* touched by awe, dismay, fear, or the like. It is not possible, Malcolm argues, first to decide that God exists and then decide how one should regard Him. It is not possible first to come to believe that He exists and then to come to have a certain determinate range of affective attitudes.

What Malcolm says here seems to me to be right, but perfectly irrelevant to his claim that 'believing in God' is non-problematic while 'believing that God exists' is problematic, and to his further claim that believing in God does not logically commit one to the belief that God exists. What his argument does show is that one cannot believe that God exists without also believing in God. But this is not to the point. It does nothing to show that 'belief in God' is non-problematic while belief that God exists or that there is a God is problematic. It does nothing to show that one could believe in God and not presuppose that God exists. We cannot believe that God exists without having one or another of a certain range of attitudes toward God. But this does not show that one could believe in God without believing that God exists, or that one's 'belief-in' could be unproblematic while one's 'belief-that' is problematic. 'All equilateral triangles are equiangular triangles' is a necessary proposition without its being the case that 'equilateral triangle' and 'equiangular triangle' are identical in meaning. 'To believe that God exists is also to believe in God' is a necessary proposition, but that it is an *a-priori* truth does not at all show that 'belief that God exists' and 'belief in God' are identical in meaning. In this respect it is analogous to 'All equilateral triangles are equiangular triangles.'

Moreover, Malcolm tells us that 'an affective attitude toward him [God] would logically imply the belief that he [God] exists.'[49] But if this is true, then there must be a distinction between 'believing in God' and 'believing that God exists'.

Malcolm has given us no reason at all to think that to believe in God does not logically commit one to the belief that God exists. Finally, if to have an affective attitude toward Him is to believe in God, and if this affective attitude toward God implies a belief that God exists, then a belief that God exists could not, as Malcolm claims it is, be problematic *while* a belief in God is not problematic. If we do not understand 'believes that God exists' because its meaning is so indeterminate, we could not know that 'a belief in God' implies 'a belief that God exists'. Moreover we could not understand what Malcolm takes to be quite unproblematic, namely 'God exists', if we do not understand what it is to believe that God exists, for we could not intelligibly *assert* 'God exists', or 'There is a God', or 'God is indeed a reality' unless we believe that God exists. Thus 'believing in God' and 'believing that God exists' are either both problematic or neither is problematic, but we cannot consistently say, as Malcolm does, that one is problematic and the other is not.

Someone might defend Malcolm by arguing that 'belief in' does not always presuppose 'belief that'.[50] I can believe in justice or believe in love between all humankind without believing that justice or such love exists. This is indeed perfectly true, but in this case, as in others, where 'belief in' does not presuppose 'belief that', we are talking about something that is an ideal or a moral conception, or something which is *merely* conceptual. But when we are talking about a concept which purportedly signifies something which is not *merely* conceptual, something which actually exists, then such a presupposition holds, or, to put the point more modestly, the onus is on Malcolm to give us the slightest reason for thinking that this familiar presupposition does not hold in such contexts. A Jew or Christian must believe that it is in some sense a fact that God exists; to believe in God is not *simply* to believe in an ideal or to use a term, like a theoretical term, that is *simply* a term which has a useful function in his *Sprachspiel*. Where what we are talking about is not an ideal or a *purely* conceptual reality, 'believing in' presupposes 'believing that'.

Malcolm's argument might be defended in still another way. To the extent that 'believing that God exists' has any determinate meaning at all, it simply means 'believing in God'. (Malcolm himself says that this is 'not an entirely unnatural use of language'.) The very use of 'believing in', when the object of belief is God, lends credence to this. Normally when we speak of persons – and God, let us recall, is in some sense 'a person' – 'belief in', as Malcolm puts it, 'primarily connotes trust or faith in'[51] the person in question; but, as Malcolm points out, 'belief in', when we speak of God, does not carry that familiar implication.[52] A man whose chief attitude toward God was fear or hatred would still be said to believe in God. But, given this turn, it is now no longer clear what the phrase 'believe in God' means. Moreover, since it is now taken as having the same meaning as 'believing that God exists', it would seem that 'believing in God' is also problematic, without possessing the clarity of 'believing in', where it connotes 'to trust' or 'to have faith'.

Malcolm does *not* tell us what he means by 'a problematic concept'; all we know is that he asserts that 'the supposed belief that God exists' strikes him as a problematic concept. I would surmise that by 'a problematic concept', Malcolm means a concept whose meaning is so indeterminate that we do not know what we are asserting or denying when we use it, or more accurately try to use it, in assertions. To put the point in a slightly different way, a concept is problematic when we do not understand what we are committed to when we employ it. It is a concept which utilises terms which have no established role or use in the *Sprachspiel*. Thus to utter 'I believe that God exists' is to give voice to an utterance that has no determinate meaning.

Note that Malcolm is not saying that the concept of God is without a determinate meaning for, after all, 'believing in God', according to him, is perfectly determinate. Moreover, if, after the devastating criticisms that have been made of his argument for it, he still holds to some form of the ontological argument, he believes that 'God exists' is a logical truth, or at least that it cannot consistently be denied without self-contradiction.[53] But if 'God exists' is necessarily true then, if one recognises it to be necessarily true, one knows that God exists. But one cannot know that God exists without believing that God exists.[54] At the time Malcolm first read his paper 'Is it a Religious Belief that God Exists?' I heard him remark to Hartshorne that though he had been impressed by, he had not been convinced by, the criticisms directed against his own very original defence of St Anselm. So presumably he still thinks that 'God exists' is a necessary truth. But if it is a necessary truth then 'believes that God exists' cannot, as he says it is, be a problematic concept.

That it is not frequently used by believers does not prove that it is problematic; and even *if* Malcolm's remarks about the ontological argument are well taken, we should still perfectly well understand what is meant by it. A man who thinks he has established by argument that God exists is a logical truth still could quite consistently assert – though this indeed would be almost redundant – that he believes his argument is correct. After all, Malcolm admits to being shaken by the arguments against his defence of an ontological argument but he denies that he was shaken enough to abandon them. Thus he gives us to understand that he only *believes* his arguments to be correct. He does not claim to *know* they are correct. A man could, and any sensible man would, only accept the ontological argument in this spirit. But then for such a man to believe that God exists would come to his believing that there were sound arguments for the claim that there is no God is a contradiction. For anyone who rejects the ontological argument and remains a Jew, Christian or Moslem, believing that God exists is a more straightforward matter. At least it is neither less problematical nor more problematical than believing in God.

In short, Malcolm has not succeeded in showing how it is possible to believe in God – to have an affective attitude toward God – without believing that God exists and he has not shown how 'belief in God' can be unproblematic while 'belief that God exists' is problematic.

VI

Malcolm has a second argument which seems to be less clearly unsuccessful only because it is less clear. He argues that, even granting 'God exists is a non-problematic concept', this does not show or in any way indicate that we must be able to adduce evidence for or against the existence of God. Someone whose religious concepts were formed exclusively from the Bible might regard this question of evidence as an alien intrusion. Such a consideration would have no contact with the religious ideas he had learned. 'It is my impression', Malcolm continues 'that this question of evidence plays no part in workaday religious instruction and practice, but puts in an appearance only when the language is idling.'[55] Here Malcolm is assuming at least the self-sufficiency and perhaps as well the compartmentalisation of the forms of life. It *may* well be true, that questions concerning evidence for God's existence do not arise in workaday religious instruction and practice.[56] But questions concerning the existence of electrons do not arise in workaday scientific practice either. Their existence is presupposed. But once their existence was a live issue and there are theoretical contexts in which it is still a question. In certain social contexts, where certain forms of life are given, questions concerning the existence of fairies, ghosts or witches do not arise in workaday situations either. Rather their existence is presupposed. But all the same questions of evidence are relevant and they can be, and in fact were, brought to bear.

It may be true that questions about the reality of God differ from questions about the reality of electrons in the temporal order of when they were doubted and when accepted. The concept of an electron was initially problematic, and only gradually came to have its present pervasive acceptance, while questions about God's non-existence did not arise (let us assume) for people whose religious ideas were formed exclusively from the Bible, though later Kierkegaardians and Barthians came to suffer the torments of doubt. But to stress this difference is to miss the crucial relevant similarity which is that in either case such presupposed beliefs can be relevantly questioned. Malcolm's remarks only show that *certain people* assume the existence of God and would be startled and offended if others questioned His existence. He does not at all show that there are no resources, even in such a Neanderthal believer's discourse, whereby God's existence could be relevantly questioned.

Malcolm agrees that if our concept of God has content (and he agrees that it must have to be viable), then we shall, if we believe in God, have some expectations as to how things will be in the world which will be different from the religious sceptics' expectations. But, Malcolm argues, it does not follow from this that such religious beliefs will 'have consequences which could be grounds for or against the existence of God'.[57] Part of the content of my belief that there is a God, Malcolm contends, might be that if I am truly repentant my sins will be forgiven. But it does not follow that this last belief must be verifiable or falsifiable if my concept of God is to have content. 'There are', as he tells us, 'beliefs and beliefs.'[58] There are various ways a belief can 'get a grip' on the world. One way to get a grip is this: a man who believes that his sins will be forgiven, if he is truly repentant, might be saved from despair. This belief gets a grip on the world by making a great difference to his actions and feelings.[59]

This seems correct enough, but Malcolm makes a puzzling remark when he says 'what he [the believer] believes has, for him, no verification or falsification.' But the 'for him' is irrelevant. Malcolm just gratuitously hauls it in. What is relevant is whether statements about a person's having such and such a belief are verifiable or falsifiable.

Later in his essay, Malcolm tries to meet the verification/falsification requirement head on. Malcolm remarks that a believer might hold a religious belief 'in such a way that no fact of experience could falsify it'.[60] Malcolm gives a case: 'as part of my concept of God I might have the belief that faith in God will cause this mountain to be cast into the sea.'[61] Such a believer believes that if the God of the Bible exists and if he has faith in this God, that a given mountain will be cast into the sea. 'But', continues Malcolm, 'if the mountain does not move shall I [that is, the believer] conclude that the belief is false; or that God does not exist? It need not be so. I might conclude instead that my faith was not strong enough.'[62] Malcolm then adds that it need not follow if I drew this last conclusion that I did not really believe that faith will move mountains. I might instead simply hold that faith will move mountains in such a way that no fact of experience could falsify it.

If the 'could' is *not* a logical 'could', as the 'could' in 'No bachelor could be married', then 'Faith will move mountains' is still verifiable *in principle* and we can still say that our concept of God has content because it is *logically possible* to state what we must expect if there is a God and what we must expect if there is no God. But if the 'could' in Malcolm's 'no fact of experience could falsify it' is logical, then 'Faith will move mountains' is equally compatible with all *conceivable* happenings and consequently such a man's concept of God is deprived of the empirical content that Malcolm agrees it requires. Malcolm has not shown how it is possible to rule out the empiricist requirements for verification/falsification for 'There is a God' and still give one's concept of God empirical content.

5

Wittgensteinian Fideism: II

I

So far I have raised difficulties about such a Wittgensteinian position, but it may be thought by some that I have not yet touched the core of such a claim. I have, it might be admitted, shown that we cannot in thinking about religion divorce it from all mysterious allegedly cosmological claims. They are indeed integral to God-talk. In denying this Coburn's analysis was implicitly reductive and not genuinely Wittgensteinian; and it is precisely attention to religious discourse itself which shows that we cannot intelligibly say that we believe in God without presupposing a belief that God exists. Again it was attention to our language that made it evident that the various forms of life were neither compartmentalised nor totally self-sufficient.

There is, however, this anomaly: in making these claims I have myself constantly, though some might feel not very consistently, played 'the Wittgensteinian game' and furthermore I have not scaled the inner bastions of Wittgensteinian Fideism, namely

(1)   that the forms of language are the forms of life,
(2)   that ultimately all the philosopher can do is perspicuously display the workings – including the interrelations – of these forms of life, and
(3)   that there is no privileged vantage point for philosophy to assess these forms of life or gain religious knowledge, for example, knowledge of whether there is a God and

what His demands on us are, if indeed He makes such demands.

I have, it may be thought, confusedly read a law into the way a word is used, unwittingly assuming in my critique of Winch and Hughes some 'transcendent rules of rationality', 'some superogatory logic' or 'epistemic distinctions' not rooted in any natural language or form of life. I have in effect engaged in a linguistic legislation which in turn serves as a mask for what in reality is a case of special pleading. But Wittgenstein, Rhees, Winch and Phillips have shown that such a drive for generality (completeness) is entirely illusory.

Like a typical metaphysician – the charge could continue – I am trying to do the impossible, namely justifiably to maintain that to commit oneself to a religious form of life such as Judaism or Christianity is irrational or illogical because such religious discourses are themselves, at key junctures, incoherent. But this is like trying to discover the colour of heat. All I can show is that from the vantage point of the forms of life I accept and operate with, God-talk is incoherent. But I can never show that it is incoherent, period. To think that I can do this is a sorry mixture of *hubris* and conceptual confusion on my part.

When I argued in the last chapter that religious utterances lack the kind of coherence they must have to make genuinely factual claims, I (to continue the objection), with an implicit *persuasive* definition of 'factual claims', go in a small circle, for my criteria for coherence rest on a culturally contingent conception of facticity. I am simply looking at the world from the point of view of a secular westerner. But that this vantage point unlocks doors to the nature of 'Ultimate Reality' or that it should be given a privileged place over other vantage points is itself a very disputable stand. Moreover, what I will take as a fact and as a legitimate categorial distinction between fact and fantasy is itself just one central feature of a given language-game – a language-game which, like all language-games, does not rest on any foundation. (The very notion of finding a foundation for a language-game would, for Wittgenstein, betray a conceptual confusion, unless we are simply going to say that the forms of life are their foundation. But that is not very helpful, to someone in search of 'rational foundations for language-games', for the

forms of language are the forms of life and his kind of perplexities about language-games would simply be transferred to
'forms of life'.)

Wittgenstein also points out that a language-game is only
possible if one *trusts* something. Doubt itself must rest on something which is beyond doubt, that is, on certain culturally
defined 'infallibilities', to use Wittgenstein's own word. If this
were not so, doubt itself would not be possible. Substantiation
must have an end and a 'language-game' is not substantiated.
'It is not rational (or irrational). It stands there – like our life.'[1]
There is no reasoning about or justifying a form of life itself.
Wittgenstein drives home his point in a striking series of remarks:

> Is it wrong for me to order my actions according to the
> propositions of physics? Am I to say I have no good grounds
> for doing so? Isn't precisely that what we call 'good grounds'?
>
> Supposing we met people who did not regard that as telling
> grounds. Now, how do we imagine this? They ask, instead of
> the physicist, some oracle. (And we consider them primitive
> because they do.) Is their asking an oracle or ordering them-
> selves by it wrong? . . . If we call this 'wrong' aren't we
> making a sortie from our language-game and attacking
> theirs?
>
> And are we right or wrong to attack it? Certainly there are
> all sorts of slogans we could support our action by.
>
> Where two principles really do meet without being able to
> reconcile each other, then everyone proclaims the others
> dolts and heretics.
>
> I said I should 'attack' the other person – but wouldn't I
> give him *grounds*? Certainly; but how far do they go? At the
> end of grounds stands *persuasion*. (Think what happens when
> missionaries convert natives.)[2]

A dyed-in-the-wool Wittgensteinian might argue that I have
confused giving grounds, making rational arguments, with persuasion when talking about whether or not to accept a religious
form of life. What needs to be recognised is that God-talk is just
one such language-game which is just there like life. It has no
substantiation and it does not need one. The very notion of
substantiation does not take hold here.

I think some of these points have at least an implicit answer in what I argued in the last chapter, but I have not answered all of them and since this Wittgensteinian challenge to my mind cuts very deep indeed and is so central in philosophy (not only philosophy of religion), I want and need to return to the argument. In particular I need to consider the claim that all philosophy can correctly do is clearly characterise the forms of life, but it can never give us knowledge of whether there is or is not a God, though it can describe the religious knowledge of the holy man. I want to argue that on the contrary philosophy, without becoming what it should not be, can and should appraise forms of life and that it can help us know whether there is or is not a God or even whether 'religious knowledge' is possible. In this argument I shall have worthy opponents in Stanley Cavell and Peter Geach, who in developing some insights of Wittgenstein and in using a philosophical method which I should judge very akin to mine, come to opposite conclusions from my own. I shall develop my own claims through a criticism of theirs.

II

In interpreting Wittgenstein, Cavell stresses that what has to be accepted when we philosophise are the forms of life. Without an appreciation of the import of this there will be little understanding of Wittgenstein's crucial insights. 'The extent to which we understand one another or ourselves is the same as the extent to which we share or understand forms of life . . . .'[3] This must be understood in a very mundane and concrete way, for to share and know the forms of life comes in a specific instance to a kind of knowledge by *wont*, namely, to know 'what it is to take turns, or take chances, or know that some of the things we have lost we cannot look for but can nevertheless sometimes find or recover . . . .'[4] Cavell goes on to point out that it is Wittgenstein's claim – a claim with which he apparently concurs – that the fact 'that we do more or less share such forms rests upon nothing deeper'; that is to say, there is, underlying the forms of life, 'no foundation, logical or philosophical', which explains them, justifies them, or 'provides the real form of which our lives and language are distortions'.[5]

Philosophers, and ordinary people in their philosophical moments, wish to 'escape the limits of human forms of language and forms of life'.[6] But they are caught up in an illusion, though it may be almost an irresistible illusion. It is Wittgenstein's task to destroy this illusion. Language does not rest upon a foundation of logic. Logic cannot show us the real form of language or of thought, for there is no such real form. There are just the multifarious, historically contingent forms of language upon which thinking depends. A search for the logic of language is a search for an illusory 'perfection or generality or completeness'. What Wittgenstein endeavours to show us is that there is no underlying logical form of language that, as a standard of intelligibility, will show us with great exactitude what can and cannot be the case. There is no such standard; there is no final and complete analysis 'toward which ordinary language longs'.

It has been thought by Marx, by Freud, and by Mannheim, that ordinary thought and language often distort our apprehension of reality. Their task was to unmask the myths generated by the folkways of man. Cavell maintains that Wittgenstein in effect shows that such an effort at unmasking 'requires a few masks . . . of its own'.[7] Wittgenstein tries to bring this sharply to our attention; he tries to lead us away from a *false* sophistication; his aim, Cavell avers, is to help us to recover 'our ordinary human existence'.[8] Wittgenstein shows us that there is no distinctive philosophical knowledge to be gained, no genuine philosophical theses to be pushed, or explanations to be given, for there is no logic to be uncovered that underpins and cuts across the forms of life. We have, when we engage in philosophical inquiry and when we think about these matters, a deep temptation to think that there must be some such knowledge, that our heterogeneous concepts must have some such foundation. Wittgenstein fights against such a 'bewitchment of our intelligence'; he 'assembles reminders' to free us from such an illusion. Philosophy – that is, good philosophy – leaves everything as it is. Cavell remarks of this Wittgensteinian doctrine. 'What it says, or suggests, is that criticism of our lives is not to be prosecuted in philosophical theory, but continued in the confrontation of our lives with their own necessities.'[9]

III

This Wittgensteinian contention is disturbing. The man tormented by certain very distinctive kinds of philosophical doubt or by the great *Weltanschauung*-problems of his time, or perhaps of any time, will be deeply dissatisfied with such contentions, though this is not, of course, to say that his dissatisfactions are well founded. He is inclined to say or at least think that if 'philosophy leaves everything as it is', that surely is the death of philosophy.

Cavell, however, in a penetrating way, gives us the other side of the coin. Do we really want philosophy to change things? We most certainly should not want philosophy 'to become merely another ideology' – in the words of George Orwell, another of 'the smelly little orthodoxes which are now contending for our souls'.[10] Cavell goes on to remark that it would be a sufficiently important change if a philosophy would develop which could prevent 'ideologies from changing the world out from under our lives . . . .'[11] Lewis Feuer to the contrary notwithstanding, it surely would be an important enough achievement for one decade if a philosophy could free us from the grip of ideology, so that we could, free from such ideological pretensions, 'grow into our future, knowing it as we go . . . .'[12]

Human beings, and philosophers in particular, take to ideologies like ducks take to water. It is, however, Cavell's claim that the insights about 'forms of language/forms of life' which we find in Wittgenstein help us to see the groundlessness of all ideological claims.

To this it might be objected that Wittgenstein and Cavell do not say or even suggest that all ideological claims are mystificatory or are all claims to be discounted; they rather want to bring us to a recognition that they are ideological and not scientific or deep 'metaphysical truths' about the condition of man in the universe.

It is not clear to me that Cavell, or for that matter Winch or Phillips, is quite so well disposed to ideological claims, but what is important here – and this is the force of the above objection – is that someone with such Wittgensteinian philosophical predilections could well argue that it is not an implication of Wittgensteinian thinking that all ideological claims are groundless but only that ideological claims have their own kind of ground. They do not have the same kind of support as factual or as scientific claims but they do have support and can be argued for. Bourgeois ideology is not without grounds and when Isaac Deutscher, to take one powerful instance, criticises it or Clinton Rossiter defends it, their claims are not typically groundless, though the argument is an ideological one. We can, as I would, argue against bourgeois ideology by arguing that another ideology, socialist humanism, is a more adequate ideology. And to such argument we expect counter-argument. The crucial Wittgensteinian reminder here is that these claims and the arguments in support of them, pro and con, are ideological – buyer beware: there are other ways, other possibilities, other world-pictures carrying other commitments. Recognise them for what they are, come to see that they are also 'necessities in our lives', and come to acknowledge once again in this new context the familiar Moorean point that everything is what it is and not another thing. Ideology is ideology and not science and not philosophy.

Sounding at a more abstract level than usual the call for the 'end of ideology', Wittgensteinian Fideists might respond by arguing that ideologies, unlike science, art, religion or morality, are not such necessities – when we engage in such talk the engine is idling and they should as *ersatz* activities be surmounted and not linked to any established form of life. Such an 'end of ideology argument' is in my judgment a mistaken one, but what is relevant here is that both claims are expressible within a Wittgensteinian framework.

What is important from a Wittgensteinian point of view is firstly to come to recognise that language, and our forms of life, rest either on conventions or (and philosophers tend to overlook this or discount its importance) on natural factual necessities and, secondly, that we can gain no philosophical overview in virtue of which we can surmount these conventions or rationalise these natural necessities. A language-game, Wittgenstein contends, is not the sort of activity for which it is possible to find a rational ground. In making us see that there is nothing to be substantiated here, Wittgenstein frees us from illusions only in the rather strange sense that he gives us to understand that the metaphysical quest or logician's quest for something underpinning these conventions or natural necessities – serving as their real foundation – is an incoherent one.

In speaking of 'conventions' here *vis-à-vis* Wittgenstein,

Cavell, rightly I believe, takes this to be the claim that the forms of life and the forms of language 'have no necessity beyond what human beings do'.[13] They are not conventions in the sense that people could make them up at will or simply decide which if any of these conventions to adopt. If we come to agree with him, he frees us from a kind of Hegelian or Russellian *philosophical Weltanschauung* in the sense that the problems of these views and the problems of philosophy generally 'are solved only when they disappear; answers are arrived at only when they are no longer questions.'[14] But in the light of what I said in the preceding paragraphs it needs to be queried whether all questions of *Weltanschauung* would be, even on Wittgenstein's own grounds, similarly dissolved. Given an identification of a philosophical *Weltanschauung* with the traditional metaphysical postures such as idealism, logical atomism, realism, solipsism and the like, the answer is Yes, but it is less obvious that the answer should be Yes where 'philosphical *Weltanschauung*' and 'ideology' are roughly equivalent.

A Wittgensteinian would not call such ideological arguments 'philosophical arguments'. However, to take such a stance exhibits that they are unwittingly operating with a *persuasive* definition of 'philosophy'. But be that as it may, Cavell, at least, does not think such ideological problems are simply problems to be dissolved by linguistic therapy, for, right after quoting Wittgenstein on what has to be accepted are the forms of life, he goes on to say:

> This is not the same as saying that our lives as we lead them – in particular, for Wittgenstein, our lives of theory – must be accepted. What he says, or suggests, is that criticism of our lives is not to be prosecuted in philosophical theory, but continued in the confrontation of our lives with their own necessities.[15]

This is a dark, yet suggestive saying. However, in what Cavell says a few pages later, it seems that he is giving us to understand that Wittgenstein believes, and that he agrees with Wittgenstein, that no ideology is of much value, that no such theoretical and visionary approach will really help us to come to grips with the problems of life and society.[16]

Yet such anti-Utopianism, such a commitment to the end of ideology, does not follow, as I tried to show above, from accepting Wittgenstein's philosophical beliefs about conventions, natural necessities and the 'forms of language/forms of life.' If one had the political temper of an Oakeshott or a Namier, plus Wittgensteinian philosophical convictions, one might come up with such an anti-ideological view. Otherwise a Wittgensteinian will say that it is not properly a *philosophical* task to engage in ideological argument involving in that sense an articulation of a 'philosophical *Weltanschauung*'. A Wittgensteinian with a historical sense can say this not only with a perfect awareness that he has persuasively defined 'philosophy' but also with a readiness to defend that persuasive definition.

A person profoundly impressed by Wittgenstein's claims about language and the nature of philosophy could very well go on to ask why we cannot accept the fundamental concepts of the forms of life as *data*, as 'irreducible' *vis-à-vis* philosophical systematising, without its entailing our 'acceptance' of these concepts as human beings and as philosophers engaged in criticising our culture and the role which various forms of life play in it? The answer to this is that we can and should accept them as *data*. Some Wittgensteinians might object to the use of 'as philosophers' here, but this seems to me a perfectly trivial dispute over how broadly we are going to use 'philosophy'. The critical point is that rational men can and do engage in such arguments, and abstract reasoning and analysis are relevant to such disputes.

However, where '*Weltanschauung*-problems' is a label for traditional metaphysical problems there can be, on Wittgenstein's view and on Cavell's, no solution to these 'problems', for in reality there are no such problems but only in such contexts perplexities felt as problems. A craving for generality or completeness – surely understandable and almost irresistible philosophical motives – drive us into these perplexities when we unwittingly become entangled in our language. We imagine a law in the way a word is used. (While we are so entangled, we actually do not *think* that this is our entanglement at all. It is not *felt* as a confusion over the workings of our language.) To gain philosophical peace, we need to overcome the spell of these entanglements. This is to be done by gaining a perspicacious

representation of our discourse, through calling to mind and
'holding steadily together' what we already know but do not
typically articulate concerning the workings of our language.
By doing this we will come to see that what in our confusion
seemed to be a great intellectual and sometimes an emotional
dilemma as well, posing for us fundamental questions about the
ultimate nature of reality, is no such dilemma at all, for our
'questions' are in reality not questions at all. We will see that no
answer is needed or possible for there is literally nothing to
answer. As Cavell well puts it: 'Socrates' interlocutors have not
found their lives, because they have failed to examine them.
Wittgenstein's have lost their lives through thinking too much,
or in the wrong way.'[17] The creatures of Wittgenstein's philosophical monologues are obsessed with a certain picture of
how things must be (say a radical empiricist picture). A man so
obsessed with such verbal pictures must be brought back to an
acknowledgement of our own common human nature and to
those conventions which have come to be our second nature. He
must come to see the massive and determinative role they play
in all thinking and living.

Now how does this apply to talk of God? Cavell argues that
Wittgenstein, like Kierkegaard, well understood that no philosophical theory could help us know whether there is or is not a
God. We have a form of language in which 'God' has a very
special, yet perfectly estabished, use. As philosophers we can
only describe it in an attempt to free someone from a certain
metaphysical picture of how this language must function, but
we have no philosophical and non-ideological grounds for criticising such a form of language and its interlocked form of life;
moreover, we can only understand it when we keep in mind its
style of functioning in actual human living. Utterances 'lose, or
cover, their meaning when they are spoken apart from
. . . the forms of life which give them their meaning'.[18]

IV

I do not wish to attack Wittgenstein's claim that there is *no*
logical form that underlies all language and is its rational
foundation. Indeed, this seems to me a profoundly correct philosophical insight. It is – or so it seems to me – another such

insight to see and show, as Wittgenstein has, that the forms of language and the forms of life are inextricably intertwined and that only by working from a participant's view or a participant-like view can we understand either. (A participant's view and a participant-like view are related as the speech of a native speaker is related to that of an accomplished non-native speaker.)

I'm not, however, at all convinced that *these* two Wittgensteinian motifs commit us to a philosophical neutralism about the forms of life. Indeed we must accept the forms of life *in the sense* that we must, in understanding ourselves and our world, *start* from them. Without such a know-how, such a knowledge by *wont*, there is no understanding of religion or anything else and hence no philosophical problems. From this, however, it most certainly does not follow that we must accept them in the sense that the forms of life are beyond criticism. Further, and more controversially, the logical priority of this knowledge by *wont* does not entail that a whole given form of life – witchcraft or astrology, for example – could not be rejected as incoherent or as irrational; and it does not follow from the above priority-view (if I may coin a phrase) that there could be no relevant philosophical criticism of our lives or that philosophy – that is, good philosophy – must leave everything as it is.

Goebbels was an intellectual of sorts and he professed the following philosophy of life: The world is a poor and pitiful place. We human beings are cowards and lukewarm men. In fact Life is dirt. It is a big Monkey-Theatre where man plays the ape. Why don't we speak the truth! Human beings: a pack of dogs![19] Around such pithy sayings, together with his escape clause that 'the intellect is a danger to the development of character,' one can build a way of life with 'Life is dirt' as a *leitmotif*. But surely such a view is not beyond relevant criticism. The Nazis helped to make Goebbels' claim that man plays the part of the ape come true. Still, is it true that all human beings are cowards or lukewarm men? Are human beings never capable or seldom capable of love, honesty, integrity or justice? Certainly human beings take what Heinrich Böll calls 'the Host of the Beast' more often than we would like to believe. In his *From Death-Camp to Existentialism*, Viktor Frankel, who most certainly had a participant's view, records how victim and victimiser help confirm that 'Life is dirt', but he also gives us some pretty good contrary evidence too. Tolstoy's view of man is more flattering than is Goebbels' but it too doesn't square with all the facts, our illusions about ourselves to the contrary notwithstanding. But, from a recognition that there is less veri-similitude in Tolstoy than our flattering picture of ourselves would naturally lead us to expect, we need not and should not flee to Goebbels' or Flaubert's picture of the human animal. In looking at such ways of life it is evident enough that we have something here that admits of examination and criticism. Empirical evidence is relevant to Goebbels' claims about human behaviour and Goebbels' evaluation of life is also open to moral counter-argument. There is no reason at all to think that such a *Weltanschauung* cannot be relevantly criticised.

It will surely be replied that I'm being grossly unfair to Cavell and to Wittgenstein. With Goebbels' mythology, we do not have a form of life, a way of life, but the revolting babblings of a sick monster. Yet, it should be said in response, the Thousand-Year Reich might very well have been a reality and had historical circumstances been different these babblings might have come to form a new or at least a remodelled form of life. That is, they might have become settled culture patterns. In the past there have been charismatic culture heroes whose ravings have had a rather more enduring impact and have been crucially instrumental in the forging of new forms of life. Is it simply the fact that Goebbels didn't succeed in getting his views accepted that makes his claims susceptible to criticism? When several people agree in attitude concerning some innovation, agree about how it is they are to act, we have the makings of a new culture pattern; where there is a cluster of these patterns, we have a new culture, but there is no reason to think that where there is such agreement there can be no relevant criticism.

Yet I am sure that it still will be felt that such remarks do not cut to the heart of the matter, for such a criticism of some particular and contingent expressions of forms of life is not like a philosophical criticism of whole forms of life. In the Goebbels case we use a moral and political point of view to criticise and evaluate a specific 'moral' and political point of view. Here we remain within a form of life. Our canons of criticism are set for us by the forms of life in question. But what would it be like relevantly to criticise morality, religion, art or science *as a whole*? (I am assuming, for the moment, what many Wittgensteinian Fideists also assume, namely that these are forms of life.) Where would we get an Archimedean point on which to stand? It is in this latter, more general way, that we should understand Wittgenstein's claims about there being no *philosophical* criticism of our lives. Further, we should also stress here that in the above case there is no *philosophical* criticism of ways of life. We hardly need a fancy philosophical theory, or even any philosophical theory at all, to criticise Goebbels. Moreover, we should not forget that it may well be the case, as Wittgensteinians believe, that in workaday criticism – moral, political or artistic – a philosophical point of view is an impediment or just so much verbiage. Philosophy cannot supply relevant standards of moral criticism: the functioning relevant elements in actual moral criticism are our specific moral perceptions, an increased factual knowledge and our common sense. Working with these, we enlarge our political and moral understanding. But we do not need philosophy for that! It only, in such a context, would distract us from the actual work of moral criticism.

Yet, whether we call our criticism *philosophical* criticism or not, we can, it has in effect been admitted, criticise our lives, evaluate mores or traditional beliefs. At least some of our forms of life are not beyond criticism and granted this is so, let us now ask: why can't philosophy be relevant here, not in the sense that it must provide either some new *Weltanschauung* – some new tablets – to criticise and replace the old or some transcendental Archimedean; but why is it not possible for philosophical analysis to point out that certain claims are *non sequiturs*, that certain claims are self-contradictory, or that certain alleged claims are without truth-conditions, while purporting to have truth-conditions? Perhaps philosophy can reasonably do much more, but why cannot it at least do that? We indeed may not need a metaphysics, even a Kantian metaphysics, but surely a little logic won't hurt, and a sharpened understanding of the concepts of truth, fact and meaning may not hurt either. Indeed these concepts, like the concept of reality, may be systematically ambiguous; this would mean that their meanings are *partially* idiosyncratic to specific forms of life. But this would only establish a partial idiosyncrasy. We say 'There is butter on the toast', '2 + 2 = 4', and 'They ought not to kill the children' are all true. What makes them true is surely very different; the criteria for truth in these different cases are not the same. Yet there is something in common here too: in order for us properly to say of any of them that they are true, they must be statements made on certain determinate occasions, they must have the highest sort of warrant available for such statements, and the person who claims they are true gives us to understand that he has no doubt about them and that he is in a position to make that claim. Moreover, if a statement of any sort is true, it is to be expected that, under optimal conditions (conditions of un-distorted communication), rational, informed and reflective people will assent to it. These features cut across the statement type in question. And this fact about our language surely counts against the claim that the forms of life are self-contained, com-partmentalised or entirely self-sufficient. In deciding whether a given statement is true these general considerations must be satisfied, though we should also take note here that these are very general and indeed rather formal features. What (for example) would specifically count as 'the highest warrant avail-able' would be very context-dependent and what is to count as 'undistorted communication' may not be beyond dispute.

There is a further point to be made. Understanding what morality or science is, we can still meaningfully ask for the pragmatic point of either activity and we can get reasonable answers to these questions. We have in a similar way and with a more practical point asked critical questions about witchcraft, astrology, belief in fairies and the like and we have arrived at answers with the progressive demystification of the world (Weber's *Entzauberung*) that led to the non-acceptance of these activities, these forms of life. These activities – speaking now of the west – once played a major role in the lives of people; that they were almost always in such societies somewhat deviant, somewhat suspect, proves little or nothing, for science also had its humble origins and once was deviant and suspect too.

People ask such questions of Christianity, Judaism or Zen and they do not always ask it from *within* the general activity religion. Yet it remains to be established that no philosophical theory could help us know whether there is or is not a God. Why is it not possible, from self-evident premises, to form a deductive demonstration of God's existence? Surely, if it would work, it would give us knowledge of God. And why are not Hume's and Kant's arguments against these claims relevant to whether we have knowledge of God? Malcolm – a paradigm case of a Wittgensteinian Fideist – even tries to show, in what appears at least to be in conflict with this general fideism, that a certain argument of Anselm's shows that it is *self-contradictory* to assert that there is no God. Others have tried to refute this and Malcolm tries to meet their criticisms. Is there not plainly here an implicit acknowledgement that philosophical argument is relevant to our knowledge of whether God exists? If one can show, as Hepburn tries to show, that Jews and Christians speak of an encounter with God while at the same time maintaining that God is utterly transcendent to the world, then has not philosophical argumentation uncovered at least a *prima-facie* incoherence in this form of life? Do we not at least need philosophical argumentation to pump the bilge of the leaky vessel of faith?

If it is said in response that it is indeed a mistake for these Jews and Christians to believe in such encounters, then how can the Wittgensteinian Fideist be so confident that Jews and Christians cannot make similar errors in coming to accept their religions? What is the justification for his claiming that his form of life, simply because it is a form of life, can never be in error, can never be something that a rational man could find reasonable grounds for rejecting?

Cavell needs to show how any argumentation for or against such a form of life is always and necessarily irrelevant before we can reasonably acquiesce in Wittgensteinian Fideism, that is, assert that what must be accepted are the forms of life and that philosophy – that is, good philosophy – leaves everything as it is, for the forms of life are self-sufficient and cannot be relevantly criticised, though from *within* them one can in a piecemeal way criticise certain of their planks or manifestations.

There is a natural and perceptive objection to what I have urged in the last few paragraphs. No philosophical theory can tell us whether there are tables or chairs or other minds or persons, so why assume or think that it can tell us whether there is or is not a God? The Kantian and Humean arguments, if correct, show that certain philosophical attempts to establish the existence of God are mistaken; they do *not* show that there is no God or that we have no reason to believe in God or that we have no religious knowledge of God. The Humean and Kantian arguments are directed at the *philosophical* attempts to justify religious forms of life rather than at the forms of life themselves.

I, of course, agree with the Wittgensteinian that it is not a proper task of philosophy to tell us, what indeed we already know, namely that there are chairs, persons, books and the like. But I do *not* agree that it is not the proper task of philosophy to tell us whether there is a God, at least in the sense that it might show us that there could not be one for the very notion is incoherent. Am I being inconsistent? I think not and for the following reason: the very concept of God, the very first-order use of the term, is problematic while this is not true in the other cases. In saying this I have in mind the following: we are indeed puzzled about the proper *analysis* of 'person' but we are not perplexed about the very intelligibility of the concept, while there indeed is a way in which believer and non-believer alike are perplexed about the elusiveness of the very concept of God. The concept of a person is, of course elusive too, but not in the way in which the concept of God is elusive. We are baffled about the proper *analysis* of the concept of a person, but it does not so utterly baffle our understanding as the concept of God does such that we wonder whether it applies to anything, whether there could be anything properly called 'a person'. But we do have just these perplexities about God. And unlike 'unicorn' it is not that we know what we mean and know there aren't any, rather we are so puzzled by the concept of God as not to know whether there could be a God, whether literally we have a genuine concept here.

Given this conceptual situation, philosophers have tried, and quite properly, to show that the concept of God is of a certain nature, and that the evidence or grounds for there being something answering to that conception is such and such. Other philosophers in various ways have challenged either or both of these claims. The first brace of claims, if correct, would give us good grounds for believing in God; the second would give us grounds, though hardly conclusive grounds, for not believing in God. Certainly the correctness of Hume's and Kant's argument do not entail that there is no God. But if all the traditional

apologetic arguments bearing the accumulated weight of cent-
uries of religious reflection and reflection concerning religion,
are conclusively refuted and no new arguments are forthcoming,
we have good grounds for denying that we know or have reason
to believe that there is a God.

If a fideist counters with 'the heart has its reasons that
reason does not know', then further problematic conceptions
have been brought to the fore. What is 'knowledge of the
heart' or 'reasons of the heart'? Are these intelligible concepts
and even if they are do we actually have such knowledge or such
reasons and, even if we do, do they give us a knowledge of God?
These are perfectly proper and not atypical philosophical
questions and if they are answered *in a certain way*, it again comes
to the claim that we have no grounds for believing that we or
anyone else knows God or has reason to believe in God's
existence.

It is a philosophical question whether the very concepts of
religious knowledge or religious belief are coherent concepts.[20]
And if they are incoherent, that is, not genuine concepts at all,
then there cannot be any knowledge of God or justified belief in
God. If there can be no knowledge of God or justified belief in
God because the concept of God is incoherent then we have the
best of reasons for believing not only that the grounds given for
believing in God by Jewish and Christian philosophers and
theologians are mistaken but also that the holy man who claims
that there is a God is likewise mistaken. Such philosophical
arguments strike both at the philosophical arguments to justify
or vindicate the forms of life themselves. If there cannot be
knowledge of God because the concept of God is incoherent, it
cannot be correct to assert, as some holy men do, 'I know that
my Saviour liveth.'

V

The very concept of a form of life is in need of dicussion. Just
what is 'a form of life' or 'a distinct form of life'? Are we simply
talking about general human categories such as art, religion,
morality, politics, science and astrology or are we speaking of
something more specific, for example, abstract expressionism,
quantum mechanics, Seventh Day Adventism or what? We are

left in the dark when it comes to a determination of what constitutes a *distinctive* and self-sufficient form of life. Yet Malcolm tells us that 'one could hardly place too much stress on the importance of this latter notion in Wittgenstein's thought.'[21] But Malcolm does nothing to clarify what it is that we are talking about when we speak of a form of life. Cavell gives a similar stress but he too is unhelpful.[22]

Wittgenstein remarks that to 'imagine a language means to imagine a form of life'.[23] And he is willing to take the language of the builder and his assistant which simply consists in a distinctive employment of 'block', 'pillar', 'slab', 'beam', as a complete language, as a genuine language-game.[24] Wittgenstein then goes on to stress in Section 23 of his *Philosophical Investigations* that there are countless kinds of sentence and the kinds that are, are not fixed but are historically variable. New types of languages, that is new language-games, come and go. He points out in this context that his term of art 'language-game' is used 'to bring into prominence the fact that the speaking of language is part of an activity, or of a form of life'.[25] Wittgenstein provides us with examples; it should be noted, however, that these language-games are *parts* of an activity or a form of life. But just which activities, of which language-games are a part, constitute a distinct form of life? To decide this is very crucial, but here Wittgenstein's commitment to clarity most certainly does not show through. Late in the *Philosophical Investigations,* where Wittgenstein remarks, 'What has to be accepted, the given, is – so one could say – forms of life?', he takes as instances of a form of life mathematics and colour-talk and stresses the conventional nature of both.[26] Here, as one commentator puts it, ' "form of life" is seen to be connected with the "bedrock" rules concerning the use of language. . .', the rules which determine in that language-game what will count as a significant sentence or what are the criteria for truth or falsity in such an activity.[27] Here they seem to be thought to be relative to the activity or practice in question. Where this is alleged to be so, 'form of life' is usually linked with very general activities, for example, mathematics and colour-discrimination. But then Wittgenstein seems to use 'form of life' in a different way as well, for presumably there could be a language, a form of life, consisting only in the issuing of orders and the reports of battle.

Wittgenstein himself tells us that there are 'innumerable' and quite variable forms of life.[28] Forms of life and language-games seem to range from specific activities to something very general like mathematics or morality. Sometimes the specific activities called 'language-games' seem to get identified as forms of life or sometimes they seem, as in the quotation above, to be parts of a language, or, more likely, parts of the general activity of speech where it is the general activity itself which is the form of life. Wittgenstein's varied examples seem to indicate that sometimes he means nothing more determinate by 'language-game' and 'forms of life' than 'things done with words'. So we are left very much up in the air as to what we are to take as a form of life: a form which is (1) also a language or part of a language, (2) conceptually self-sufficient and (3) can require or receive no justification or foundation.

What does seem to me uncontroversial, important and true in this obscure talk is something which George Pitcher brings out about the dark saying 'the forms of language are the forms of life', namely that to speak and understand a language is to engage in certain modes of behaviour; that is 'it is a matter of being able to *do* a variety of things, to act or behave in certain ways – and to do so under the appropriate conditions.'[29] Still, if 'form of life' is to take anything at all from ordinary usage, there must be many ways of doing things with words which hardly count as a form of life or as a language-game. Surely, as we did above, to identify 'forms of life' and 'language-game' with 'things done with words' would constitute a *reductio* of Wittgenstein's view. But then of the many things done with words, the many games we play with language, what does count as 'a form of life'? How distinctive and conceptually self-sufficient must something be in order to count as a form of life? I'm not asking for sharp boundaries here. Of course, one would expect a penumbra, but what more definitely is the core concept of a form of life? Cavell does little to enlighten us here when he speaks of 'forms of life' as 'the whirl of organism', for example, 'our sharing routes of interest and feeling, modes of response, senses of humor and of significance and of fulfilment, of what is outrageous, of what is similar to what else, what a rebuke, what forgiveness, of when an utterance is an assertion, when an appeal, when an explanation . . .'[30]

How can this range of rather different things all bear the weight of 'what must be accepted, what can have no philosophical justification, is the forms of life'?[31] Malcolm and Cavell both tell us (and Winch suggests the same thing) that the very notion of justification must be elucidated by reference to forms of life; we justify something by appeal to the ways of doing things exhibited in forms of life. But we cannot justify a form of life itself. As Malcolm puts it: 'As philosophers we must not attempt to justify the forms of life, to give reasons for them.'[32] We can only point out 'This language-game is played' – that philosophy 'leaves everything as it is'.[33]

This *may* indeed be true for *some* forms of life, but why for all – particularly if 'forms of life' includes fairly specific activities: distinctive ways of doing things with words? Why should it be true, or is it true, that all our routes of interest, modes of response, notions of explanation, conceptions of rebuke are immune to philosophical criticism? This certainly seems highly unlikely. We need a very careful and very detailed argument to give us some grounds for believing it. And an essential prolegomena to such an argument is a clarification of 'a form of life' (*Lebensform*).

As we have seen, in practice Wittgensteinians seem to have in mind a very wide range of things. Toulmin's 'modes of reasoning' (forms of life) are very general activities like science, morality and religion; Winch seems sometimes to have that in mind too and sometimes something more specific, for example, Judaeo-Christianity, Azande magical practices and the like. Yet sometimes even more specific activities are involved. Where this is so, the appeal to the forms of life can even be used to back up thoroughly ethnocentric and partisan claims. Consider this notorious example. Peter Geach asserts, without any supporting argument at all, that 'If an argument has true premises and a heretical conclusion then a logical rule that would make it out formally valid is simply a bad bit of logic.'[34] Geach simply *assumes* that a heretical conclusion is a false conclusion. There must, he believes, always be some fallacy in any proof against Roman Catholic dogma. To such an arrogant and bald assertion an *ad-hominem* argument is perfectly proper as an initial move: Geach's Catholic faith together with his at least apparent acceptance of the Wittgensteinian doctrine that what must be accepted are the forms of life has stood in the way of his sense of logic and his sense of reality. There are literally thousands of different faiths most of which claim to be the 'One True Faith', and many of these systems of salvation have quite different forms of life. Roman Catholicism could even quite naturally be thought of as a Jewish heresy. What is regarded as heretical and what is not, or whether anything at all is regarded as heretical, depends on where one stands and *who* one is. What reason has Geach to believe that what the Roman Catholic Church regards as heretical is heretical, except, of course, from the limited perspective of the Roman Catholic Church? To this it might be replied that 'heretical', like 'small' or 'hard', is a relative term, for it must, in order to be adequately understood, always be filled out as 'heretical from *x* point of view', where the variable *x* must take as its values names for doctrinal systems.[35] But, even if this is so, as it appears to be, it still does not follow that Geach has said something that is acceptable, for what reason does he have for regarding what the Roman Catholic Church regards as heretical doctrine as false doctrine? If 'heretical' is such a relative term, Geach's claim would become doubly difficult unless he would wish to argue, implausibly, that 'false' is also a relative term. Moreover, to make his initial claim plausible he must give reasons for those beliefs. Otherwise his claims are little better than Heidegger's claim that truth is to be found by following Hitler's dictates.[36]

It will not do for Geach to tell us that he accepts these matters on faith, for he made this claim as a bit of philosophy. He made it specifically as a claim about what constitutes a good or 'bad bit of logic'.[37] For Geach to plead here that he plays a certain language-game, that he is immersed in Roman Catholic forms of life, and that what is given and what must be accepted are the forms of life is most surely a *reductio* of Wittgenstenian Fideism. If all such specific practices are regarded as self-sufficient, philosophically uncriticisable forms of life, then we have certainly achieved, in philosophy, an incredible absurdity. If this is what Wittgensteinian Fideism leads to then it should be unequivocally rejected, for it also means that all argument and reasoning between different sects, faiths and ideologies would be *a priori* impossible. But there is no good reason for believing that we are as badly off as that. At the very least Wittgensteinian Fideists must produce some very cogent reasons for such claims. The burden of proof is on them.

More fundamentally still, if we have premises known to be true and if from these premises, by procedures generally acknowledged to be valid, we derive a heretical conclusion, we have a very good reason to believe the heretical conclusion is true. Geach's claim that our logical rule *must* in such an eventuality be wrong – 'a bad bit of logic' – is simply the irrational evasion of a man who must hold on to his faith no matter what.

Cavell, who does not suffer from such dogmatism, might reasonably reply that a Wittgensteinian Fideist need not be comitted to anything like Geach's absurd dogmatism. 'Forms of life' need not be construed so narrowly. But then, it is natural to ask, how much wider should we construe them? And with this we are back to our earlier questions: what, after all, is a form of life? What are we to take as such a self-contained activity? Which social practices are forms of life? We are not told. Suppose our 'form of life' which must simply be accepted and not criticised is Christianity. Then indeed a Christian can relevantly criticise Roman Catholic or Lutheran or Seventh Day Adventist practices and dogmas. But the Christian 'form of life' itself is immune to relevant criticism. A Jew or Moslem with different forms of life cannot relevantly criticise a Christian. Moreover, they cannot relevantly criticise each other and a Christian cannot relevantly criticise their religious beliefs and practices. *But* this is only a slight improvement over Geach, for on such Wittgensteinian assumptions it is *a priori* impossible for there to be a relevant discussion between a Christian and a Jew concerning the respective merits of their religions. There can on such a view be no argument about whether Jesus Christ is or is not God. All we can do is engage in persuasion. There are, when the argument is on this level, only the self-sufficient forms of life – forms that cannot properly be called rational or irrational – which must simply be accepted or rejected. Yet to say that a man became God incarnate most surely *appears* to be a claim about how the world goes. It most surely appears to be the case that about this it cannot be true that both Christians and Jews are right. Why should we say – with easy evasion – that different language-games are played here, different forms of life are accepted and that we must simply accept them or reject them, but that we cannot relevantly reason about their adequacy?

Again it might be thought that our unit is still too narrow. We should not speak of the Christian, Jewish, Islamic or Mormon forms of life but of the monotheistic form of life. But a difficulty similar to the one we have just considered pops up again here. Not all theists are monotheists. Given the monotheistic form of life, we could, from this perspective, argue for or against Christianity or Judaism. But we could not argue about the comparative adequacy of Christianity and Hinduism. Moreover, there are the old Germanic gods. Are they simply to be ignored since no one plays that language-game any more? It is difficult to be content with this, but again, given Wittgensteinian Fideism, any argument about the comparative merits of the Germanic and Christian conceptions of deity would be impossible. We could only describe the different forms of life of which they are a part. But, is it so evident that the old Germanic religions are on a par with Islam, Christianity and Judaism? Perhaps, but it hardly is an *a-priori* certainty, as it would have to be if Wittgensteinian Fideism were true.

However, we should question the basic assumptions on which such claims rest. Ninian Smart, who very much stresses 'the higher order neutrality of the philosophy of religion' and who claims that we must understand religious doctrine in terms of its function in the whole religious practice of which it is a part, argues, in careful detail in his *Dialogues of Religion*, that there are relevant arguments between faiths as different as Judaism and Therevada Buddhism.[38] Therevada Buddhists are agnostic about supernatural beings, Jews are not; Hindus do not believe in the ultimate reality of a Personal Creator, Christians do. It most certainly appears that one or another or all of these parties are wrong here. No grounds have been given for saying they are all playing self-contained, self-sufficient, perfectly adequate language-games that cannot possibly be criticised. As is evident from Smart's book, argument between faiths is complex and seemingly intractable. But there are relevant points of contact and conflict. And telling considerations can be brought for and against these beliefs.[39] Only if the concepts of coherence and consistency are utterly internal to each form of life such that all criteria of appraisal are *sui generis* is it the case that Smart is trying to do something that cannot be done. But by now we should be very sceptical about that. Smart is not just having different forms of life have a whack at each other.

There is still another way we may look at the concept of a form of life in talking about religion. We might say that our unit for a 'form of life' is something very general like religion, morality, art, science and the like. If we say that, we escape the above difficulties but we encounter new ones. 'Religion' is certainly a very open-textured term; the several sets of practices, for example, Buddhism, Shinto, Tao, Islam, Judaism and Christianity, that are called 'religion' are very different. Some Jews and Christians believe that Buddhism or Confucianism should not really be regarded as religions; they are, they claim, rather simply ways of life, basically sets of ethical and prudential beliefs. It is also true that some Buddhists think that the very central doctrines of Christianity and Judaism are peripheral to 'True Religion', for they are not, according to them, conducive to salvation. There are indeed striking differences between all the various activities labelled 'religion'.[40] Even the notion of 'salvation', if we regard all religions as systems of salvation, is in the various religions very different. People, including sociologists of religion, do not agree about what 'religion' is, much less about what 'True Religion' is; religion is what W. B. Gallie calls an essentially contested concept, but this betokens a far more subjective concept than Gallie will acknowledge, for where there can *in principle* be no *rational resolution* about what is 'True Religion', then there most certainly can be no genuine argument concerning which of these religions are true religions, but only disagreement and conflict masked as argument.[41] *If* we take religion, science, morality, art as our units for 'a form of life', we have pressed together within each of them activities which are very heterogeneous indeed.

However, even if we accept religion as one of our units for 'a form of life', a Wittgensteinian Fideist will still continue to encounter grave difficulties, for we can and should argue, as did J. S. Mill and William James, about the 'utility of religion'. We are not simply limited to neutrally characterising that form of life. Philosophers can and do ask: Do we or do we not need religion? Would our lives be pointless or even impoverished, would morality topple, would life together in society become impossible, if people ceased to be religious? Is some religious belief essential to give sense to a person's life or can, and should, people learn to live, as Marx and Freud thought, without religious beliefs? These are difficult questions, unclear questions, but no adequate grounds have been given by Wittgensteinian Fideists that no argument at all can be given concerning these questions.[42] They can and, of course, will argue that these questions cannot be raised without being themselves part of a form of life. Once this is thoroughly taken to heart, they will claim, it will be realised that the above questions cannot be rightly asked, as though there were standards all things must match up to. But this again assumes that there are no such general standards of consistency, coherence or truth and it further assumes what I have challenged, namely that all criteria of appraisal are *sui generis* to particular forms of life.

As J. M. Cameron, a religious philosopher not uninfluenced by Wittgenstein and Kierkegaard, has well stressed, it is a philosophical prejudice to believe that whatever can be said can be said clearly. (This, of course, doesn't mean that we shouldn't try to be as clear as we can.) If these very general activities (for example, religion, science, law, morality) are 'the forms of life', no good argument has been given for the claim that we must simply accept them and that we cannot possibly relevantly criticise them.

In short, 'forms of life' and 'forms of language' are incredibly vague phrases, but in any of the senses discussed above, there are no adequate grounds for the belief that these forms of life must just be accepted and cannot be criticised philosophically. Such a rejection of Wittgensteinian Fideism can go hand in hand with an agreement with Wittgenstein that logic is no ideal language which gives 'the real logical form' of either our everyday or scientific statements. His criticisms in his *Philosophical Investigations* of any variety of logical atomism or any kindred approach seem to me devastating. But Cavell is mistaken in thinking that an acknowledgement of this commits one to the belief that philosophy cannot relevantly criticise forms of life. Moreover, one can believe that putative statements like 'And God raised the Lord and will also raise us by his powers' must, in order to be genuine statements of fact, be statements to which questions of evidence are relevant, without being committed to an ideal language method or to any belief that there is 'a real logical form' that underpins the forms of life.

Patrick Sherry in his careful and important 'Is Religion A "Form of Life"?' may have, in part following J. F. M. Hunter, teased out something more of what Wittgenstein means by 'forms of life'.[43] Sherry takes him to mean 'basic human activities and responses like hoping, feeling certain, measuring, giving orders, asking questions, and greeting people, and indeed using language generally.'[44] These on Wittgenstein's account are the fundamental facts – the givens – from which philosophy must start. There is no getting back of them and showing their rationale or rational justification. Rather, Wittgenstein tells us, 'What has to be accepted, the given, is – so one could say – forms of life?'[45] We reach a point in the search for justifications in which no more can be said and we must simply say: '. . . this is simply what I do.'[46] Sherry captures a number of Wittgenstein's essential points in the following passage:

> The refrain 'This is what I [or we] do' is one frequently encountered in Wittgenstein's later philosophy. Usually it is introduced to counter what he regards as a mistaken hankering after justification (cf. R.F.M. ii. 74). Wittgenstein insists that explanation must at some point give way to description (P.I. 109) and that it is sometimes silly to ask for reasons for things: 'Do we live because it is practical to live?' (R.F.M. v.14). 'Does man think, then, because he has found that thinking pays . . . Does he bring his children up because he has found it pays?' (P.I. 467). No, for sometimes we must just say 'such is human life.' Giving grounds comes to an end some time, but 'the end is not an unfounded presupposition; it is an ungrounded way of acting' (*On Certainty*, 110). This brings us to bedrock: 'The limits of empiricism are not assumptions unguaranteed or intuitively known to be correct; they are ways in which we make comparisons and in which we act' (R.F.M. v.18).[47]

In short, on this Wittgensteinian account, justification comes to an end with these forms of life. I have tried to show that there are serious difficulties in connection with this, but I should also like to raise an additional difficulty, pressed by Sherry, namely that if his above account of Wittgenstein's obscure conception of a form of life is well taken, then religion cannot be a form of life, though it 'includes several forms of life . . .'.[48] That is to say, religion would include the forms of life of hoping, feeling certain, loving, repenting, meditating, forgiving, praying, cursing, confessing, singing hymns and the like. What we should see is that religion is a collection of forms of life.

Given such a reading of 'forms of life' and the relations of forms of life to religion, Wittgensteinian Fideists would have to be arguing that 'forms of life and language-games like hoping, praying, worshipping, feeling certain about things, and telling stories cannot and should not be justified.'[49] That is to say, these are the things which do not stand in need of justification and indeed are activities where the very idea of justification does not take hold. But, as Sherry points out, this will not do, for while it *may* very well be the case that it is pointless to ask for a general justification of hoping, feeling certain, loving or forgiving, it remains the case that the distinctive and particular hopes of Christians, for example, hopes for the forgiveness of his sins and for the resurrection of the dead, or the kinds of love and forgiveness characteristic of Christianity, do stand in need of justification. To talk about justifying hope *sans phrase* seems silly, but to talk of justifying the rationality of hoping for a resurrection of the dead does not appear to be at all unreasonable. Sherry's comment here seems to me decisive:

> When Wittgenstein said that forms of life are 'given' and beyond justification or criticism, he meant that it is absurd to ask for a justification of hoping and so on in general, since 'this is simply what we do.' But this doesn't mean that we can't ask for a justification in *particular cases*, e.g., by asking whether a hope or an expectation is likely to be fulfilled. Likewise, when Wittgenstein said 'this language-game is played', he meant, among other things, that it is simply a fact of nature that people tell jokes, give or obey orders, make up stories, and report on past events. It would indeed be silly to ask for a justification of such practices; but *individual cases* can be appraised in various ways – jokes can be funny or crude, orders pointless or immoral, and reports of events untrue or graphic.[50]

While Cavell, Sherry and Hunter carefully explicate the

actual nature of Wittgenstein's elusive conception of 'a form of life' and probably succeed in capturing it, Vernon Pratt in his *Religion and Secularization*, while latching onto a notion that probably was not Wittgenstein's, actually comes up with a conceptualisation of a form of life which is significant in its own right and might well be something that Wittgensteinians could utilise.[51]

Pratt points out that neither Winch nor I distinguish between what Winch calls 'modes of social life', such as science and religion, and 'a form of life'. A 'form of life', Pratt remarks, is 'the life-style of a culture – of which the social structure and functioning of Winch's (or, better Evans-Pritchard's) Azande would be one example; and another, the form which civilization takes in contemporary Western Europe'.[52] He goes on to add, 'to describe a "form of life" would thus be to describe a culture: its class structure (if it has one), how power was distributed, the way in which the satisfaction of basic needs was institutionalized, the methods employed in maintaining order, the art which flourished, and so on.'[53]

A person might be engaged in several modes of social life and indeed they might conflict with each other, but, aside from someone such as an anthropologist doing field-work in some primitive society, most people are only involved in one form of life.

Pratt grants that I have made out a good case for not regarding modes of social life (with their partially distinctive vocabularies and conceptions) as self-sufficient palatinates.[54] But this does not begin to show that forms of life, as he has characterised them, do not set distinctive criteria of intelligibility, reality and rationality. Modes of social life do not set the meanings of many key terms used within their domains, for they are used in other modes of social life as well. 'Wise', 'powerful', 'loving', for example, are not only used in religious contexts. But, by contrast, to talk of a form of life is to talk of a culture as a whole with its own distinctive language. It is not, to put it conservatively, implausible to claim 'that concepts have meaning in virtue of being embedded in a particular form of life'.[55]

To speak of the conceptual self-sufficiency of whole cultures with their distinctive embedded languages is indeed a more plausible Wittgensteinian Fideist move, but it too is not free from serious difficulties. Magical beliefs, as Evans-Pritchard points out, are so ubiquitous in Azande culture that they affect everything one does and provide such a general orientation toward life as a whole in that culture, that they surely deeply affect (indeed pervade) the life-style of that culture. Similar things must be said for belief in God in Christendom during the Middle Ages. Yet, as we have seen, such conceptions are not beyond criticism in terms of conceptual resources within each culture and conceptual resources that may cut across cultures. Belief in God or belief in witchcraft may commit believers to inconsistent beliefs or to incoherencies. The concept of truth and the concept of consistency with its related concept of coherence are, as we have seen, not utterly form-of-life dependent. If Ruth Bendict's characterisation of the Dobuans is at all accurate or Evans-Pritchard's characterisation of the Azande is accurate, both the Dobuans and the Azande have beliefs, embedded into their very social structure and central to their lives, which could not possibly be true: which, in that important sense, commit them to illusions. But then such forms of life could not be beyond rational criticism and comparison.

VI

The dialectic of this argument should not yet come to an end, for there is another side to the matter that needs to be examined. Why – returning now to Wittgenstein's own conception of a form of life – shouldn't the notion of 'forms of life' be vague, by definition non-denumerable? If we take to heart what Wittgenstein says about completeness and family resemblance isn't this just what we should expect? Complaining against it on this score is like complaining against 'game' on the same score. A calculus-like language would be a human catastrophe. Moreover, when I ask for the 'pragmatic point' of an activity like religion am I not in effect assuming unrealistically that there are formal criteria of pragmatics *überhaupt*? Isn't that a myth? Can we do anything other than to assemble reminders about these forms of life and point out that to understand what morality, science or religion is entails understanding their divergent and diverse rationale? The real force of their procedures is (1) to ensure that there will be as little *Weltanschauung* in philosophy as possible and (2) to point to the fact that after we have a perspicuous representation of religious discourse, philosophical criticism of religion is gratuitous in all but the case of the 'knight of faith' and there the relevant criticisms are all existential and not in Wittgensteinian terms 'philosophical'.

Surely there is a sense in which we want as little *Weltanschauung* in philosophical *analysis* as possible but why cannot philosophy legitimately be concerned to articulate and defend a general outlook concerning man and his place in nature – an outlook which consciously incorporates certain values and has as one of its aims the alteration of human life? This is indeed a *Weltanschauung* but what of that, since no adequate grounds have been given for believing that such an activity is impossible, irrational or undesirable? Historically speaking philosophers have been engaged in this task and they have served as critics of other *Weltanschauungen*.[56] What good grounds are there for changing this form of life – we call philosophy?

Indeed let us not forget that philosophy includes – and essentially includes – analysis as well. But it is a mistake to think it must limit itself to that. The mistake involved in saying it is not the task of philosophy to articulate or criticise *Weltanschauungen* is comparable to the mistake involved in asserting that philosophers should do meta-ethics only, never normative ethics. What is valuable in such a slogan, for example, to do moral philosophy properly is to do meta-ethics and only meta-ethics, is (1) the stress on elucidation as the first step and often in a given bit of philosophising the only necessary step and (2) an implicit warning not to confuse these activities. Indeed it is sometimes true that after an elucidation has been carried out nothing more needs to be done; but this is not invariably true and, at the very least, there remains a wide range of normative arguments only some of which are existentialist.

To regard this critical normative inquiry as an essential element in philosophy does not at all involve an intention to search for formal criteria of pragmatics *überhaupt*. I suspect such a notion is scarcely intelligible, but whether intelligible or not, it is hardly at issue when, in reading James and Mill, Freud and Jung, Marx and Pascal, we trace out their conflicting and challenging arguments about the utility of religion. In the light of the deeply embedded human interests, needs and the capacities of the human animal, is religion something that human beings no matter what their condition, no matter what their society, need and should have? Pascal and Jung, on the one hand, and Marx and Feuerbach, on the other, come down on different sides of this issue, but, with the possible exception of Jung, they all understood religion very well – they only questioned its value – the rational point of continuing to have such a human activity.[57] It is in this sense that we are concerned with the 'pragmatics of religion'.

Understanding admits of degrees and of kinds. As we saw in discussing Winch, there is a sense in which we could not understand religion unless we understood something of what it involves as a participant would understand it. We could no more understand religion, if we did not have this participant's understanding, than we could understand bridge without *such* an understanding of bridge. But, as one might intelligibly assert that bridge is a stupid, pointless game, so one might intelligibly, though perhaps falsely, make harsh judgments about the value and point of religion in human life. Marx's and Engels's critique of religion may be unjustified but it is perfectly intelligible.

Let me now turn to the first objection. I do not, of course, object to 'forms of life' being open-textured and I do not think language is calculus-like or should be treated as if it were. I doubt if any light will ever come from the formalisers about any non-logical, non-metamathematical philosophical perplexity. But 'form of life' is a term of Wittgensteinian art and it is too minimally articulated to bear the great weight Wittgenstein, Winch, Malcolm Cavell and Phillips put on it. I find it, in ways I have tried to indicate, very useful to regard language in a Wittgensteinian way as an activity, and it seems to me correct to cut, as Wittgenstein does, the artificial barrier between words and *Lebenswelt* by stressing, even with the obscurity of 'forms of life', that the forms of language are the forms of life. But we have *not* been shown, what is *prima facie* implausible, that philosophy cannot criticise the forms of life but can only perspicuously display them. Indeed philosophers must first understand religion and this involves understanding the workings, 'the logic', of religious discourse. But they should appraise the truth-claims of religion as well.

VII

I will now consider, as a kind of coda to my discussion, what might be taken as a principled objection to the basic philosophical methodology I have used in attacking Wittgensteinian Fideism. The objection would smoke out, as Kierkegaard did with Hegel, what the objector would take to be central, unjustified assumptions of my own. A critic might commence by pointing to this cleft – I indeed must maintain only an apparent cleft – in my thinking. While like a Wittgensteinian I claim there is no general criterion of meaningfulness underlying ordinary discourse in virtue of which it might be shown to be inconsistent or be corrected by some other form of discourse; still, even without such a criterion, I maintain that it is possible philosophically to criticise and assess whole modes of *first-order* discourse, including religious discourse, as in some fundamental way unintelligible or incoherent. But how could this be? Am I not really being inconsistent or incoherent here myself? And in order to avoid inconsistency or incoherence must I not invoke some form of the very ideal language method I disavow? How else can I intelligibly make such criticisms of a form of discourse? How else could I show that certain types (kinds) of ordinary utterance are not in good logical order as they are? If one rejects the idea that underlying ordinary discourse there is some correct form for intelligible propositions, then one cannot but in consistency take Wittgenstein's position that every kind of sentence is in order as it is. The task of a philosopher cannot be to correct the form of a proposition – to put it in correct logical form – or to criticise it, for there is no such underlying correct logical form. The proper philosophical task can only be to understand it.[58]

This objection could be deepened and extended in the following way. I claim to appeal to and to discover by such an appeal that religious discourse has become a kind of incoherent, *ersatz*-metaphorical discourse in which terms like 'person', 'act', 'love', 'good' become so stretched as to be eroded of all intelligible content. *But whose ordinary language am I talking about?* Am I not simply assuming that there is a core of primary, ordinary uses which are paradigmatic for what is 'ordinary discourse' or 'non-stretched discourse' and that this paradigmatic core gives us our criteria for what is intelligible and what is not? Have I not failed to note Wittgenstein's insight that 'our language can be seen as an ancient city: a maze of little streets and squares, of old and new houses, and of houses with additions from various periods; and this surrounded by a multitude of new boroughs with straight regular streets and uniform houses.'[59] Have I not forgotten, my critic could reiterate, that ordinary language has a vast range of different and developing and intertwined uses and that, as Malcolm points out, 'Wittgenstein studied any use of language real or imaginary, that may illuminate a philosophical problem.'[60] Where is the justification for picking out certain bits of that language and taking them as paradigmatic for all uses of language? Isn't my procedure perfectly arbitrary? If one is consistently to philosophise from ordinary language one will not select such arbitrary paradigms, but, where the engine is not idling, one will simply look and see how the various language-games are played. Description will replace all assessment and even analysis.

I have in effect shown, the objection could continue, how different talk to and of God, and talk of 'the reality of God', is from talk of 'the reality of physical objects'. But I confusedly think I have done something more that cuts against Wittgensteinian Fideism and in favour of some form of scepticism. When I would have us believe that the latter talk of reality (that is, talk of physical objects) and not the former corresponds to objective reality, I am implicitly and unjustifiably holding on to certain arbitrarily selected paradigms. I could only make out this claim if there were some check on what is real and what is unreal which is not found in natural languages or conceptually parasitical extensions of them and which in some sense transcends them. But I am thoroughly sceptical of any such transcendence of what has been misleadingly called natural languages.

There is, however – the objection could run – no such criterion; there is no way of intelligibly asserting that religion, as a whole, or God-talk or any other mode of discourse as a whole, is a mistake or is incoherent. Mistakes and incoherencies occur but they are specific mistakes or incoherencies *within* a religious framework; moreover, the very criteria for whether such a mistake or an incoherency has occurred is to be found within religion itself. Philosophy cannot be for or against religion – it cannot reveal, as I try to do, the 'groundlessness of religion', it can, where it knows its place, only elucidate it. It will forever remain impossible to show that the believer's religious discourse and therefore his religious form of life and faith is *intrinsically* incoherent, or unintelligible.

It is just here with this challenge that I feel the most powerful threat to the basic theses of this book. If these criticisms cannot be met, there is, I believe, a fundamental error in my own reasoning. I feel here my philosophical commitments are pulling in several directions, for often I am tempted to argue in just this Wittgensteinian way – it sometimes seems to me so very right – and yet when translated into the concrete, when applied as Winch does to the Azande magical beliefs and when applied to talk of God, it seems to me to have absurd consequences. (Even Winch seems dimly to sense this when he speaks of the paradoxes of a protagorean relativism – paradoxes which he quite fails to overcome.) Yet surely we cannot stand apart from our forms of life with some criterion of conceptual propriety which is not rooted in these very forms of life? Hence my ambivalence. But ambivalent or not, if I cannot surmount these criticisms, my basic theses have been undermined.

First, if it is true that I am inconsistently Wittgensteinian, then I am indeed inconsistently *Wittgensteinian*. That is to say, if it is true that at some points I am led to assert that some types of ordinary usage are not correct usage, and if no Wittgensteinian could consistently assert that, then I am no Wittgensteinian. I agree with what Austin has made a platitude: though ordinary discourse is the first word, it is not necessarily the last word. I would add (making a very unAustinian point) that whole types of sentences used for particular purposes may be incoherent and that in the case of certain central segments of God-talk they actually are. Ordinary usage is only sometimes in order as it is.

Such an approach does not commit me to some logical atomistic theory of logical constructions or ideal language method but it does commit me to some claim – to put it crudely – that when we reflect on our various linguistic activities, we find, when it comes to talking about what there is, that some of these activities are epistemologically more fundamental than others. It is my claim that the epistemologically more fundamental ones, the ones that are culturally universal and essential for all understanding, are the ones that tell us about what some philosophers in a grandiose way call 'physical reality'.[61] Every tribe plays that language-game. And it is these clusters of claims which are open to test – to confirmation and disconfirmation – and it is with them that we have clear cases of both a definite sense and reference. It is indeed true that without a natural language we could not understand such meta-talk as I have just engaged in and it is also true that without such a language there could be no understanding of what it is to test the reality of something – what counts as an observation of an event, process, determinate thing and the like.[62] I am thus contending that when we reflect on the various 'forms of life' – the various linguistic activities that we actually engage in – we will find that some are 'ground floor', that is, determinative of what can be seen, after a careful reflection on one's language, as constitutive of or at least as an irreducible element in talk of what there is. The other forms of discourse are in various ways parasitic on it and if in trying to assert the existence of something we make assumptions which run counter to it, we say something which is incoherent. Yet this is hardly what philosophers such as Quine, Sellars and Rorty have characterised and criticised as foundationalism.

However, these remarks are vague, simply asserted rather than argued for and they remain programmatic. I believe something like this could be successfully argued and I think my remarks about the verifiability principle will do something to support such a claim, but I do not wish to rely on such a controversial claim at this point, but simply to indicate that if the arguments I am about to give in this coda fail and no other arguments of that type would meet the objections I have raised to my procedures, I would fall back on such a basic programmatic commitment.

One might be tempted to speak here of Nielsen's 'empiricist dogma' or 'positivist article of faith' or something of the sort. But I think this would be a mistake. First, I have arguments for such a modest empiricism which are open to assessment. And I would, of course, be willing to abandon my thesis if there were superior counter-arguments against them and against the plausibility of the thesis. Second, I think the specific arguments I and others have raised about specific claims of religion have such a force that it is more reasonable to question the general Wittgensteinian thesis that every form of discourse is all right as it is then to reject these arguments. After all, unless Wittgensteinian Fideism is itself to become a dogma, it must stand up to some kind of test.

I do not, however, think I need to be pushed to such contested and some, no doubt, would say barren ground, for I think I can show how independently of such a commitment I can consistently philosophise from ordinary language *and* properly criticise whole modes of *first-order* discourse as being in certain fundamental respects unintelligible or incoherent.

First, it should be noticed that it is one thing to say that ordinary language is inconsistent or incoherent and it is something else again to assert that of *a certain mode* of discourse: talk of God, talk of fairies, talk of ghosts and the like. I am only maintaining the latter. I do not think any coherent sense has been given to the former claim and I think that Ziff has shown in his *Semantical Analysis* that people who talk that way are talking nonsense. But to claim that every form of discourse is all right as it is, rests, as I have argued, on a compartmentalisation thesis, for example, religion sets its own criteria for what is intelligible, that is both unjustified, if my arguments have been at all correct, and inconsistent with Wittgenstein's claims that various forms of language are crisscrossed and involuted. My loyalty to his technique rests

(1)   on his arguments that language should be regarded as an activity – something that people do – and not as a calculus, and

(2)   on his claim that no general criterion – the ideal language of a logician or some metaphysical criterion – can replace or undermine natural languages in determining what it makes sense to say.

But to hold such a position is perfectly consistent with saying that there are certain segments of our language which are in certain respects unintelligible and that this can be seen by reflection on the actual workings of our language.

Malcolm maintains for himself (it is not evident that Wittgenstein would maintain this) that when a philosopher investigates a concept of ordinary language and comes to conclusions at variance with ordinary language, the philosopher can be quite certain that he must have made a mistake. This is at least plausible for the range of cases Malcolm considers. (Note they are what have become the *traditional* epistemological doubts.) If an idealist or sense-data philosopher says that it is logically impossible to see physical objects or if someone says that knowing how another person feels is a conceptual impossibility, we may recognise *that* they are in error (though not *what* exactly their error consists in) by noting that such sentences as 'I see my wallet now, it's on the sofa' or 'He is in a terrible state of depression' have a perfectly straightforward unproblematic ordinary use and hence cannot be self-contradictory or conceptually out of order. Where there is no hesitation about or perplexity about the actual use of such *first-order* sentences, Malcolm's claim is at least persuasive. But Malcolm suffers from a one-sided diet. No one would feel so confident about 'God is my strength and my hope' or 'My soul shall not perish'. With such sentences there is perplexity about the *first-order* sentences themselves. We do not know when, if ever, they are used to make either true or false statements, yet they purport to be statemental. Moreover, to say that they are not bits of ordinary language is plainly to make an arbitrary stipulation about what is to count as 'ordinary language'.

Such a response on my part does not meet but instead reinforces the criticism that in philosophising from ordinary language, I have, in criticising *first-order* religious discourse, arbitrarily selected certain common-sense paradigms as the key to intelligible speech and have simply rejected large segments of God-talk because they deviate from these paradigms. But I have not done anything so arbitrary or indeed arbitrary at all. Certain key segments of religious discourse *purport* to make true or false statements – assertions about what is the case, for example, 'God made the world and sent His only begotten son to save mankind'.[63] If we select for comparison with such God-talk certain paradigms such as 'There are clouds in the sky', 'Hans caught three fish', 'Women die sometimes in childbirth', which are bits of discourse used pervasively by believers and non-believers alike, we will see that there is an important difference between them and such God-talk. The propositions expressed by the use of such sentences have had their repeated use throughout cultural space and time. In very different cultures with radically different languages these sentences have their more or less rough equivalents. Peoples of all cultures, everywhere and everywhen, agree that statements made by the use of such sentences reveal to us what is the case. (This is not to deny that they make other and sometimes seemingly conflicting claims as well. But they do agree on such statements.) These forms of speech are the ones taken by everyone to be unquestionably informative. If anything tells us what is the case, they tell us what is the case. But, as Malinowski in effect shows, there is no such cross-cultural agreement concerning religious claims. Yet conceptual analysis reveals that non-anthropomorphic religious claims – claims which purport to be true or false and to be *tellings that*, not *tellings to* – are not empirically testable.[64] That is to say, they do not have the logic of statements used to make assertions about what is the case. It is also true that there are participants of the culture in which God-talk occurs who have no understanding of them beyond a Ziffian sense of the linguistic regularities into which they enter. They are completely unable – as was Wittgenstein himself – to say 'Yes they are true' or 'No they are false' or 'Maybe they are true'. They have no understanding of how these declarative religious utterances can be used to make statements – true or false.

Given this sociological fact, given the Malinowskian anthropological fact previously referred to and given the admitted logical peculiarities of these key religious utterances, it is not so clear that I have selected arbitrary paradigms for comparison with religious discourse.[65] In fact my paradigms are not arbitrary at all, for I have taken core cases of utterances that have an unquestioned factual status (if they don't have factual status nothing does) and thus can make substantive claims concerning the cosmos, if any utterances can, and I have shown that religious utterances – utterances purporting to make such substantive claims – function very differently than they do. If we couple this with the fact or putative fact that neither believer nor non-believer can show what it would be like to have religious knowledge or justified religious beliefs: to know whether religious claims are true or false or to have good grounds for believing them to be true or false, then the two contentions taken together give us good grounds, if they are true, for claiming that my range of paradigms is not arbitrary, for an examination of how they function reveals what language users, believers and non-believers alike, take in their actual practice to be such substantive statements and it also reveals how far key religious utterances, with a similar *surface* grammar, deviate from that norm.

Someone might counter that religious utterances are *sui generis* and about a mystery. Since this is so, why, after all, accept that commonly accepted norm? Why stick so exclusively to these ground-floor paradigms when the subject of our religious discourses is such an ultimate mystery?

To this it should be replied that with these core paradigms we have a norm which is common currency both in the language in question, namely English, and in the languages of the entire human family, while the very conceptions built·into God-talk, and not just the philosophical and theological accounts of this discourse, are widely disputed and not culturally ubiquitous. There is no one who can intelligibly deny that we can know what time it is, whether there are stones or trees or whether there is a difference between day and night, but many would deny that anyone, including manifestly holy men, ever have religious knowledge or even justifiable religious beliefs, for example, know or rightly believe that there is a God and that He guards the destinies of man. Thus philosophers, *qua* philosophers, should not rest content here with the knowledge – this language-game is played.

On Fixing the Reference Range
of 'God'

If my arguments so far have been near to their mark, the
dialogue between belief and unbelief and the concerns of traditional philosophical theology cannot be so easily put aside as
certain fideists, and indeed as certain sceptics as well, would
have it. Most importantly, there is no sound argument, providing a short way with dissenters, which shows that *first-order*
religious discourse and religion itself are and can be in no
conceptual disarray. No such short way with dissenters is
rationally justified.

Ziff, as we have seen, argued that there are certain conditions
associated with the concept of God which make God an intelligible though difficult concept. What we have said in the last
chapter and what we have said in criticism of Ziff does not
gainsay the fact that we have *some* understanding of the con-
-ditions, including the problematic conditions, of which Ziff
speaks. Thus, the concept of God is to some degree intelligible.
But, as we have also seen, the degree of intelligibility here
appears to be of a very low order. It may even be that the
conditions for the employment of 'God' do not even form a consistent set. Finally, it appears to be the case that, though 'God'
is supposedly a referring expression, we still have no idea at all
of how, even in principle, we could be taught the meaning of the
term 'God' extralinguistically when 'God' is used non-

anthropomorphically. Given that 'God' is a name or at least some kind of referring expression, this is, to say the least, an anomaly. And if, as Michael Durrant has powerfully argued, it is neither, there are, as he also shows, radical difficulties and incoherencies in the alternative, less intuitively plausible conceptions. While orthodox believers *intend* to be asserting a fact when they say 'There is a God', 'God exists', 'God does in reality exist', or 'Something and one thing only is omniscient, omnipotent and infinitely good', they seem not to be able to say what would or could, even in principle, count toward establishing either the truth or the falsity of such statements. Though 'God' and 'There is a God' are part of the corpus of English in a way 'The central meaning process is difficult to measure' or 'The ground of all and all cannot transmute itself into Being-for-itself' are not, yet for all that, such God-talk is in a certain important respect problematic.

In order for us to understand what we are saying when we speak of God, our concept of God must have some empirical anchorage: a factually necessary being – the most plausible of the candidates for an appropriate necessary existence – must have some empirical criteria if it is to be regarded as a coherent concept. That is to say, it must be at least possible to state what, at least in principle, would count for or against the truth of the statement that something is transcendent to the world and completely independent of the world. Positivists have argued that such a statement is not confirmable or disconfirmable, even in principle and have concluded that such a statement is therefore devoid of factual significance. Many would challenge that 'therefore', others would make determined efforts to supply an empirical anchorage for God-talk, and still others would argue that religious utterances have a radically different function in the *Sprachspiel*. We have already seen something of what Wittgensteinian Fideists would say about the latter. It is to the former arguments, as well as to some distinct arguments for the latter, that I shall now turn.

I noted in chapter 2 that there is a perfectly plausible sense in which religious utterances are intelligible. We can make grammatically well-formed religious utterances in English, Italian, German and so on, and religious terms have an established use in our language. But we also saw in chapter 2 and in my discussion of Wittgensteinian Fideism how in another sense there is perplexity concerning their intelligibility, a perplexity which would be relieved if we were able to exhibit a method of verification – some kind of empirical test – for key religious propositions. Yet it is just the likelihood of achieving this that is so very problematical. Consider a Russellian restatement of some key theological propositions:

(1) Something is the one infinite creator of all other things.
(2) Something is transcendent to the world and the world is dependent on it.
(3) Something is an infinite, eternal, uncreated, personal reality, who has created all that exists other than himself, and who has revealed himself to his human creation as holy and loving.
(4) Something is the source and ground of all existence.
(5) Something is absolutely unproduced.
(6) Something holds in himself the reason for his existence.
(7) Something does not depend on anything for his existence.
(8) Something is self-caused and self-justifying.
(9) Something is the substance of the cosmos and is gracious.
(10) Something made the world and governs it.

These putative statements have been taken as key statements in the theistic theological tradition. They have been thought to be key links in our God-talk. Most of them must be true if our quest for God is not to end in failure. Yet it appears at least to be very problematic if any empirically identifiable state-of affairs counts for or against their truth. If you think any of these statements are false, what in your opinion establishes or even tends to establish their falsity? If you think they are true, what in your opinion establishes or even counts toward establishing their truth? It is far from clear that anything does or could. They appear to be factual statements but they seem, at least, to lack truth-conditions.

Those who have argued for the factual unintelligibility of 'God governs the world' or 'The substance of the cosmos is gracious' have had an important but fairly specialised point in mind. Considerations of the above mentioned sort have prompted them to deny the factual significance of such claims. I shall now turn to a detailed examination of these considerations.

Antony Flew has put the general difficulty that many people feel about the *meaning* of these religious claims with considerable vigour in the form of a challenge – a challenge that by now has been dubbed 'Flew's challenge'. It could well be put like this: An alleged theological or religious assertion is a *bona-fide* factual assertion if and only if the person making the alleged assertion is prepared to specify what actual or conceivable turn of events would be incompatible with it and what actual or conceivable evidence would count against its truth.[1]

Flew asks of putative assertions such as 'God loves mankind' or 'God gave us an immortal soul' what at least conceivable turn of events would be incompatible with their being true or what at least conceivable evidence would count against their truth. If nothing could, then these statements are pseudo-factual statements, statements which some people (usually believers) believe to be factual, but statements which are actually devoid of factual content or significance. Yet believers, or at least many believers, do make such pseudo-factual statements. Rabbi Fackenheim's reasoning here is paradigmatic. Consider his remark 'that there is no experience, either without or within, that can possibly destroy religious faith' and his very typical apologetic point: 'Good fortune reveals the hand of God; bad fortune, if it is not a matter of just punishment, teaches that God's ways are unintelligible, not that there are no ways of God.'[2] This manner of reasoning is not idiosyncratic to Fackenheim. Many Jews and Christians seem to reason in this way – particularly when pressed. But if this is so – Flew's challenge goes – then certain of their very crucial putatively factual religious assertions are in reality devoid of factual significance.[3]

One can attempt to meet Flew's challenge in a number of ways. The most direct way is, of course, to meet the challenge head-on by showing how in principle such key religious assertions are factual assertions, that is, how they do specify what at least conceivable turn of events would be incompatible with them and what at least conceivable evidence would count against their truth.

Now, there is surely one way to do this, one way to answer

Flew's challenge, that is so very obvious that one wonders, perhaps fearing one's own naïveté, whether Flew could have possibly overlooked it. Asked to specify what would count against the assertion 'God loves mankind', we could say 'God hates mankind' or 'God is really jealous of human beings' counts against such a religious claim.

But it will surely be felt that there is something fishy here, for we are using religious statements to confirm a religious statement, but the confirming statements are as puzzling as the assertions to be confirmed. Surely what is needed, Flew would no doubt argue, are straightforward non-religious, non-theological empirical statements to serve as evidence for the religious statement. But this does smoke out an assumption in Flew's challenge. That is to say, a central assumption in Flew's challenge is that a religious assertion is a *bona-fide* factual assertion if and only if we can specify in non-religious, non-theological terms what at least *conceivable* turn of events would be incompatible with it or what at least conceivable evidence would count against its truth. Religious statements purporting to make factual assertions must be at least confirmable or disconfirmable in principle by non-religious, straightforwardly empirical, factual statements.

Why should we accept this restriction? Why must theological and religious statements be confirmable or disconfirmable by such straightforward empirical statements? Why, to be *bona-fide* factual and religious assertions, must they have such clear non-religious consequences? As Gareth Matthews has appropriately remarked,

> This might be a reasonable demand if we had already established that, e.g. geometrical assertions have clear non-geometrical consequences, that physical assertions have clear non-physical consequences, that ethical assertions have clear non-ethical consequences, etc. But in the absence of any such established conclusions, (such a claim) appears to be discriminatory against theology.[4]

Yet isn't there a point in being discriminatory against key religious and theological statements of the type we have been mentioning? The class of geometrical assertions for which we do not ask for non-geometrical consequences are all analytic statements; when we have geometrical statements which are not analytic, as in applied geometry, we expect non-geometrical consequences. Ethical statements are commonly validated or justified by non-ethical, purely factual statements, for example, 'Since he had a stroke, he ought to step down as premier of the country'. But a characteristic feature of purely *factual* assertions is that they must be confirmable or disconfirmable empirically. A statement would never unequivocally count as a factual statement unless it were so confirmable or disconfirmable, unless, some at least conceivable, empirically determinable state-of-affairs would count against its truth or count for its truth. But, if the assertion and the denial of the religious statement in question is equally compatible with any conceivable, empirically determinable state-of-affairs, then the religious statement in question is devoid of factual significance. It parades as a factual claim but in reality it is not. Flew's challenge is just this: believers regard certain of their very key religious claims – claims upon which the rest depend – as factual statements; but if they actually are factual, then it must at least be logically possible to describe two states both of which have distinct empirical content one of which actually obtains when the religious statement is true or probably true, the other when it is false or probably false. That is to say, if a certain empirically determinable condition obtains, the statement is true or probably true; if another such condition obtains, it is false or probably false. If it is not possible to conceive of any such conditions, then the putatively factual religious statement in question is neither true nor false. Flew challenges the believer to state these conditions of confirmation or disconfirmation, but it is characteristic of a vast amount of modern belief that its *putative* factual statements do not satisfy these conditions. The central religious beliefs of Christians and Jews, or at the very least of sophisticated Christians and Jews, are of this kind.

A believer may indeed, and quite properly, not wish to engage in natural theology; he may be a theological non-naturalist, that is to say, he may not believe that it is either possible or desirable to support his religious claims by appeal to empirical phenomena or by philosophical or theological argument. But, theological non-naturalist or not, if certain of his most crucial religious claims are factual claims, as he believes them to be, then they must, as we have noted, be at least confirmable or disconfirmable in principle. It is not a question of proving his statements to be true, but of showing that they have *the kind of meaning* he believes them to have – of showing that they have *factual* content, for if they are devoid of factual content, religious claims are (1) not what believers have thought them to be and (2) they are then, at the very least, without the kind of veracity that mankind has generally thought they possessed. Hepburn is surely correct in stressing that we should not identify religion with its doctrinal formulae and there may well be, as Santayana stressed, important elements in religion which survive the dissolution of central doctrinal beliefs. Yet the doctrines remain crucial and are importantly *presupposed* in many things that religious people do. If religion becomes moral poetry – simply a set of aspirational ideals – and, *if it is recognised as such*, much of its appeal, its great power to take hold of us and to transform our lives, will be irretrievably lost. Given what Judaism, Christianity and Islam have been, there are certain putative facts of a very extraordinary sort that a believer, to be a believer, assumes; certain key religious statements state these alleged facts; and one cannot consistently both believe that religious statements like 'God loves man' or 'God sustains the universe' are factual statements and deny that they are subject to empirical confirmation and disconfirmation.

Matthews gives the theological non-naturalist another innings. The theological non-naturalist could concede that not all religious statements are compatible with all conceivable states-of-affairs in the empirical world; they cannot be and still be factual. But we must be extremely careful what we conclude from this. The theological non-naturalist might concede that certain of his key religious claims, since they are intended by him as factual, must be subject to empirical confirmation and disconfirmation. To be factual statements there must at least be some conceivable but empirically identifiable states-of-affairs with which they are incompatible. But we must not forget that one can understand that a given claim is incompatible with some conceivable states-of-affairs without claiming to know what the incompatible states are.[5]

We could not understand what is meant by a given factual statement and still *not* understand what conceivable states-of-affairs it is incompatible with, for we would not then know its truth-conditions, and if we did not know that, we would not know what it stated. But anyone of us could, on the authority of someone else, accept that a given type of sentence is used by some people to make factual statements and thus must be incompatible with some at least conceivable states-of-affairs without claiming to know what states-of-affairs such statements are incompatible with; but we would still not understand what facts such statements asserted, for we would not understand what factual content they had and thus we would not find them factually intelligible. (Indeed we would even have to take it on faith that they had a factual content. We would in such a situation understand the sentence used to make such statements as we understand 'Orange ideas are last in line'; that is to say, we would understand it as being a part of the corpus of English, but we would not understand it, as it is intended to be understood, namely as a factual statement. More will be said in support of this in section II.) Now it surely isn't important that a *given person* knows how to confirm or disconfirm a factual statement; what is crucial is that it be capable in principle of such confirmation or disconfirmation and in that way be subject to confirmation and disconfirmation. But believers, or at least sophisticated believers, generally use their key religious sentences in such a way that no idea is given as to what in principle would be incompatible with their assertion or denial. It isn't just that some plain fideist doesn't know what would count for their truth or falsity; no-one does, not even the theological experts. It is this that keeps such statements from having factual significance.

To speak of God understanding what they are incompatible with, as Matthews does, is to go in a vicious circle, because it is just the factual intelligibility of a claim like that that is in question. And we cannot say, again as Matthews does, that it is a matter of faith with us that claims like 'God loves mankind' are factual, for if we cannot understand what it would be like for it to be a fact that God loves us or that there is a God, we do not understand *what* it is we are to take on faith. When we speak of having faith in any proposition p, we presuppose that p is intelligible and is indeed a genuine proposition. We can take its *truth* on trust but not its *intelligibility*, for unless it is intelligible to us, we do not understand what it is we are to take on trust.[6]

II

I. M. Crombie in two notable essays makes a determined effort to meet Flew's challenge. Unlike Hare and Braithwaite, but like Mitchell and Hick, Crombie believes that certain key theological and religious statements are statements of fact and, as such, they must at least be confirmable or disconfirmable in principle.[7] Christianity, as a human activity, involves much more than believing certain matters of fact, but it does involve belief in what the believer takes to be certain very extraordinary facts. Christians, whether they have an interest in natural theology or not, do have certain allegedly factual religious beliefs. They assert that there is a God, that he created this world and that he is our judge. These putative factual beliefs are presupposed in the other things that the Christian, Jew or Moslem does. They may be awkward 'facts' for him, but he must believe them none the less, for they underlie his entire activity. When we state such 'facts', we make what Crombie calls theological statements, though, as Crombie is quick to point out, his characterisation involves a wide use of the word 'theological' for they are the kind of statements which all Christians make. Unlike 'God is a necessary being', or 'God is pure act' or 'God is absolutely simple and immutable', they are made by plain believers as well as theologians. They cover what I call religious statements as well as what, on a narrower conception of 'theological', would be called purely theological statements, for example, 'God is pure actuality'. For the course of my discussion of Crombie I will accept his quite unexceptionable vocabulary.

Here Flew is met head-on: 'God sustains man and will finally redeem man' is thought by Crombie to be factual and confirmable or disconfirmable in principle. Christians and Jews must believe that there exists a being who somehow sustains the cosmos but who still is transcendent to it; and they must show how such a belief is empirically testable; that is, they must show

how an assertion or a denial that there is such a non-spatiotemporal individual is not equally compatible with any-thing and everything that might conceivably happen in the world.

How does Crombie make out his case?

In his 'The Possibility of Theological Statements', Crombie makes some remarks about the subject 'God' that seem to me immune to the trenchant criticisms that Blackstone has made of his views.[8] Early in this essay Crombie points out that para-doxical features inherent in God-talk make it apparent that we are *not* talking about a reality 'which falls within our normal experience or any imaginable extension of our normal exper-ience'.[9] God, Crombie argues, 'may not be identified with anything that can be indicated'.[10] We learn from the very paradoxical features of God-talk that, if religious statements are about anything, they are about a mystery. A god who is not mysterious would not be the God of Christianity, Judaism and Islam. Yet believers are convinced that they can know some-thing of the mystery 'God' refers to because they have a Revel-ation, that is, a communication made to them in terms they can understand. There is a sense, Crombie argues, in which we cannot know what it is that theological statements are about, but there is another sense in which we can know enough about God for our speech about him to have an intelligible use.[11]

Yet, Crombie continues, it isn't enough simply to know the mythology in which such talk is embedded. 'God' occurs in the mythology, but if we are ever to understand it as anything other than mythology, we must finally take the hard way and discover that to which 'God' refers without benefit of mythology.[12] In our earliest ways of thinking about God, God, like the Homeric gods, was almost a super-human being – a kind of cosmic Superman – and his grace and his wrath were something con-crete, but our theological concepts have been progressively detached from such a fictitious celestial being. With this grad-ual demythologising the concept appears to have been slowly but unwittingly deprived of all factual content.

Crombie concedes that it 'is indisputable that there is no region of experience which one can point to and say: that is what theological statements are about'.[13] But this, he reiterates, does not show that theological statements have no use, for their very elusiveness is a partial definition of the use they have: it is 'a consequence, indeed an expression, of the fact that all theological statements are about God, and God is not part of the spatio-temporal world, but is in intimate relation with it.'[14] 'God' differs from ordinary proper names not only in the fact that, like 'Mussolini', it has certain descriptive phrases regularly associated with it, but also by virtue of the fact 'that its use is not based fundamentally, as theirs is, on acquaintance with the being it denotes'.[15] 'God', one is inclined to think, is an improper proper name. 'God', we are told, stands for an individual. But what can be made of this claim when the 'normal criteria of individuality are not held to apply in this case'?[16]

The descriptions that are sometimes offered as uniquely characterising him ('the first cause', 'a necessary being') are such that nobody can say what it would be like for something to conform to one of them and thus they lack identifying force.[17] How, then, can we fix the reference range of 'God'? If 'God created the world' is to be a factual statement 'we need to be capable of envisaging specimen situations which fall within the range and specimen situations which fall outside it.'[18]

Crombie wisely remarks that the anomalies inherent in theological statements could well be taken, *not* as attesting to their logical incoherence, but as implying that the 'formal properties of our statement alone' could also be taken as attesting to the fact that theists 'believe in the existence of a being different *in kind* from all ordinary beings'.[19] To believe, as believers do, that God is a transcendent, infinite and incomprehensible being in an incomprehensible relationship to the universe, is, among other things, to believe that there exists an *object* of discourse which is particular but not indicable.[20] To put the matter this way will not by itself, Crombie recognises, solve any problems but it will make it crystal-clear what the believer is *not* talking about.

To conceive of the object of the believer's God-talk, we must be willing to conceive the possibility of an object which is 'neither similar to, nor in any normal relation with, any spatio-temporal object'.[21] 'God', a believer believes, refers to a mystery beyond experience. Yet the believer also believes that there are faint traces or indicia of this Divinity 'to be detected in experience . . . .'.[22]

How much more can we fix the reference range of 'God'? We have been given some negative clues about what we are not talking about, but the *via negativa* cannot carry us all the way to the promised land. We must, Crombie contends, to make sense of Jewish–Christian talk *about* God and *to* God, be able, in a positive way, to say something about what it is that Jews and Christians are talking about or to. But if we listen attentively to God-talk in its living contexts, we will, Crombie argues, come to discover its reference range.

Our concept of the Divine, vague as it necessarily is, 'is the notion of a complement which could fill in certain deficiencies in our experience, that could not be filled in by further experience or scientific theory-making; and its positive content is simply the idea of something (we know not what) which might supply those deficiencies.'[23]

What are those deficiencies in experience that lead us to speak of the Divine? We cannot, Crombie argues, be completely content with the idea that we are normal spatiotemporal objects. We cannot adequately describe a human being as we would 'a chair, a cabbage or even an electronic calculating machine'. We need additional concepts like loving, hoping, dreaming, and so on, which do not admit of a full characterisation in purely physical terms in the way walking or digesting do. The agent's experience of such things *cannot* adequately be characterised in terms that are appropriate to spatiotemporal objects; 'part of our experience of ourselves is only describable with the aid of concepts of a non-physical kind.'[24]

This, Crombie argues, should *not* lead us to a Cartesian dualism; 'we should not derive from this the grandiose view that we are spirits. . .'.[25] What we should recognise from this is that it gives us 'the notion of a being independent of space, that is a being whose activity is not at all to be thought of in terms of colliding with this, or exercising a gravitational pull on that'.[26] We have no *lively* idea of such a spirit – such a being independent of space – but our inability here is not like our inability to conceive of a being corresponding to a meaningless or self-contradictory description. It is not like 'round-square' or 'asymmetrically democratic potato'.

'Spirit' is not an expression which affronts our logical conscience or leaves us with no clue at all. There are many different grades of 'not knowing what is meant by . . .' and our ignorance of the meaning of 'spirit' (that is, of what something would have to be like to conform to the requirements of this world) is not absolute.[27]

Given such dual aspects in our own nature, we have, according to Crombie, some inkling, in our own experience, of the reference range of God-talk.

Because as agents we, or many of us at any rate, are not content to view ourselves merely as physical objects, but as something in some sense distinct from or different from physical objects, we have come to feel alienation, we have come to view ourselves as strangers and sojourners upon the earth, and we have out of our needs posited 'a spiritual world to which we really belong'.[28]

Given that we are beings with a spiritual aspect, we have been led to conceive, though surely not with any clarity, of beings – pure spirits – who are perfectly what we are imperfectly. The smattering of spirit which we find in ourselves is an ambiguous pointer to a perfect spirit – a spirit which we cannot conceive – from which our imperfect spirituality comes.

But isn't this notion of 'spirit' an illegitimate, reified abstraction? Perhaps we cannot adequately describe human actions in the terms appropriate to describing the movements of a ball or other physical objects or even movements of the human body, but this does not at all justify the claim that we have an idea of 'a spirit', or of a 'non-spatiotemporal object', or 'non-spatiotemporal person'. 'Spirit' is not the name of or a label for a distinct kind of being or entity. As Crombie well puts the objection himself: 'We should all regard it absurd to speak of beings which were pure digestions; not the digesting of animals, but just digestings. Is it not equally absurd to speak of things which are pure spirits; not the spiritualizing of animate physical objects, but just spirits?'[29]

In response to this Crombie makes a point which is central to his whole analysis. Crombie agrees that if our claim is that we know what we mean by 'spirit' in the way we know what we mean by 'digestion' the above objection is decisive. But the theologian need not and should not commit himself to any such claim, for 'spirit' has a different role to play in religious discourse than it has in everyday life. 'Spirit' so functions theologically that in Berkeley's words 'we have no idea of spirit'; that is to say, we do not know what in its theological use 'spirit' stands for or denotes. Crombie only rejects as extravagant the claim that we have no notion whatsoever of how the word is used in such a setting. To use the word properly in a theological setting involves the deliberate commission of a category-mistake under the pressure of religious convictions that require for their expression such a deviation from what in non-religious circumstances would be our normal linguistic practice. It is indeed true that we cannot have any clear conception of such a spirit, but the word does have a use in religious and theological discourse. In fact it is the case that the theological and religious use of 'spirit' – and this use defines such meaning as it has for us in religious discourses – involves a category-mistake, but it is not *simply* a category-mistake that results from logical or linguistic confusion 'but one *deliberately* committed to express what we antecedently *feel*; and, if we antecedently feel something, the category-transgression we deliberately commit to express that feeling has some meaning – that, namely, which it is designed to express.'[30]

Crombie is surely right in saying that something may be intelligible though we have no clear and distinct conception of it, but the problem is whether we understand *anything* of 'pure spirit'. Does 'a pure spirit' have a use any more than 'a pure digesting'? I don't think so. 'Pure spirit' parades as a referring expression, but unlike 'the spirit of man' or 'her spirit was down', we have no grasp at all of what we are talking about here.

But, it will be replied, Crombie frankly grants that we do not know the meaning of 'spirit' in its religious use; he readily admits that he has 'no idea of spirit'; he even recognises that such a use of 'spirit' involves a category-mistake. Yet Crombie thinks that all the same, by this deliberate committing of a category-mistake, we express that of which we have some inkling through our understanding of ourselves 'only in so far as we are spiritual'. But we have no understanding of ourselves *only* as spiritual beings. Crombie himself can make nothing of man 'as a committee of two distinct entities, body and soul'. We understand what it means to speak of our spirits being down or of our being in high spirits, but since 'spirit' is not a label for a distinct entity or being or process, we have no more idea or notion of ourselves 'only in so far as we are spiritual' than we have an idea or notion of an engine 'only in so far as it is an engine and not a piston, valve, carburettor, and so on'. It isn't that we have aspects or parts here which are distinguishable but not separable, but that as we have no idea of an engine as something distinguishable from its parts, so we have no idea of a spirit as something distinguishable from a man, donkey, chimpanzee, and so on. We have no idea of ourselves 'just as spirit', so this cannot serve to give us even an inkling of what a pure, bodiless spirit is. It is not that we lack a clear and precise conception of it: that is indeed tolerable; it is rather that we have no understanding of it at all. There is no 'human aspect' or 'human part' which 'spirituality' or 'spirit' names or labels that can, even in principle, be conceived of as something separately identifiable from the behaviour of an animate human being or other animal and thus can serve as a model for an appropriate, though vague, understanding of what is meant by 'pure spirit' or just 'a spirit'.[31]

Crombie is no doubt correct in arguing that the category-mistake involved in such talk of 'spirit' does not result from pressures derived from logical theory, but results from an attempt to express what we antecedently but obscurely feel. He is also no doubt right in arguing that such a conception can 'survive a clear realization of the logical anomalies of such a belief'.[32] But, after all, what is it that we do feel? Well, as Crombie puts it, we feel our alienation, our estrangement; we feel like strangers, sojourners on the earth. We, or at least some of us sometimes, no doubt do *not* feel 'at home' in our world; the contemporary world as well as the not so contemporary world has been a place where men have frequently experienced estrangement; we dream of some perfect isle where there is no death, no hate, no feeling of not belonging, and so on. Here 'another world' is intelligible though fanciful, just as anthropomorphic gods are intelligible; it could serve as our model of 'the spiritual world, to which we really belong'. Utopia may be unrealisable but it is not inconceivable; but, again once we move away from anthropomorphism, we fly into unintelligibility. We can understand what it is to talk of blessed isles, but we do not understand what it is to talk of a non-spatiotemporal world. But, as Crombie stresses, no civilised person believes that such blessed isles or spirits exist and we can no longer accept the old anthropomorphic conception of God. What we would believe in, if we were to believe in such anthropomorphic spiritualities, is intelligible enough; it is just a gross superstition. To avoid superstition, but to preserve belief, we abstract once too often and get a concept of 'Spirit' and 'a non-spatiotemporal being' that is devoid of sense; but when we engage in our characteristic religious activities, the old anthropomorphic picture reasserts itself and our words do have an intelligible use. We unwittingly shuttle back and forth between these two contexts and easily but conveniently conceal from ourselves that we do not understand what we are talking about.

It is indeed true that it is not just conceptual puzzlement but emotional need that prompts us to make a deliberate category-transgression, but the category-transgression in both cases points to a logical confusion. We have a use of 'spirit' and 'spiritual world' that is quite intelligible but involves *no* opting for some 'non-spatiotemporal object' or, for that matter, 'a purely mental entity or part', whatever that could mean. We have no inkling or indicia in experience which point, no matter how opaquely, to a pure spirit. We have no clue to it at all. Thus our dissatisfaction with viewing ourselves as non-spiritualising organisms and our need to acknowledge a spiritualising aspect in our own actions give us no clue to what it is we are talking about when we speak of that mystery 'beyond experience' which is the divine. It gives us no understanding at all of the extralinguistic reality – the semantics – of 'the Divine' or 'God'.

But God is not only a spirit, he is infinite spirit. Let us assume that in one way· or another I have been mistaken in my argument that Crombie has not given us an intelligible model for understanding 'spirit' in 'God is a spirit' or 'God is spirit'. But even so, as Crombie well recognises, he is not out of the woods yet, for even assuming, for the sake of the argument, that we understand the noun, let us now ask: 'Do we understand the adjective?' More specifically, do we understand the phrase 'infinite being'? (We certainly understand 'an infinite number of natural numbers' but 'an infinite being', 'an infinite particular', is another kettle of fish.) Again we can say some negative things about the use of 'infinite being'. An infinite being is unlimited; there is nothing to which such a being must conform. Yet since we cannot know God, we cannot acquire a precise sense of 'infinite being'. But for all that, 'infinite being' might have an intelligible use.[33]

This term, Crombie argues, gets its sense by contrast with this universe and the things within it. Many people, who are fully aware that we cannot prove that this universe has an origin outside itself or even give good evidence for that belief, still maintain that there is something about the universe that prompts us to ask where it comes from. This gives us our inkling in experience, which enables us, in an indirect way, to fix the reference range of 'God'. To understand 'infinite' as well as 'omnipotent' and 'creator', when applied to God, we must have these feelings of the finitude and the contingency of things, we must have the conviction that the universe is, in some sense we can scarcely understand, a created, dependent, derivative universe.

If we have these feelings, then we must by contrast be able in some sense to conceive of a non-derivative (that is infinite) being. This is the closest we can get to understanding such a being. In speaking of the universe as finite, contingent or derivative, or, less technically, in making the judgment that there must be something behind all the passing show, we are exhibiting our 'intellectual dissatisfaction with the notion of this universe as a complete system'.[34] The concept of God, the concept of an infinite being, is that which makes contrast with what we conceive the world to be like when we feel its limitations or imperfections. To speak of God is 'to refer to the postulated, though unimaginable, absence of limitations or imperfections of which we are aware'.[35]

To make clear his meaning Crombie gives us an analogy. In writing an essay one might feel that a given sentence one has just written does not correctly express what one wanted to say, without, at the moment, being able to say what 'the correct version of the sentence' stands for. But one would still recognise it and welcome it if it came. We are in a similar boat about the universe. Our sense of finitude and contingency gives us an intellectual dissatisfaction with the universe; that is, it gives us a sense of its impermanency and createdness, but we still cannot say what would characterise 'a non-contingent universe'. None the less as *that which* would in some sense fill out these gaps or deficiencies in our experience, we have, Crombie argues, some very obscure notion of the reference range of 'God'. To ask for more is to neglect the otherness and *essential mysteriousness* of God. A God who is not mysterious would not be the God of our religions.

There are some crucial differences between these cases which may render Crombie's analogy useless. From past experience with other sentences, we do indeed know what it is like finally after a struggle to get the correct version of a sentence. There may have been a time in which people did not have such an idea of a correct version of a sentence, but just felt somehow dissatisfied with some of the sentences they wrote and kept working at them until they no longer felt that way. Gradually there emerged, from situations like that, the rather vague conception of 'getting the right version of the sentence' so that now when a sentence we write seems to us somehow wrong, as mine frequently do, we have through all these past cases an admittedly very amorphous concept of what it is to get the correct version of a sentence. Only we do not know, in *this particular* case, what 'the correct version of the sentence' refers to. But we know in general what we are talking about when we talk about the correct version of a sentence. But, as Peirce once observed, universes are not as numerous as blackberries. In other cases, we have not been able to contrast 'a finite, dependent universe' with 'an infinite, non-dependent being'. We have never been able with other cases of universes independently to identify or indicate such an 'infinite being', so we do not understand what is supposedly being referred to or pointed to by such terms. We speak metaphorically of their 'pointing out of experience' but we have been given no idea at all of what 'to point out of experience' means, much less of what 'to point out of experience in a certain direction' means.

But the analogy apart, what does it mean to speak of an 'intellectual dissatisfaction with the universe as a complete system'? Why qualify it with 'intellectual', why not 'emotional'?

In speaking of 'the universe' we have an umbrella term for all the finite, contingent things, processes and events that there are. Why should it be a surprise or an intellectual problem, given some minimal reflection about what a thing is, that there should be an infinite or at least an indefinite number of things that came into existence and some day, no doubt, shall cease to be? And why should it be a surprise to us that in the final analysis we can only describe what they are? Why should this give us any licence for the very odd phrase 'the universe is irrational' or 'the universe is dependent'? Why should it give us an intellectual dissatisfaction with the universe? I should think that we should rather be intellectually puzzled as to what it could *mean* to say of the universe that it is or could be other than this.

But as a harassing, disturbing kind of *emotional* perplexity, carrying with it certain verbal pictures, it is possible to understand what it would mean to say that one had a certain dissatisfaction with the universe as a complete system. We (or at least we westerners) in talking about things (occurrences, processes and the like) in the universe have learned to look for further things, again within the universe, upon which the things we examined depend, and then in turn we look for still further things upon which these things depend without any apparent *a-priori* stopping point. Given this cultural practice, we may, in certain moods anyway, also want to ask that question about *the totality of things*, especially if we as children have been told that everything depends on God, that he is behind 'the whole passing scene' and the like. We have an anthropomorphic but intelligible picture here which will carry us along, but we can't get behind it or beyond it. It is plain enough that our question is not a rational question. It only strikes us, or strikes some of us in certain moods, as a rational, literal question because we have an emotional investment, resulting from powerful early conditioning, in so talking about the universe. We should not speak here, as Crombie does, of an intellectual dissatisfaction, but of an emotional one born of our natural infant helplessness and our early indoctrination.[36]

That there is no intellectual problem here but an emotional harassment, felt as a philosophical problem, is evident enough when we reflect that we do not understand what we are asking for when we ask for a non-derivative, non-contingent, infinite being, by reference to which we might contrast ourselves as derivative, contingent or finite beings. But without a nonvacuous contrast, without the ability to say what would and what would not be an instance of whatever it is we are supposedly talking about, we do not yet know what we are talking about. Crombie sometimes concedes this, or at least *seems* to concede it, when he says we have no idea of such a being, or confesses that such a reality is incomprehensible, for if we have no idea of it and if it is incomprehensible, then we indeed have no understanding of it and it is for us a meaningless notion. Furthermore, we cannot have an understanding of one half of the pair of concepts finite/infinite, derivative/non-derivative, contingent/non-contingent without having an understanding of the other.

But, Crombie could reply, we do after all have an understanding of our contingency, finitude, derivativeness, for we, or at least some of us sometimes, have in a very vivid way feelings of contingency, finitude and derivativeness. And thus we must have *some* understanding of what it means to speak of a non-finite, non-dependent being. Crombie could concede that he should not have said or suggested that an idea of such a being is altogether unintelligible.

The argument is slippery here, but let us, for the sake of the argument, accept Crombie's rejoinder. But accepting it, it still does not at all carry us to an understanding of some object of discourse that is an infinite, non-spatiotemporal, non-indicable individual. It does not show us what would or logically could satisfy these conditions. What gives us the *illusion* that we know what we are talking about here is that ordinarily, when we feel our contingency and finitude, we contrast it with something that in a physical sense, and in a quite non-metaphysical sense, is permanent. We look up at the vast starry skies and reflect on the fact that we are by contrast, infinitesimal, momentary creatures. We seem, and in a way are, as nothing by contrast with 'the ageless stars'. We feel to the full our mortality, our contingency, and our finitude and there is something perfectly physical, but still in a non-metaphysical way mysterious and grand with which we can and do contrast our finitude and contingency. We can, alternatively, if our grip on reality is not so good, perhaps conceive of a superhuman but quite spatiotemporal being, who is not contingent, dependent, derivative, finite *in the way we are*. This conception of a cosmic Popeye also gives us our sense of finitude and contingency and gives us our necessary contrast to ensure that our concepts of finitude and contingency are intelligible. But, as Crombie stresses himself, belief in such superhuman beings is a gross superstition. In trying to distinguish our developing religious beliefs from such superstitious beliefs we abstract once too often and come up with a pseudo-concept devoid of factual content and thus, when we assert that what this concept supposedly refers to actually exists, we have said something that is without factual intelligibility. Yet it is this pseudo-concept that Crombie has found so necessary for non-superstitious theistic belief. Crombie has tried hard to meet Flew's challenge but he has not succeeded in doing it.

III

I have not invoked in my above arguments all of the considerations that Crombie uses in elucidating the logic of God-talk. Crombie, in attempting to show that certain crucial God-statements are indeed factually intelligible, invokes the doctrine of analogical predication, the authority of Christ, and a theory of eschatological verification. I have elsewhere tried to show the defects in the concepts of eschatological verification and in such an appeal to authority. And Crombie's use of analogy has been subject to devastating criticism by Blackstone.[37] But Crombie's claims which I have just examined are quite independent of the above mentioned claims. I have stressed these distinct, logically independent claims and have tried to show that even with them Crombie has not been able to establish how it is that his key theological statements have factual content. Yet they are Crombie's central arguments for delimiting the reference range of 'God'. If they collapse Crombie's account would be thoroughly gelded.

There remain, however, some additional arguments that might be used to give force to Crombie's claim to establish the factual status of theism.

Crombie has some important things to say about the role of parables in religion. The Bible abounds in parables and they are essential for our understanding of the claims of religion. 'Parable', Crombie admits, is used by him in an extended sense.

The description of Christ's action of riding into Jerusalem on an ass on Palm Sunday would in Crombie's terms count as a parable, for it helps us to understand something about the extraordinary nature of the Messianic King and the non-political nature of the Messiah's kingdom.[38]

Our knowledge of what God is like is only given in parables. Our understanding of many sentences like 'God is wrathful toward sinners' or 'God is our merciful Father' can only be understood within the parables of our religion. But we also come to understand that our parables do not tell us, in any literal fashion, what God is really like, for example, how he is merciful, wrathful, and so. But we *trust* the *source* of our parables. We trust, take on faith, that our images given in the parables are faithful: that the parables are faithful, that they refer us, and refer us in a *certain direction* 'out of experience . . .'.[39] They point to an incomprehensible reality, totally out of our own or anyone else's experience, which is the underlying reality that we approach through a faithful parable.[40]

Why do we accept these parables as *faithful* parables – as parables which truly 'point out of our experience'? If we are Christians, we do this because we trust Jesus and he authorises the parables. Jews and Moslems would accept other religious authorities as authorising certain parables as faithful, reliable parables. We, as knights of faith, simply trust the source of our parables. We trust (have faith) that our parabolic language refers beyond the parable to a God whom we cannot positively comprehend. But, if we are Christians, our trust in Jesus leads us to believe that we will not be misled by the parables as to the nature of the underlying reality referred to in the parables.

This talk, tempting as it may seem to some, will not do. Unless we understand what is meant by saying, outside of the parable and quite literally, that there is a God and he is merciful, how could we possibly trust that Jesus or any other religious authority is either guiding us rightly here or misleading us in the parable, for we could not, if we did not understand the utterance literally in its non-parabolic context, know what could count as being misled or as failing to be misled by Jesus or by anyone else?[41] Without some independent way of indicating what we are talking about when we are talking about God, we cannot understand what is meant by saying that the image or the parable *is or is not* faithful. And we cannot take on trust what we cannot understand, for we cannot know *what* it is we are supposed to take on trust. If, as Crombie avers, we can *only* talk about God in images, then we cannot intelligibly speak of faithful or unfaithful images any more than we can speak of married or widowed stones. And to add insult to injury, we must note that the phrase 'parables referred out of our experience' like 'unconscious toothache' has no use. Wittgenstein gave 'unconscious toothache' a use; Crombie has *not* given 'referred out of our experience' a use.

It might be replied that in general we know what it is like to be misled. We know it to be a distressing, unpleasant and disheartening experience. We, in trusting Jesus, at least trust that we won't have this experience. We can know something about Jesus and we can trust that he will not mislead us about God. But this misses my last point. It is just this that we are unable to do, no matter how much we may *want* to, for only if we can understand what is meant by 'God' could we take anything about him on trust. In this way faith cannot precede understanding.[42]

Crombie, like Hick, makes a further argument that is important in trying to establish the factual status of theism. (I have dealt with this argument in more detail elsewhere with specific reference to Hick, so here I shall be brief.)[43] The argument I have in mind is Crombie's appeal to eschatological verification. To put the matter metaphorically first: we see now through a glass darkly but after our bodily death we shall see face to face. It is a mistake to argue, as some have, that Crombie here uses a theological concept to explicate a theological concept.[44] An atheist can, and some did, believe in immortality. Let us grant – what in reality is very problematic – that immortality is an intelligible notion, and furthermore let us even grant that it is true that man is immortal. But even granting that, we still have not got to the promised land, the concept of eschatological verification still will not do the job it was designed to do by Crombie. Consider the putative statement 'God is merciful'. Crombie asks:

Does anything count against the assertion that God is merciful? Yes, suffering. Does anything count decisively against it?

No, we reply, because it is true. Could anything count decisively against it? Yes, suffering which was utterly, eternally and irredeemably pointless. Can we then design a crucial experiment? No, because we can never see all of the picture. Two things at least are hidden from us; what goes on in the recesses of the personality of the sufferer, and what shall happen hereafter.[45]

But presumably in the hereafter, we would be in a position to know, or have some grounds for believing, that the suffering was, or was not, utterly, irremediably and eternally pointless, for then we would be in a position to see all of the picture.[46] But how could we even then be in such a position? No matter how long we lived in the hereafter, after any point of time, we would *not* have good grounds for asserting or denying the suffering was *eternally* pointless. We could never – and this is a conceptual and not an empirical point – be in a position to see things *sub specie aeternitatis* and grasp what the whole picture is like. At any point in time, the believer or the non-believer could justly claim that we could not make such a judgment because the whole picture wasn't in. In fact we couldn't know or even have reasonable grounds for believing that a fair sample has been taken. But even if we drop the requirement that the suffering be seen to be *eternally* pointless Crombie's account has still not been saved.

Suppose we were somehow to discover after our bodily death that there is no suffering which is utterly and irredeemably pointless, then according to Crombie we would have good evidence for believing in God. How so? Someone might well agree that there is no utterly and irredeemably pointless suffering and still assert that he doesn't understand what is meant by 'God' and so he doesn't understand what it means to say that God is merciful. After all the sentence 'In spite of the fact that there is no God there is no utterly and irredeemably pointless suffering' is not a self-contradiction. What, after all, is meant by the subject term 'God'? How could suffering or the lack thereof do anything to show how there might exist an object of discourse which is particular but not indicable? If we could understand what 'God' meant, Crombie's remarks might help us to give sense to 'God is merciful', but since we do not understand what 'God' means, we cannot understand 'God is merciful'.

To this Crombie might well reply: 'Indeed I haven't shown how "There is no utterly pointless and irredeemable suffering" allows us to conclude that God is merciful or to understand the word "God", but I did not try to. Furthermore, I grant that I have not shown how, on purely intellectual grounds, one could conclude that naturalistic interpretations of such experiences are inadequate. That cannot be done. But I have done what I set out to do, namely to meet Flew's challenge. I have shown under what conditions I would be prepared to give up my claim that God is merciful. I have shown how such a claim is falsifiable "in principle".'

But I do not see how Crombie has met Flew's challenge. If the statement and denial that God is merciful are both equally compatible, as they have been shown to be, with the statement 'There is no utterly pointless, irredeemable suffering' and with any possible empirical statement, which reports experiences we have or might *conceivably* have in our bodily life and in our non-bodily life (whatever that may mean), then we have not shown, as Crombie must, how the assertion or denial of the mercifulness of God has *different* factual content, and thus we have not shown how such religious statements can be used to make factual statements, for it is the believer's claim that 'God is merciful' asserts something different from 'There is no merciful God'. It is not enough that different strings of marks are used, but different factual assertions are supposed to have been made – statements with different experiential consequences. But Crombie has not been able to show how this is so; and as a result he has not been able to show that his God-statements have the kind of intelligibility that he claims for them.

Crombie, like Hick, is perfectly prepared to admit that both naturalistic and non-naturalistic interpretations of our religious experience are perfectly possible and quite plausible. He *trusts*, he says, that the non-naturalistic, theistic interpretations more adequately depict the facts. But this, he claims, is for him, and should be for all believers, a matter of *faith* and not a matter of knowledge. But if my above arguments are correct it could not possibly be a matter of *faith* for him, for he has not succeeded in establishing that his theistic beliefs are indeed beliefs of the sort he takes them to be, for he has not shown how they are expressible in factual statements, and thus he has not shown how they form an intelligible alternative to naturalism. He is in the same boat as the Edwardian who steadfastly denied that young ladies sweat – they only glow. The Edwardian shows by his speech that he no doubt has a different attitude toward young ladies than the plainest of plain men, but he doesn't show that he has different factual beliefs about them.

IV

There is one further line of argumentation that Crombie avails himself of that might be taken as establishing the factual status of theism. The claim that a sentence is used to make a factual statement if and only if it is verifiable (confirmable or disconfirmable) is, Crombie argues, a confused conflation of two distinct claims. Once they are separated, we should come to see that we have no good grounds for *denying* that our key religious or theological claims assert facts, have the logical status of factual statements.

What are these two quite different claims? The first one is the claim that a statement of fact 'must be verifiable in the sense that there *must not be a rule of language* which precludes testing the statement'. Whether we can *in fact* test it does not matter, but it must be *testable* in principle; that is, there must be no logical ban on verifying it, as there is (or so let us assume) on verifying moral statements like 'You ought not to kill puppies just for the fun of it' and on analytic statements like 'Puppies are young dogs'. To try to verify these statements, Crombie argues, is to show that you do not *understand* what they mean. That is to say, there is a logical or conceptual ban against verifying them. But if something is a factual statement there *can* be no logical ban on verifying it, but whether or not it is *in fact* verifiable is quite another matter. Crombie only makes a claim about a necessary condition for factuality. He maintains that there can be no *logical* ban on verifying a statement if that statement is to count as a genuine factual statement. If a statement is a factual statement then it must be the case that there is no *logical* ban on verifying it (confirming it or disconfirming it).

The second claim – a claim that must not, if clarity is prized, be confused with the first – is that *for any individual* fully to understand a statement, he must know what a test of it would be like. If he has no idea how to test whether a person had mutton for lunch, then he does not know what 'having mutton' means. This, Crombie argues, has nothing to do with the logical status of the expression in question, but merely with its 'communication value' for the person in question. To count as a factual statement, a statement need *not* be verifiable *in this* sense or have such communication value. We would say, however, that if utterances did not have 'communication value' we could have no fair idea as to what would make them true and what would make them false.

Crombie argues that our key religious statements are only unverifiable in this *second*, quite harmless, sense. *But since they are about a mystery this is just as it should be.* But they are verifiable in the *first sense* and this is enough to ensure that they have *factual* meaning. Recall that there is no *linguistic rule* to the effect that there can be no test for 'God is loving' or 'God made man in his image and likeness'. The Christian argues that we cannot confirm or disconfirm that 'God is loving' or 'God created man in his image and likeness' because, since our experience is limited in the way it is, we as a matter of fact cannot get into the position of verifying such claims. But there is no *logical ban* on verifying them. They are perfectly verifiable in principle. This being so, they have factual meaning and after the death of the body we shall then in fact be in a position to verify such claims. This is enough to preserve their factual status.

Within the parable, 'God is merciful' and 'God loves us' even have communication value. The communication value is derived from similar utterances with a different proper name. Within the parable we understand such talk, but we do not know the 'communication value of such utterances *outside* of the parable'. But, Crombie argues, given the hiddenness, the wholly otherness, the mysteriousness of God, this is just what we should expect. As Kierkegaard has well argued, any being who did not have these features could not be God. Talking within the framework of the parable – the Biblical stories for example – we work in a context of 'admitted ignorance', but we accept this language because we *trust* its source. We do not know how our parable applies, but we believe – have faith – that it applies 'and that we shall one day see how'.[47] The religious man – if he knows what he is about, that is if he understands his religion – does 'not suppose himself to know what he means by his statements'. He does not suppose himself to be the Holy Ghost. But it is also incorrect to claim that he falls back, when pressed, on complete agnosticism, for he can turn for a check – for a test – to the person of Jesus, the mediator, and to the concrete process of living the Christian life. There, in the anguishing struggle to pare away 'self-hood', he will encounter divine love directly. Thus these key religious and theological statements are verifiable in principle; there is no *logical ban* on verifying them. They meet the minimum requirements for being factual statements, so it is a mistake to say that they are cognitively or factually meaningless on the very grounds that Flew and the logical positivists mark out as relevant for determining factual intelligibility. In fact we should say that within the proper religious contexts they even have communication value. 'Seen as a whole', Crombie can conclude, 'religion makes rough sense though it does not make limpidity.'[48]

We have already discussed the specific difficulties in trying to move from what we understand *in the* parable to understanding how the parable could refer to that which is 'out of experience'; and we have discussed the difficulty in trying to appeal to authority, Jesus's or any other's, to settle questions of meaning. We can, as Hepburn has shown, know a lot about Jesus and about Christian living, but this does not, and cannot, take us to God unless we *already* understand what 'God' *means*. No matter how much we love and trust Jesus, his saying 'There is a God. Love Him with your whole heart and your whole mind' cannot *mean* anything to us unless we already understand the meaning of 'God'.[49] It would be like Jesus telling us to put our trust in Irglig when we had no idea of what was meant by 'Irglig'. But what is new in Crombie's above arguments, and what must be examined, is Crombie's claim that there is no *logical ban* on verifying (confirming/disconfirming) 'There is a God', 'God loves us', 'God is merciful' and the like. *Perhaps* there is no such ban, but they still have not been shown to be verifiable (confirmable/disconfirmable) in principle, for we do not have any idea of what it would be like to confirm or disconfirm such claims. We do not understand at all what it would be like for such claims to be either true or false or probably true or probably false. It isn't that these utterances just lack 'communication value' for some (say non-believers), but since believers and non-believers alike have no idea of what would or could count as confirming them or disconfirming them, neither a believer nor a non-believer can know what it *means* to say that they are used to assert facts.

Now, Crombie could reply that to argue in this way is to miss his point. When Schlick and Carnap put forth the verifiability criterion as a criterion for what is to count as a factual statement, they were talking about verifiability *in principle*. To speak of 'verifiability in principle' is to speak, as they stressed, of the *logical* possibility of verification. When you say, Crombie could continue, that we cannot specify what would or could count as a verification/falsification or confirmation/disconfirmation of these theistic claims, your 'cannot' is a *factual* 'cannot'. You just mean that, as a matter of fact, we can think of none, but you do not rule out, by definition, that there might be some such verification. Thus you cannot consistently say that it is *logically impossible* to verify them, as it is in the case of moral statements, imperatives, analytic statements, and the like. Since it makes *sense* to look for evidence for these claims, they remain verifiable (confirmable or disconfirmable *in principle*) and thus they do have a *factual meaning and content*, even under a criterion of meaning like that of Carnap or Schlick.

I think – as does Carnap – that there is such a ban or at least an implicit ban on verifying non-anthropomorphic God-talk.[50] The crucial, yet inessential, difference between analytic statements and theological statements in this respect is that in the case of these non-anthropomorphic theological statements the ban is not so obvious. We know that it is a conceptual blunder to try to verify whether 'Bachelors are really unmarried' or 'Wives are really women'. Given an understanding of the constituent terms, we know there can be no question of confirming or disconfirming such statements. But this is not true for 'There are matzos in the centre of the sun' or 'There are beings as folksy as Johnson on Mars'. There is no way of detecting whether these statements can, as a matter of fact, be verified from examining the meanings of the constituent terms in such sentential contexts. Thus, unlike analytic statements, we have not ruled out the logical possibility of their verification. But consider now such sentences as 'There is an infinite being' or 'A being transcendent to the universe and not spatiotemporally related to the universe directs the universe in an incomprehensible way' or 'There is a reality in all ways greater than nature'. Such sentences, sentences which are (according to Crombie) an integral part of a non-anthropomorphic theism, are sentences which, given the meanings of their constituent terms, cannot be used to form statements which admit of the logical possibility of verification/falsification or confirmation/disconfirmation. Where 'infinite being' is being used non-anthropomorphically, there can, *logically* can, be no observing an infinite being. To understand this term, in the only way we can understand it, is to understand that there can, logically can, be no way of indicating or identifying what it purportedly refers to. The same is true of 'being transcendent to the universe', 'not spatiotemporally related to the universe', 'directs the universe in an incomprehensible way' and 'greater than nature'. Yet, if Crombie is correct, such talk is not just a part of the theologian's febrile chatter about 'God', but is embedded as well in a sophisticated religious man's talk of God. But Crombie's own remarks about such phrases *in effect* show that to understand the conventions governing such talk is to understand that such sentences cannot be used to make statements capable of confirmation or disconfirmation. (Of course, as we have seen at other places in his argument, he speaks as if such statements were verifiable; but we have shown that none of his arguments show that there are traces of indicia in the world pointing to an infinite individual transcendent to the cosmos.)

This is so because it is *logically* impossible to specify what 'God' refers to such that we can ascertain what must be the case so that we can distinguish between it being the case that God exists and it being not the case that God exists. To understand the syntax of 'God' (in non-anthropomorphic employments) is to understand that we cannot specify what 'God' refers to in empirical terms. To speak of specifying his effects when we are logically debarred from specifying him makes no sense at all. To speak of *indirectly* verifying x makes sense only if it is at least *logically* possible directly to verify x. Putative God-statements are *in principle* unverifiable if there is no possibility of specifying the referent of 'God' in empirical terms. In this crucial way questions about confirmation/disconfirmation of God-talk and questions about specifying the referent of 'God' hang together. Only if the latter is possible is the former possible.

The fundamental thing to be noted here is this: God is *not* for a believer some kind of theoretical construct. God is *not* consciously conceptualised by the believer as a mystifying term we insert into our discourse to allay anxieties. Rather 'God' is supposed to be some kind of referring expression standing for an infinite, non-spatiotemporal, non-indicable individual, utterly transcendent to the cosmos. When we reflect on the meanings of these terms, we recognise that it would be logically impossible to verify that such an alleged individual exists. Anything that we could apprehend or could be acquainted with would *eo ipso* not be such a reality.

The above line of argument indicates that there is a logical ban on the verification of such putative God-statements; it is only not so obvious and not so explicit as it is in the case of some other types of statement, for example, analytic statements. Furthermore, we are easily led into mistakenly thinking that there is no such ban, for there are different uses of 'God', including anthropomorphic uses of 'God', where 'God created the heavens and the earth' or 'God governs the world' are factual (confirmable or disconfirmable) and known to be false. But given the non-anthropomorphic uses of 'God' that Crombie so patiently details, such sentences are not used to form statements which are logically possible to verify. Crombie has not shown how his key theistic claims, when construed non-anthropomorphically, have factual intelligibility and yet, as he rightly claims, their having such intelligibility is crucial to the soundness of the fundamental claims of Christianity, Judaism and Islam.

Empiricism, Theoretical Constructs and God

I

Empiricism in religion has not had its final hearing. There is a 'Quinean move', and 'interpretative move' and what I shall label a kind of 'naïve empiricism' that still needs to be heard. I shall start with 'naïve empiricism' first and then proceed to the other two moves.

A rather commonsensical philosopher – a kind of naïve empiricist – recalling the refinements of the theology and falsification debate might argue in this manner: suppose certain very extraordinary events suddenly and inexplicably began occurring in great numbers, for example, suppose all over North America it turned out that sick people get well whenever they sincerely with their whole heart and mind ask God for help. Suppose further that this happens even when they have diseases that doctors believe are quite incurable. Those who have faith, that is those who can really bring themselves to believe in God, and who ask God for help in this manner get well, those who are without unwavering faith do not. No known medical account of how they could have got well exists. There is not, let us suppose, even a plausible psychosomatic account. Further suppose that no naturalistic explanation is found for their getting well when they pray and yet these happenings go on regularly for several generations. If these extraordinary but quite empirically describable events were to take place, would it not then become reasonable to assert that there is a God or that there probably is a God who answers the prayers of those who truly beseech him? More generally, if there were areas in our experience which did not *in fact* admit of naturalistic explanation, would this not go some way to confirm theistic beliefs and disconfirm or at least weaken naturalistic ones? Wouldn't a man be a pretty poor empiricist who did not attend to and modify his beliefs in a theistic direction on the basis of such experiences? ·

I may be a pretty poor empiricist, but I do not think that such events, if they were to transpire, would count for a non-anthropomorphic God-assertion. I do not think that it would establish such theistic beliefs or even give them an empirical anchorage. The naturalist in such a fantastic circumstance could readily admit, and should indeed readily admit, that these are extraordinary events of a thoroughly baffling kind. At present he has no explanation for them at all. Maybe he never will have; but, it seems to me, he would be right in asserting that he sees no reason for saying that *in principle* there can be no naturalistic explanation of such events. There may indeed be events for which we have no naturalistic explanation and there is no compelling reason to believe that at any given time or perhaps even ever there will be a naturalistic explanation for everything.[1] A naturalist or atheist should assent to that.

However, there is another claim, frequently confused with it, which he most certainly should question. That claim is this: 'There is some turn of events, for which, for some *principled* or theoretical reason, no naturalistic explanation can, logically can, be found.' His questioning here should be of a distinctive sort. It should not be a matter of assessing the grounds for believing such a putative statement to be true, for no clear sense has been given to such a word-string. Given the above bizarre experiences, the naturalist could most properly reply: I don't have an explanation for them and perhaps I never will but I don't see how they can be said 'to point out of experience toward a Being transcendent to the cosmos', for 'point out of experience' has no use in the language and 'a Being transcendent to the cosmos' is said to be a referring expression and yet we have not been told what would or could count as its referent. We have no idea how to identify such a sponsored referent or what would count for or against there being such a referent. Thus such an objection does not touch the kind of difficulties that have been raised about the intelligibility of God-talk.

II

Still working within what broadly may be characterised as an empiricist framework – after all, there are empiricists and empiricists – there is another counter-argument with a Quinean flavour to the type of argument I made in my last chapter.[2]

On the very same grounds as the grounds I have used to criticise Crombie, I would have to say – so the argument runs – 'There are electrons' and 'Photons exist' are either unintelligible or without factual significance. But such a claim is surely absurd. In short, there are theoretical terms in science that do not admit of complete elucidation in terms of what Carnap and Hempel call an 'empiricist language'. One cannot indicate or point to what these theoretical terms stand for.

Unless I wish to be thoroughly absurd, I must certainly allow that it is not meaningless to talk about photons, but if I allow such talk then should I not in consistency also admit that 'There is a God' or 'God exists' have factual content? Moreover, it is unrealistic and unreasonable to examine statements like 'There are electrons' or 'All men have an Oedipus complex' in isolation. We must not forget Quine's reminder 'that our statements about the external world face the tribunal of sense experience not individually but only as a corporate body'.[3] Such an argument would have it that it is also true that to understand such statements we must see how they function within the body of a theory. It makes no sense to try to confirm them or infirm them in isolation. They are only so testable when they are examined as part of a whole conceptual system.

The same conditions, they argue, apply to religious utterances. We should not, as both Crombie and I have done, examine religious statements in isolation, but only either in the body of a whole theory – as in some theological system – or, more plausibly, I should think, as part of the whole activity of some given religion. Furthermore, we cannot directly confirm or disconfirm high-level theological or religious statements such as 'There is a God' or 'God created the heavens and the earth' or 'God loves man'. Apparent disconfirming evidence can always be plausibly met by adding or altering various subsidiary hypotheses or subsidiary theological statements. We can always make an adjustment somewhere in the system. But exactly the same thing is true of any theoretical principle in science. In both religion and science, if enough of these subsidiary claims fail or are thought to fail, the whole system or the whole religion is given up (people do lose their faith), but it is never a matter of disconfirming or infirming key religious statements taken in isolation. Such statements, as their analogues in science, are *relatively immune* to confirmation or disconfirmation. But it is still not the case that *within the system* there is nothing that counts as an empirical check of religious claims. Certain high-level statements can in no way be directly confirmed or disconfirmed, but other statements within the system can, so that it is not the case that religious language is devoid of an empirical anchorage. But fundamentally it is the system as a whole which is up for test.

There are several issues that need to be untangled here. I shall consider the easier ones first. There can, as we have seen, be no *logical* ban on directly confirming or disconfirming (infirming) high-level religious or scientific statements, *if* they can be *indirectly* confirmed or infirmed. Quine does not question that such statements can be indirectly confirmed or disconfirmed when taken as part of a system of statements. But the above Quinean argument does nothing to show that it is *logically* possible directly to confirm or disconfirm key central segments of such God-talk. Yet if my arguments in the last chapter have been correct, it is *logically* impossible directly to confirm or infirm such central segments of non-anthropomorphic God-talk. But then it is also impossible indirectly to confirm or infirm them, for 'indirectly' could only qualify 'confirm' or 'infirm' if it had an intelligible opposite. But if it is logically impossible 'directly to confirm or infirm them', then 'indirectly confirm or infirm' is deprived of its putative intelligible opposite.

What should be said in reply to such an argument is that it was a mistake to introduce the terminology of 'direct' and 'indirect' here. Rather what the Quinean should have said is that what counts as confirmation or disconfirmation in such a context is the testimony of lower-level statements as statements in a religious system. This is what counts as a test here and this is what establishes the empirical anchorage for religious claims. Remember it is the whole religious system that is being tested and not individual religious statements. There is no step-by-step testing of individual statements.

This is certainly a plausible remark to make. However, it makes several quite questionable assumptions and it is these that need critical inspection. Part of the difficulty with this Quinean move is involved in the phrase 'system' and the analogy between science and religion or science and theology. Usually people who make these Quinean claims are philosophers who work in the philosophy of science and their paradigms for 'system' come from mathematics and science (usually physics). But religions and even theologies are hardly – at least in that sense – systems. They are not neat or even unneat hypothetico-deductive–predictive systems. Rather religions are activities, essentially social activities as Durkheim stressed, with rites and loosely related doctrinal claims. The doctrinal formulae of religion indeed fit together and they are not unconnected with the ritual of the religion in question. But these different types of religious sentence are not in tightly related inferential patterns. One can accept some parts and still reject other parts. And there is no clear sense of what is 'the whole of the system'. In fact there is no unproblematic use of 'system' here. Christianity and Judaism do not have axioms, theorems, or rules of formation and transformation. We must not forget that religion is an activity and not a theory or not just a theory – and that theology, particularly natural theology, though it claims to be a science is not, to put it conservatively, a discipline with an unproblematical scientific status. Moreover, it is risky to treat 'God' as having the same logical status as the theoretical terms of science. 'God', unlike 'neutrino', is not a theoretical term or a theoretical construct. It has, at least as the world religions have developed, a very different use in the language. 'God' presumably refers to an infinite, non-spatiotemporal individual who is transcendent to the universe. A Jew or Christian cannot view his God *simply* as a heuristic device to use in facing the problems of life or in achieving social solidarity and selflessness; in fine, he cannot regard his religion merely as the conceptual framework he adopts. Rather he must believe that 'God' actually denotes what he takes to be 'an ultimate reality' whose existence cannot depend on human conventions. Perhaps the believer is mistaken. Perhaps there is no such reality, but in believing in God it is this that he takes as the object of his religious faith. By contrast, a theoretical construct is something for which no question can (logically can) arise about whether the theoretical term, which is its sign-vehicle, stands for a reality either in or 'out of' the world. Where such questions are in order we cannot be speaking of something which is merely a theoretical construct. But such questions are in order vis-à-vis 'God'. It is not self-contradictory or even a deviation from a linguistic regularity to ask whether there is really a God. Similarly, whereas in the case of 'electron' there is reason to believe that what is being talked about is part of the furniture of the universe, these realities cannot be treated as being simply theoretical constructs and the logical possibility of such realities being observed cannot be ruled out. But, where 'God' is used non-anthropomorphically, it is logically impossible to observe or perceive God.[4]

It is not a matter of finding out how 'God' functions in the theory, for religion is not a theory, or at least not primarily a theory or sometimes even at all a theory, but a complex, loosely knit activity. Discussions of what I have called 'Wittgensteinian Fideism' have brought out how without a participant's understanding or a participant-like understanding of that activity, there can be little understanding of 'God'. Yet even with it the concept of 'God' still remains very problematical. These various differences destroy the point of the analogy between science and religion or science and theology. Robin Horton may very well be right in maintaining that many primitive religions are a kind of ersatz scientific system functioning in those cultures very like science does in ours. But religion has so developed in industrial societies that by now it is very unlike science.

Someone might resist and maintain that 'God', as the concept is employed in industrial civilisations, after all is not so very unlike a theoretical entity such as a neutrino. Many Jews remain thoroughly sceptical and yet are wedded to Judaism. For them, as for certain Christians, 'God' is a 'construct of the human heart'. In that way 'God' indeed is not a theoretical construct. But the crucial thing to see is that we are still talking about a construct – something which from a logical point of view still remains for them a heuristic device to dramatise their conception of the Highest, of that which is most exalted and most worthy of devotion.

As radical theology in effect attests, there are indeed those within the Jewish tradition and even within the Christian tradition who would make such claims. We are reminded of Feuerbach's remark that what today is atheism tomorrow is religion. But my point quite simply is that this is indeed *radical* theology and such a shift is a *radical* shift in religious stance, for it is, as Santayana clearly recognised, a naturalistic and indeed an atheistical *reconstruction* of religion and not an attempt perspicuously to display – to interpret – the actual use of 'God' in the mainstream or even near-mainstream Jewish and Christian tradition. Santayana playfully called himself 'a Catholic atheist' but in spite of the fact that he deliberately immersed himself in the stream of Catholic religious life, he never took the sacraments. He neither literally thought of himself as a Catholic nor did Catholics regard him as a Catholic.

Think of what a Jew or Christian could say and still remain a Jew or Christian. Consider: 'No question of the reality of God can arise for God is *not* a reality transcendent to the world but simply, though profoundly, a moral myth we tell ourselves to make sense out of an otherwise senseless existence.' This may be a profound remark but it is not a remark that a knight of faith could possibly make. 'God' is not used in Jewish or Christian discourses either as a label for a theoretical construct or as a 'construct of the human heart'. God in Jewish or Christian religious discourses is not taken to be a fictitious or mythical being. A believer may indeed maintain that our images or concepts of God are myth-ridden but he cannot say that in believing in God we are believing in a myth. His scepticism must always be qualified.

To save something of religion or even to save what a secularist might take to be 'the heart of religion', one might, through suitable stipulations, come to use 'God' in a new way such that it is now taken to be simply a symbol for our ultimate concerns.[5] We could reconstruct the Jewish and Christian religions in this way. But this is to do something entirely different than what the Christian or Jewish theologian or philosopher set out to do, for now we are no longer even trying to elucidate 'God' but we are recommending a new use for 'God' that would radically alter the use it actually has and make Judaism and Christianity into something very different from what Jews and Christians take it to be.

Some might feel that *vis-à-vis* the Quinean move, I have not gone to the heart of the matter. What I have ignored is the Quinean claim that statements cannot be confirmed or infirmed in isolation but that our statements about what there is face the tribunal of sense-experience not individually but as a corporate body. It is only when, after repeated examination, a number of claims fail that a whole religion is given up. The last part of this claim is surely correct. The problem of evil beautifully illustrates it. If one has good reasons for believing in the God of the Jews, Christians and Moslems, one can meet Humean objections about evil. But, given the weakening of faith on other grounds, the Humean challenge about evil becomes powerful.

There is, however, reason to be sceptical about the claim that statements must face the tribunal of sense-experience as a corporate body rather than individually. Here, such Quineans may well be caught up in 'the myth of the whole'.[6] Why in such a loosely organised activity as religion must it be the whole system which is tested? Even a Christian might have his doubts about the Trinity, original sin or the virgin birth and still believe that there is good evidence or good grounds for believing in a creator of the heavens and the earth and for many other crucial elements of Christian doctrine. And for many former Jews or Christians who have become sceptics, it is the very centrally placed religious claims of Christianity that cause the trouble rather than peripheral claims or claims near the experiential periphery. That is to say, *if* the sceptic could accept or make sense of the central ones, he could accept the peripheral ones without any difficulty. If he could believe in God, he could believe that he ought to hold the Sabbath sacred or that Jesus inexplicably cured the sick. It is the central religious doctrines that he needs some evidence for or at least needs to know what it would be like to have evidence for them. If there were such evidence, he could readily enough accept many of the peripheral beliefs. If, to paraphrase James Joyce, he could accept those absurdities he could accept many other absurdities less central to the framework. One can believe that Jesus was a deep spiritual leader, that he was born in Nazareth and that he preached brotherly love and cured people in a mysterious way and still find the claim that 'Jesus is God incarnate' utterly incoherent.

Religion and even Christianity is not such a seamless web as this Quinean approach would give us to understand. There are no sound reasons for accepting the claim that only or even typically whole systems are confirmed or infirmed. It may be that we can only understand such utterances in context, as part of a language-game, but in that language-game individual statements are up for test in isolation or relative isolation and some seem to be utterly untestable and make no coherent links with those which are testable. A kind of Hegelianism which would deny this is suspect even when it comes from a distinguished logician. At least we have been given no adequate reason for accepting it.

III

So those philosophers of religion, such as Crombie, Hick and Wilson, who would be empiricists in religion, stick, and rightly so, to questions concerning the confirmation of certain key religious claims.[7] Their problem is, how are we to make sense of them by showing that they are at least in principle confirmable or infirmable? Jews, Christians and Moslems believe their key theological and religious claims to be factual, but they are perplexed, as I am perplexed and as Flew is, about the logical status of such God-talk. Given the fact that naturalistic accounts and theistic accounts seem equally compatible with all experiences actual and conceivable, it is far from evident how there could be any other than a purely terminological difference between the man who asserts and the man who denies the existence of God. Their difference appears to be quite comparable to the difference between the man who asserts 'Jane sweats' and the man who replies 'No, Jane doesn't sweat she only glows'. Thus empiricists in religion, try, and to my mind quite properly, to specify certain experienceable states which, if they were actually to transpire, would count for theism and against atheism. Crombie's and Hick's doctrine of eschatological verification was developed in order to show how theists do not simply differ in verbal-picture preference from atheists, but differ substantively over a matter of fact, for example, over the existence of and nature of God, where affirmations and denials of Divine Existence make some difference in experience in the hereafter. The naturalist says something that is mundane and down to earth. The theist wants to say something about an ultimate mystery such that what he says in some intelligible sense goes beyond what the naturalist can say. But given the above state of affairs it looks as if the theist succeeds only in using a different and more perplexing notation. My tactic with such empiricists in religion has been simply to track down their varied and often subtle claims to have described a conceivable *experienceable* turn of events which would count for the truth of theism and against atheism. If my arguments have been correct, they have not succeeded in doing that; they have not succeeded in showing that 'There is a God' and 'There is no God' or 'God loves all mankind' and 'God is indifferent to the affairs of men' and the like are not equally compatible with any and every conceivable experienceable turn of events that might, logically might, transpire. This shows, given the theory of factual intelligibility we both share, that their key religious claims cannot have *the kind* of intelligibility and logical status they claim for them. We differ in our choice of picture-preferences and we differ in our attitudes but not about what there is.

Given this state of affairs, the non-believer can quite properly claim:

(1)   that the believer does not succeed in asserting anything more when he speaks of God than the non-believer does when he talks in purely secular terms; and

(2)   that there is good reason to reject the believer's picture-preference and accept the non-believer's picture-preference because the believer's is more mystifying and obscurantist than the non-believer's. The believer wants to say something more but fails to say anything coherent which conveys any information about what

there is that is not already conveyed in the non-believer's remarks.

IV

It might be responded that even if all my objections against empiricist and cognitivists in religion are sound, I have only given good evidence for the claim that there is no possible *decision-procedure* for these theistic claims: there is no possible way of deciding which are true or probably true. But I have not shown that the believer's statements are meaningless.

To this my reply is that I have not said or implied that they are meaningless; indeed I have stressed that they are meaningful. I have only shown – given non-anthropomorphic uses of God-talk, talk involving what is thought to be a transcendent reference – that they are *factually* meaningless or, if you prefer to put it that way, devoid of factual content or factual significance. They simply do not come off as factual statements. If there can be no conceivable tests which would, either directly and indirectly, singly or in conjunction with other statements, give us empirical grounds for asserting the theistic claims and retracting the non-theistic ones or retracting the theistic claims and asserting the non-theistic ones, then these claims are without factual content, that is, they do not succeed in making factual claims or claims about what there is. But this is not to say that they are meaningless *sans phrase*. They could have emotive meaning as the positivists believed or they could be pseudo-factual propositions with the kind of sense appropriate to ideological claims.

Against what I have just said it might be countered that I am still too much of a *verificationist* and that I am too rigid in my classification of types of statement. There are, it will be maintained, factual statements that are in no way confirmable or disconfirmable (infirmable) even in principle. I treat 'empirical fact' as if it were a pleonasm, but it most certainly is not. There are empirical facts and non-empirical facts.

Here I must confess that I am, with regard to *factual* statements, an unrepentant verificationist and I do believe that in an important sense 'empirical fact' is a redundancy. I have elsewhere argued for that and I have argued, as well, that there are independent grounds for accepting a weakened version of the verifiability principle as a criterion for *factual* intelligibility.[8] Here, I shall simply throw out this challenge: can we give a case of a statement whose factual status is accepted by all parties as quite *unproblematic* which is not at least confirmable or disconfirmable in principle? I do not think that we can. And *if* we cannot does this not at least give some *prima-facie* plausibility to the contention that a statement to be *factual* must be at least confirmable or disconfirmable in principle?

V

There is a rather different tack that might be taken here. One might give up the claim that theists and non-theists are making *rival* factual assertions and one might assert instead, as Basil Mitchell does at the end of his review of *Religious Experience and Truth*, that theism 'in its *cognitive aspect*, should be regarded as a conceptual scheme which offers, like any metaphysic, a systematic interpretation of human experience and must be judged by criteria of consistency, coherence and capacity to illuminate'.[9]

This interesting *aperçu* of Mitchell's, which is an expression of what I have called the interpretative move, very much needs elucidation, systematic development and defence. Yet there are difficulties in any such view which need careful attention.[10]

If we follow Mitchell, Judaeo-Christian belief at least appears to become something very different than traditional believers have taken it to be. It can no longer be the case that believers are asserting a fact, namely, that there is a God, that atheists are denying or that agnostics question, that is, agnostics believe that it could be a fact that there is a God but wonder if such a religious claim is really true. But, on Mitchell's view, the *cognitive* difference between belief and unbelief or between religious belief and religious belief, for example, Hinduism and Islam, is like the difference between two people who talk about the same thing in different languages. Another analogy – perhaps an analogy that Mitchell would be happier with – is that for him the difference between belief and unbelief is like the difference between phenomenalism and physicalism or nominalism and scholastic realism, as these differences are seen by analytic philosophers like A. J. Ayer. It finally is all a matter of what conceptual framework, what universe of discourse, you want to choose. There are and can be no substantive differences on such an account (for example, Ayer's) between the phenomenalist and the physicalist or between the atheist and the believer. There is only a difference in how we are going to speak and how we are going to organise or represent the facts. But if this analogy is apt, does it not become evident that Mitchell's proposal, in the last analysis, comes down to nothing more than a dressed up version of the claim that the theist and the atheist have different picture-preferences?

Consistency and coherence are indeed necessary conditions for good physical or biological science, for a good normative ethics, or for a good system of any sort, but they are not sufficient conditions. There are plenty of paranoid systems with a tolerable degree of coherence and consistency; a sufficiently intelligent paranoid could construct a perfectly coherent and consistent but utterly fantastic system. Many a poor soul who believes he is Napoleon, Stalin or Hitler can make out a consistent, coherent case for himself, if we will only share with him certain initial assumptions. But these crazy systems, it will be replied, lack the power to illuminate. It will be maintained, however, that by contrast the conceptual schemes and the great metaphysical schemes of the past have this power to illuminate.

There is a crucial ambiguity here that must be brought to light. How, if at all, do such systems illuminate? I want to say never *qua metaphysical* systems. But this is a dark saying that needs explanation. In most of the great metaphysical systems – pre-eminently in Plato and Aristotle, Scotus and Occam, Kant and Schopenhauer – we find brilliant conceptual analyses, that is, arguments of the same kind (though often in a radically different idiom) that we find in the works of anti-metaphysical analytic philosophers. But the way these analyses have a capacity to illuminate has little or nothing to do with the acceptance or rejection or even the understanding of these great metaphysical systems or schemes. Plato's metaphysical system, like that of Plotinus, is best viewed anthropologically as a bit of tribal folklore. But, as any reader of *The Republic*, *The Protagoras* or *The Theatetus* knows, there are in Plato brilliant and illuminating conceptual elucidations. But the striking illumination we gain from these analyses can be assimilated and used without a commitment to Plato's metaphysical system.

However, as Passmore has stressed, there are other things in these metaphysical philosophers as well.[11] These metaphysicians are, in Passmore's terms, also sages. In the traditional metaphysicians I have mentioned and many more – including such lovers of mystagogy as Plotinus, Schelling and Heidegger – there occur penetrating, riddling, but insightful remarks about life. But such remarks also occur, and usually in a far more articulate and penetrating form, in the great works of literature. There is far more wisdom and a profounder coming-to-grips with the problems of human existence in the works of Tolstoy, George Eliot and Camus than in Plotinus, Schelling or Heidegger.[12] Some will reject this. Some think that Heidegger is a brilliant literary psychologist masquerading as a metaphysician and some even believe that in psychological insight alone there are certain passages in Heidegger that are seldom matched in literature. I think it would be very difficult to sustain this claim. But whether I am right or not in my judgment about the novelists and the metaphysicians, the sage remarks and insights into the human condition of such writers as Plotinus, Schelling and Heidegger have no *logical* connection with their metaphysical systems. Such psychological passages often do illuminate, but in a radically different manner than in the way in which philosophical analysis illuminates. Yet, consider the metaphysical systems themselves – the grandiose, but obscure conceptual schemes – how do they have the capacity to illuminate? Do they really give us any illumination at all? What vision or understanding can we or do we gain from them? *The Bible*, *The Bhagavad-Gita*, *The Upanishads*, exhibit a powerful moral vision and depth of insight into our human lot along with some nonsense, superstition and crudities. The vision and insight is precious, but, as Santayana so well realised, such insight is perfectly available to the atheist. Yet taken as grand metaphysical schemes do the metaphysical systems of the past or the existentialist schemes of the present, so justly parodied by Günter Grass, have a capacity to illuminate?[13]

The answer is that they do not. What they do is mystify, obfuscate and obscure and give the man caught up by them the *illusory* belief that the sage remarks gain a profound but mysterious support from the metaphysical superstructure. The two sets of remarks do come from the same volumes; sometimes even a given paragraph will have a mingling of both. The unwary are deluded into thinking that in some way the metaphysical superstructure gives the sage remarks some unfathomable, but absolutely crucial support, that is somehow quite independent of the whims of mortal will. The neophyte and plenty of others too have the very mistaken belief that if they will only study the system long enough, learn finally to penetrate the obscurities, see the rationale that remains hidden in these metaphysical thickets, that they too will finally discover a deep rationale or justification for living in a certain way and for viewing life in a certain way. Here we have the irrational, metaphysical heart of philosophical rationalism. There is no *such* illumination in metaphysical systems, in theological systems, and in the living religions.

VI

Someone who has thought about 'seeing as' and Jastrow's ambiguous 'duck–rabbit' might wish to push Mitchell's claim in the following direction: though 'There is a God' or 'God loves all mankind' are not even verifiable in principle, they are still cognitively meaningful, for they are used to signal that the sincere user of that utterance looks at the world in a certain way: that he will interpret everything that happens as if there were a God who loves all mankind.

This rather popular move perplexes me in at least three ways:

(1)   just what does it *mean* and how could it be an answer to the question 'Does "God exists" mean ". . ."?'

(2)   how could it ever be adequate to a religious man's intentions,

(3)   what of the morality of such an appeal?

Indeed given that a man understands what 'God exists' or 'God loves all mankind' *means* – that he understands what kind of truth-claim is being made – he could understand what it would be like to interpret everything that happens as if there were a God who loves all mankind. But for the man who is puzzled about what it means to assert 'God exists', this interpretative point of view does not help at all. For if he does not understand 'God' he will not understand what it is to interpret or look at the world in a theistic way. The interpretative point of view just does not come to grips with this logically prior question of *meaning*.

There is a further difficulty here. 'Jones sees it as a duck and Fred sees it as a rabbit' is very different from 'Jones interprets events atheistically and Fred theistically', for one can turn the Jastrow figure on one side and say (demonstrating one's point by ostension), 'There it looks like a duck' and bring in a duck, if need be, to show the resemblance. But nothing like this can be done to show what it would be like to 'look at' or 'view' events atheistically or theistically.

Someone who understood what it *meant* to say that God exists but thought that the assertion was false or rather far-fetched, still might, like Ivan in *The Brothers Karamazov*, argue that people ought to interpret the world theistically or act as if God existed. Indeed a man might say, 'I don't know whether God exists and I don't think anybody does either, but I'm going to live *as if* He does; I am even going to interpret events in a theistic manner.' *Given* an understanding of what 'God exists' *means*, that position is perfectly intelligible. I could readily understand a fideist making such a claim. But I could not understand how a Jew or a Christian (fideist or non-fideist) could, while remaining a Jew or Christan, say: 'God exists' *only means* 'Behave agapistically and with humility', 'Go to synagogue (church)', 'Read the Bible and fast on the Day of Atonement (Lent) and so on'. This is an *utterly secular* rather than a religious reading of 'God exists'. Whatever language-game is played by believers with 'God', this is plainly not it. And this is also my answer to my second question, can the interpretative view be adequate to a religious man's intentions. My answer is that it could not.

It also seems to me to be true that such an argument is extremely questionable on moral grounds. If the world of the Grand Inquisitor were the real world, if man would despair without a belief in God, if life would have no point without a belief in God, then perhaps one should, if one understood that talk, act as if God existed and interpret the world in theistic terms. It indeed distresses me to say this. 'Part of me' says: truth is too precious to be overrun here. But, after all, how could one show truth to be an *intrinsic* value?[14] Under *such* circumstances why make such a thing of truth?

There is, however, no need to accept this cruel dilemma in the first place. It is not true that without a belief in God life is without point and morality is groundless. Whatever ground morality has, it has it in complete logical independence of belief in God. 'God is good', 'God is the Highest good', are in Jewish–Christian discourses analytic. But 'God' does not mean 'good' any more than 'puppies' means 'young', for to say 'a good wife will try to understand her husband's aspirations' is most certainly not to say, what is nonsense anyway, 'a god wife will try to understand her husband's aspirations'. 'Good' does not mean 'God'; 'There is no God but the napalming of children is evil' is not a contradiction. Furthermore, given this independence of meaning, and given that good is a defining characteristic of God, there is and can be no understanding of 'God' without a logically *prior* understanding of 'good' any more than one could understand 'puppy' if one had no understanding of 'young'. And while for a believer the loss of faith *may* be a shocking, soul-searing loss, it still remains the case that human love, happiness, companionship and understanding are of value even in a Godless world.[15] Even in such a world the torturing of children remains vile. Indeed certain 'world-renouncing' or 'otherworldly' ideals, ideals Steppenwolfian personalities are inextricably committed to, become absurd with the 'death of religion'. But other ideals, ideals of human happiness, solidarity and achievement, retain their point. The bliss of religious ecstasy is lost but the joys of life, refined and non-refined, are perfectly available in a Godless world. Such experiences give sense to the remark that even in a world without God such actions can have a point.[16]

VII

Perhaps a better face could be put on Mitchell's claim. We should not lose sight of the fact that Mitchell is talking about the *cognitive aspect* of theism. Some believers, though by no means all, are in the very nature of the case committed by their *faith* to an unconditional acceptance of the key claims of their religion. They can no more take them in a tentative way than a lover can be tentative about his love for his beloved. It is certainly true that the Christian, to take one example, does not believe in a God against whom he can bring charges. He could not in a Jamesian fashion characterise his religious beliefs as his 'working hypotheses'; they cannot for him be simply his 'conceptual scheme' and he cannot think of his religion simply as his *Weltanschauung* or the *Weltanschauung* of his tribe. This does not at all catch his *attitude* toward his religion: the attitude of faith is one of *unconditional trust* in God. But, as Mitchell has brought out in another context, such remarks are about the *pragmatics* of belief: they tell us about the attitudinal reactions of religious believers to religious utterances, but they tell us nothing about the *logical status* of the utterances themselves. A wife, desperate for her family's well-being, might passionately aver of her husband, 'He won't drink again'. This is logically a prediction, it is not like his expression of intention 'I won't drink again'. Indeed 'He won't drink again' may well express the heartfelt wishes of his wife and it could be accepted by her with unswerving and unquestioning faith. But all the same – in spite of its emotive aspects – it has the logical status of a prediction open to confirmation or disconfirmation. That is its *cognitive* aspect. Similarly the non-tentative way the believer takes his religious claims in itself establishes nothing about their logical status.

What is relevant, and what is involved in our prior discussion, is just what logical status such elements in the conceptual scheme do have. What kind of statements are metaphysical statements? They are not analytic; and, Mitchell makes quite evident, they are not empirical either. But then they cannot be factual, for they are not verifiable (confirmable or infirmable) in principle, but if they are not factual statements, then it cannot be a fact that there is a God, that He shall raise the quick and the dead, that He made the world and governs the world. But then the Christian loses his central conception of a transcendent infinite power to whom he can turn in his hour of need.

If Mitchell gives up any claim that key religious utterances have a factual status, then his key religious or theological utterances, expressive of 'a systematic interpretation of human experience', cannot state facts, cannot be assertive of what there is. If this is so, it appears that Mitchell is indeed open to the charge that he has reduced theism to a *mere* conceptual scheme touched with emotion. But if this is all it is, he has deprived it, in order to escape perplexities about its claims, of any possibility of making a substantive claim about what there is. By such man-oeuvring, we can indeed avoid scandal to the intellect, but only at the price of emasculating theism.

Mitchell can only rationally resist this criticism by claiming that 'God governs the world' or 'God shall raise the quick and the dead' are indeed, as interpretations of human experience, factual substantive claims but that they are not even verifiable in principle. But now we are once again back to the classic arguments about whether all factual statements are in principle verifiable (confirmable or disconfirmable). Only if I am mis-taken in my claim that to be a *factual* statement a statement must be at least confirmable or infirmable in principle, can Mitchell *perhaps* give some acceptable sense to his claim that these statements are metaphysical statements that provide a fundamental interpretation of our experience. But without this, Mitchell's manoeuvre is without merit. In short its tenability is completely dependent on the intelligibility and tenability of the fundamental claims of philosophical rationalism. The tenabil-ity of such a metaphysical view of the world is a necessary but not a sufficient condition for the tenability of such an interpret-ative point of view.

Notes and References

Introduction

1. See my 'Can Faith Validate God-Talk', in *New Theology Today*, no. 1, eds M. Marty and D. Peerman (New York: Collier-Macmillan, 1964); and my 'Religious Perplexity and Faith', *Crane Review*, 8 (Autumn 1965).

2. See my *Reason and Practice* (New York: Harper and Row, 1971). For a briefer, though very simplified statement, relating it to things I say in this book, see my 'Religious Skepticism', *Free Inquiry* (February 1981).

3. I use the term 'analytic tradition' with some ambivalence. I am within the analytic tradition in the broad sense that Richard Rorty is in the analytic tradition. I write with the style of argumentation characteristic of that tradition but I do not accept many of its doctrines or restrictions about what philosophy should be. See Richard Rorty, *Philosophy and the Mirror of Nature* (Princeton, NJ: Princeton University Press, 1979), pp. 8–9. See also his 'Philosophy in America Today', *Analyse und Kritik*, forthcoming.

1. Perplexities about Religion

1. Axel Hägerström, *Philosophy and Religion* (London: Allen & Unwin, 1964) Part III, and William Kennick, 'The Language of Religion', *Philosophical Review*, vol. 65 (January 1956).

2. Kai Nielsen, 'Linguistic Philosophy and "The Meaning of Life"', *Cross-Currents*, vol. XIV, no. 3 (Summer 1964), and 'Linguistic Philosophy and Belief', *The Journal of Existentialism*, vol. VI (Summer 1966).

3. Tillich and his many followers talk this way at great length and with considerable obscurity. I once with less obscurity tried to make out such a case for 'the essence of religion'. I mention my own essay, for it is a good example of how bankrupt this position can be. See Kai Nielsen, 'Religion and The Human

Predicament', *The Humanist*, vol. xviii, no. i (January–February 1958). For some powerful counter-arguments against such views see William Warren Bartley, *The Retreat to Commitment* (New York: A. A. Knopf, 1962).

4. William Alston (ed.), 'Religion and the Philosophy of Religion', *Religious Belief and Philosophical Thought* (New York: Harcourt, Brace & World, 1963) p. 12.

5. There is a problem, which I choose to skip over at this early point, about how exactly to put my point here. It could be said that 'God' should be in the lower case when preceded by an article. One could admit there is a god and yet deny that God exists. But 'There is God' is deviant and revealingly deviant and it could reasonably, though I think mistakenly, be argued, as Plantinga has, that 'God exists' on some uses anyway is analytic. Yet we can still ask: 'Is there a so-and-so or the so-and-so that "God" supposedly denotes?'

6. This assumes, of course, what later will be examined, namely that the premises are intelligible. Someone could object that unless you know what 'a necessary being' means – and we don't – you don't know that you have a statement when you use that expression, and you can speak of valid logical form only with respect to statement–schema or statements. (See n. 39, p. 196.)

7. This Wittgensteinianism is indeed a dark saying. Robert Hoffman in a personal communication has objected as follows:

Quite beside my personal feeling that the later Wittgenstein doesn't solve problems but only poses them, I believe that your using the expression 'the forms of life' can only obscure matters. The expression is not self-explanatory and unless the reader is familiar with a lot of fairly difficult writing on the subject, he'll not know what 'a form of life' is, much less how 'the forms of language are *the* forms of life' [my italics]. I think that to rely on Wittgenstein's jargon is to play with the fire of shibboleth, which sheds little light.

I am in some measure in sympathy with Hoffman here. I didn't mean to endorse this statement of Wittgenstein's as my later chapters on Wittgensteinian Fideism should make perfectly apparent. But I did want to use it here as a statement of a way of arguing against my own methodological assumptions.

8. This is an assertion of a position, hardly an attempt to establish it. In attempting to estabish it one would surely have to consider Nidditch's arguments concerning the denial that almost any so-called mathematical proof is a proof. See P. H. Nidditch, *Introductory Formal Logic of Mathematics* (London: Cambridge University Press, 1957) pp. lff

9. Ian T. Ramsey, *On Being Sure in Religion* (London: The Athlone Press, 1963) p. 23.

10. Ibid.

11. Ibid, p. 90.

12. Ninian Smart, *Reasons and Faiths* (London: Routledge & Kegan Paul, 1958) p. 17.

13. I argue that such religious talk is incoherent in my *Contemporary Critiques of Religion* (London: Macmillan, 1971) and in my *Scepticism* (London: Macmillan, 1973). In my 'Agnosticism', in Phillip P. Wiener (ed.), *The Dictionary of the History of Ideas*, vol. 1 (New York: Random House, 1973) I argue that similar arguments were perceptively made in the nineteenth century.

2. *The Intelligibility of God-Talk*

1. This has been powerfully argued by I. M. Crombie in his 'The Possibility of Theological Statements', in Basil Mitchell (ed.), *Faith and Logic* (London: Allen & Unwin, 1957) pp. 31–48.

2. Rudolf Bultmann, 'What Sense Is There to Speak of God', *The Christian Scholar*, vol. XLIII, no. 3 (Autumn 1960) 66–7.

3. Rudolf Carnap, 'The Elimination of Metaphysics Through The Logical Analysis of Language', in A. J. Ayer (ed.), *Logical Positivism* (Glencoe, Illinois: The Free Press, 1959) p. 66.

4. Paul Edwards, 'Some Notes on Anthropomorphic Theology', in Sidney Hook (ed.), *Religious Experience and Truth* (New York University Press, 1961) p. 242.

5. It could be argued that the making of such inferences from 'God created the world' establishes nothing about 'God', for we also can make inferences from 'Irglig created the world' or 'A Trig created the world'. The deductive relationships are determined, not by 'God' or 'Irglig' or 'A Trig', but by the meanings of the rest of the words in the sentence. On the contrary, it shows something about 'God' and 'Irglig', namely that they are words that could properly take that place in such a sentence, for

'In created the world' or 'Yellow created the world' or 'Very created the world' are not intelligible. We understand that 'God' is a certain word which has a proper place in certain sentences. That 'x created the world', as far as usage goes, takes some values rather than others shows that 'created the world' is in some sense an intelligible expression and that 'God' is one of the admissible values for the variable 'x'.

6. John Passmore, *Philosophical Reasoning* (London: Duckworth, 1961) p. 83.

7. Paul Ziff, 'About "God"', in Hook, *Religious Experience,* pp. 195–202.

8. The articles by Hick, Clarke, Schmidt and Edwards all occur in Hook, *Religious Experience.* The articles by Hoffman and Glickman appear in *Sophia.* Robert Hoffman, 'Professor Ziff's Resurrection of the Plain Man's Concept of God', *Sophia,* vol. II, no. 2 (July 1963), and Jack Glickman, 'Hoffman on Ziff's "About 'God'"', *Sophia,* vol. VI, no. 3 (October 1965).

9. I have in mind Hume's argument in *An Enquiry Concerning Human Understanding,* Section X, Pts I–II, and P. H. Nowell-Smith, 'Miracles', in A. Flew and A. MacIntyre (eds), *New Essays in Philosophical Theology* (London: Macmillan, 1955) pp. 243–53. But to see that things are not all that obviously settled here, see C. D. Broad, 'Hume's Theory of the Credibility of Miracles', in Alexander Sesonske and Noel Fleming (eds) *Human Understanding: Studies in the Philosophy of David Hume* (Belmont, California: Wadsworth Press, 1965); Chapter 2 of Ninian Smart, *Philosophers and Religious Truth* (London: S.C.M. Press, 1964); and Richard Swinburne, *The Concept of Miracle* (London: Macmillan, 1970).

10. It might be objected that the burden of proof should not be on Ziff to show that there are no miracles. The burden of proof is the other way. Among other things 'miracle' must be made understandable. What could it mean to say 'the laws of physics were suspended' or that 'something occurred which was contrary to natural regularities'? These are indeed obscure notions, but it isn't plainly evident that a miracle is unintelligible, and simply to assume that there can be no miracles is to ignore the obvious theological counter-move that it is natural for a theologian to make when Ziff makes such a claim. It is this that keeps his argument here from being air-tight. See here the

references in note 9 to Broad and Smart and, perhaps most important of all, to Swinburne.

11. Paul Ziff, *Semantical Analysis* (Ithaca, New York: Cornell University Press, 1960) p. 197.

12. C. B. Martin, *Religious Belief* (Ithaca, New York: Cornell University Press, 1965).

13. W. Norris Clark, 'On Professor Ziff, Niebuhr and Tillich', in Hook, *Religious Experience*, p. 224.

14. Note that while the jargon is different we seem not to be so very far from Russell's theory of descriptions here.

15. Paul Ziff, 'About "God"', in Hook, *Religious Experience*, p. 198.

16. Ibid., p. 199.

17. Ibid.

18. Ibid.

19. Ibid.

20. Ibid, p. 200.

21. Here I shall not consider all of Hoffman's arguments for it seems to me that they have been clearly refuted by Glickman. See Hoffman, 'Ziff's Resurrection', 1–4, and Glickman, 'Hoffman on Ziff', 33–9. I shall also discuss in the paragraphs following this citation what I take to be Hoffman's rather inadequate response in his 'On Being Mindful of "God": Reply to Kai Nielsen', *Religious Studies*, vol. 6 (1971) 289–90.

22. Ziff, 'About "God"', in Hook, *Religious Experience*, p. 201.

23. Hoffman, 'Ziff's Resurrection', 2–3.

24. This, of course, does not mean that Hoffman is not making a correct claim about meaning. Later I shall argue that with suitable qualifications such a claim ought to be made. But without such an argument he has not refuted Ziff.

25. Glickman, 'Hoffman on Ziff', 39.

26. Someone might object that unless what is meant by 'logically possible' here can be specified independently of the notion of 'in principle', we do not have an adequate understanding of that claim. An analysis of 'logically possible' would indeed be very difficult but that is true for many other working terms, including 'true'. But this, as we have learned from Moore, does not mean that we do not know the meaning of the term in question or that we cannot satisfactorily operate with it. We can translate into the concrete and in that way specify what

we mean here. Consider the following sentences: (1) 'A married man is a husband.' (2) 'Nixon eats faster than Fullbright.' (3) 'Nixon sleeps faster than Fullbright.' (4) 'Johnson carried the Statue of Liberty to Vietnam in the palm of his hand.' Anyone who understands English knows no question of (1)'s confirmability or disconfirmability can arise. There is a *conceptual ban* on verifying (1). Thus it plainly is not even verifiable in principle. (2), by contrast, plainly is, for we can describe its truth-conditions; the same holds for such an absurdity as (4). Moreover, (2) and (4) are such that there is plainly no conceptual ban on looking for evidence for their truth or falsity as there is on looking for evidence for the truth or falsity of (1). (3), by contrast, is *not* such that one plainly exhibits one's failure to understand English if one looks for evidence for its truth or falsity. It is correct to say we do not know what (if anything) would count for its truth or falsity and thus we do not know or have grounds for believing it is verifiable (testable). It is not even clear whether it has a use (except as a philosophical example) in the language and if it has no use, no intelligible question can possibly arise about verifying it, and thus it is not verifiable in principle for it makes no sense to try to verify it. But since it is not *crystal-clear* that (3) has no use, we cannot be confident that there is a conceptual ban on looking for evidence for its truth or falsity. But such indeterminate cases, including more obvious ones like 'He sees with his eyes', do not mean that the distinction is unworkable or inadequate. It only means that sometimes we do not know how to apply it or even whether to apply it. For further argument in that area see my 'God and Verification Again', *Canadian Journal of Theology*, vol. xi, no. 2 (1965).

27. John Hick, 'Meaning and Truth in Theology', in Hook, *Religious Experience*, p. 203.

28. Ibid, p. 204.

29. Ibid, p. 205.

30. Paul Edwards, 'Some Notes on Anthropomorphic Theology', in Hook, *Religious Experience*, p. 242.

31. For a justification of that claim see J. N. Findlay, 'Can God's Existence Be Disproved?', in Flew and MacIntyre, *New Essays*, pp. 47–56.

32. Edwards, 'Anthropomorphic Theology', p. 243.

33. The contention here is *not* that we typically apply 'loving' or 'just' only to embodied agents (assuming that is not a pleonasm). Rather the claim is that 'being just' or 'being loving' is something that someone does. It is appled to actions. The claim I am making is that 'bodiless action' is without factual intelligibility. There is nothing that counts for or against the truth of 'There was bodiless action in Haiti'. It might be argued that God can act justly or lovingly without a body because he can act through (by means of) other persons with bodies, for example, 'Gustavus Adolphus' justice shows God's handwork'. But this won't help for we still do not understand 'he can act', that is, 'God acts though bodiless' in the above sentence.

34. On reading this in an earlier draft, Hoffman wrote to me: 'So the verifiability criterion of meaningfulness returns in formal dress. It couldn't get itself accepted to the philosophical banquet table when dressed as "confirmation or disconfirmation", but in the more formal attire of "truth conditions" it's legitimate enough to get in the back way.' But, in arguing, as I did and as Edwards did, from cases where it is plain – even without invoking the verifiability criterion – that the word-strings in question (for example, 'bodiless action') are meaningless, and then, in showing that statements involving, directly or indirectly, a notion of bodiless action are meaningless *because* unverifiable, I provided indirect support (vindication) for such a criterion. I didn't simply assume it. Moreover, I asserted in the very next paragraph that what I said at that point was still 'fundamentally question-begging'.

35. Ziff, 'About "God"', in Hook, *Religious Experience*, p. 197.

36. Edwards, 'Anthropomorphic Theology', p. 243.

37. Ibid, pp. 244–5. Even if it is a 'theological howler' to claim that there is such a Creator of the universe entails there was a time when the universe did not exist, Edwards's point here would still stand. The point is that both sentences are problematic. If one entails the other, we are still no better off in understanding either.

38. Ibid.

39. See my 'Metaphysics and Verification Revisited', *The Southwestern Journal of Philosophy*, vol. vi, no. 3 (1975), and my 'Facts, Factual Statements and Theoretical Terms', *Philosophical Studies*, vol. xxiii (1975) (Maynooth, Ireland).

40. Ziff, 'About "God"', in Hook, *Religious Experience*, p. 199.

41. I return again to this point – a point which surely needs further argumentation – in my chapter 'On Fixing the Reference Range of "God"' and my article 'Metaphysics and Verification'. I also have discussed this point at some length in my *Contemporary Critiques of Religion* (London: Macmillan, 1971).

3. *The Challenge of Wittgenstein*

1. D. Z. Phillips, *The Concept of Prayer* (London: Routledge & Kegan Paul, 1965); Peter Winch, 'Understanding a Primitive Society', *The American Philosophical Quarterly*, vol. 1 (October 1965).

2. Ludwig Wittgenstein, *Lectures and Conversations on Aesthetics, Psychology and Religious Belief*, (ed. Cyril Barrett) (Oxford: Blackwell, 1966). Hereafter referred to as Lectures on Religious Belief.

3. Ludwig Wittgenstein, 'A Lecture on Ethics', *Philosophical Review*, vol. 74 (1965) 3–12, and G. E. Moore, *Philosophical Papers* (London: Allen & Unwin, 1962).

4. Wittgenstein, *Lectures on Religious Belief*, p. 59.

5. Ibid. For at least a *prima-facie* conflicting interpretation see F. Gerald Downing, 'Games, Families, the Public and Religion', *Philosophy*, vol. XLVII (January 1972) 38–54. Downing rightly stresses that for Wittgenstein there cannot be an essentially 'private-language' and that for him 'language-games' are not isolated or sharply demarcated. But this is compatible with the sense of being *sui generis* stressed here.

6. Wittgenstein, *Lectures on Religious Belief*, pp. 70–2.

7. Ibid, p. 71.

8. Ibid, p. 60.

9. Ibid.

10. Ibid, p. 53.

11. Ibid, p. 54.

12. Ibid, p. 55.

13. Ibid, pp. 56–7 and 62.

14. Ibid, p. 56.

15. Ibid, p. 57.

16. Ibid.

17. Ibid, pp. 57–8.

18. Wittgenstein, 'Lecture on Ethics', 12.

19. Wittgenstein, *Lectures on Religious Belief*, p. 58.
20. Ibid.
21. Ibid.
22. Ibid.
23. Ibid.
24. Ibid.
25. Moore, *Philosophical Papers*, p. 312.
26. Ibid.
27. Recall in this connection what Wittgenstein says in his conversations with Schlick and Waismann: 'At the end of my lecture on ethics, I spoke in the first person. I believe that is quite essential. Here nothing more can be established. I can only appear as a person speaking for myself' (p. 16). And also ponder in this context the remark about 'reason' he made to Rush Rhees:

In considering a different system of ethics there may be a strong temptation to think that what seems to us to express the justification of an action must be what really justified it there, whereas the real reasons are the reasons that are given. These are the reasons for or against the action. 'Reason' doesn't always mean the same thing. . . . (p. 26)

28. Wittgenstein, *Lectures on Religious Belief*, p. 63. W. D. Hudson in his 'Some Remarks on Wittgenstein's Account of Religious Belief' in A. Vesey (ed.), *Talk of God* (London; Macmillan, 1969), gives an analysis of Wittgenstein's account that is very different from the one given here. However, his elucidation of 'pictures' has been effectively criticised by Michael Durrant, 'The Use of "Pictures" in Religious Belief', *Sophia*, vol. x, no. 3 (July 1971) 16–21.
29. Wittgenstein, *Lectures on Religious Belief*.
30. Ludwig Wittgenstein, 'Lecture on Ethics', 9. It should not be forgotten that this lecture on ethics was given in 1929 or 1930 while the lecture on religion was given in 1938. This was a period when Wittgenstein's conceptions were changing. In the earlier lecture his views were closer to his views in the *Tractatus*. We cannot just assume the views in both essays are the same.
31. Ibid.
32. Ibid., 10. It has been thought by some that in his lecture in religious belief Wittgenstein is rejecting the claim that any

'non-literal assertion', if intelligible, must be expressible in a literal way. My claim is that whichever move he makes he gets into serious difficulties.

33. Ibid.

34. Ibid.

35. Ibid, 11.

36. Ibid, 12.

37. Ibid, 16. It might be objected that I am forgetting here that 'nonsense' is used by Wittgenstein as a term of art. The expressions he is talking about here, it may be contended, are merely nonsensical in a technical way. But this doesn't mean that in an ordinary sense of 'nonsense' that they are nonsensical. However, Wittgenstein seems to mean, when talking about religious utterances, that they are nonsensical in a more ordinary way; they are not simply nonsensical in the way the propositions of his *Tractatus* are said to be nonsensical, for it is not the case with 'God created the heavens and the earth' that we have something that allegedly can be *shown*, but çannot be *said*. Rather we are here saying something that in an important sense is not understood. The doctrines of the *Tractatus* are such that we can weigh up their merits and demerits, but such religious utterances are utterly mystifying. See here George Pitcher, *The Philosophy of Wittgenstein* (Englewood Cliffs, New Jersey: Prentice-Hall, 1964) pp. 154–7.

38. Wittgenstein, 'Lecture on Ethics', 16.

39. D. Z. Phillips, 'Philosophy, Theology and the Reality of God', *Philosophical Quarterly* (September 1963) 346.

40. Rush Rhees's remarks on Wittgenstein's lecture on ethics. See *Philosophical Review*, vol. 74 (1965) 26.

41. Wittgenstein, *Lectures on Religious Belief*, p. 72.

42. Wittgenstein, 'Lecture on Ethics', 15.

43. There is, of course, much more to be said about such issues, some of which I have said in my 'Religion and Commitment' in William Blackstone and Robert Ayers (eds), *Religious Language and Knowledge* (Athens, Georgia: University of Georgia Press, 1971); my 'In Defense of Atheism', in Howard Kiefer and Milton Munitz (eds) *Perspectives in Education, Religion and the Arts* (Albany, New York: State University of New York Press, 1970); and in my *Ethics Without God* (London: Pemberton Publishing, 1973). It has been thought by some that at least the form of my

argument is crudely empiricist. I hope that later chapters show that it is empiricist but not crudely empiricist. I have also said crucial methodological things about such issues of empiricism in my *Reason and Practice* (New York: Harper & Row, 1971), particularly in Chapters 21 and 31 through 36.

4. *Wittgensteinian Fideism I*

1. The scattered but central sources here are as follows: Peter Winch, *The Idea of a Social Science* (London: Routledge & Kegan Paul, 1958); 'Understanding a Primitive Society', 307–25; G. E. Hughes, 'Martin's *Religious Belief*', *Australasian Journal of Philosophy*, vol. 40 (August 1962) 211–19; Norman Malcolm, 'Anselm's Ontological Arguments', *The Philosophical Review* (1960) and 'Is it a Religious Belief that God Exists?' in John Hick (ed.), *Faith and the Philosophers* (New York: St Martin's Press, 1964); Peter Geach 'Nominalism', *Sophia*, vol. III, no. 2 (1964); Stanley Cavell, 'Existentialism and Analytic Philosophy', *Daedalus*, vol. 93 (Summer 1964); J. M. Cameron, *The Night Battle* (London: Burns & Oates, 1962); 'What is a Christian?', *The New York Review of Books*, vol. VI (26 May 1966); Robert Coburn, 'A Neglected Use of Theological Language', *Mind*, vol. LXXII (July 1963); R. F. Holland, 'Religious Discourse and Philosophical Discourse', *Australasian Journal of Philosophy* (1956); D. Z. Phillips, 'Philosophy, Theology and the Reality of God'; D.Z. Phillips in his *Concept of Prayer, Faith and Philosophical Enquiry* (London: Routledge & Kegan Paul, 1970), and *Death and Immortality* (London: Macmillan, 1970) gives us a detailed paradigmatic statement of Wittgensteinian Fideism.

2. Norman Malcolm, 'Anselm's Ontological Arguments', vol. LXIX, *The Philosophical Review* (1960).

3. Ibid.

4. Axel Hägerström, *Philosophy and Religion* (London: Allen & Unwin, 1964) p. 216.

5. I do not necessarily lay all these *aperçus* at Wittgenstein's door, but all of them can clearly be found in one or another of his disciples.

6. Hughes, 'Martin's *Religious Belief*', 211–19.

7. Ibid, 214.

8. Ibid.

9. Ibid.

10. Ibid, 214–15.

11. Ibid, 215.

12. Ibid.

13. Ibid.

14. Ibid.

15. Ibid.

16. Ibid, 215–6.

17. Coburn, 'A Neglected Use of Theological Language'.

18. I doubt if Coburn would consider himself a Wittgensteinian Fideist and, taking into account his *other* writings, I doubt that he should be so characterised. I only wish here to consider whether his central contentions in 'A Neglected Use of Theological Language' could readily be utilised in the service of Wittgensteinian Fideism.

19. Ibid, 371.

20. I do not mean that I am suggesting that there are contexts in which these questions are literal questions for which there is 'cosmological information'.

21. Coburn, 'A Neglected Use of Theological Language', 373.

22. Ibid, 374.

23. Ibid.

24. Ibid, 381.

25. Ibid.

26. Sidney Hook neatly exposes some of the verbal legerdemain in such conversion by stipulative redefinition in his essays 'Modern Knowledge and the Concept of God' and 'The Quest for "Being" ' in his *The Quest for Being* (New York: St Martin's Press, 1960).

27. See 'The Hiddenness of God and Some Barmecidal God Surrogates', *The Journal of Philosophy*, vol. LVII (28 October–10 November 1960) 689–712; 'Professor Malcolm on God', *Australasian Journal of Philosophy*, vol. 41 (August 1963) 143–62.

28. The central essay here is his 'Understanding a Primitive Society', 307–25. But see also Winch, *Social Science*.

29. Winch, 'Understanding a Primitive Society', 308.

30. Ibid.

31. Ibid.

32. Ibid.
33. Ibid, 309.
34. Ibid.
35. Ibid.
36. Winch, *Social Science*, p. 100.
37. Leslie Fiedler, 'Introduction' to Simone Weil's *Waiting For God* (New York: Capricorn Books, 1951) pp. 3–4.
38. That 'determinate reality' is a pleonasm has been argued in a powerful way by Axel Hägerström in his *Philosophy and Religion*. It is surely to be hoped that the rest of Hägerström's writings in Swedish will soon be made available to non-Swedish readers.
39. I also make such assessments in my 'On Speaking of God', *Theoria*, vol. xxviii (1962, Part 2); 'Religion and Commitment', in Blackstone and Ayers, *Problems of Religious Knowledge*; 'Eschatological Verification', *Canadian Journal of Theology*, vol. xi (1962); 'God and Verification Again'; 'On Fixing the Reference Range of "God"', *Religious Studies* (October 1966).
40. Winch, 'Understanding a Primitive Society', 319.
41. Winch, *Social Science*, pp. 100–1. James Kellenberger believes that Winch and I are talking at cross-purposes, for in talking of 'intelligibility' I am talking of meaning (what it makes sense to say) while 'Winch is talking about intelligibility in the sense of rationality (in fact, he tends to use the two terms interchangeably) . . .' (p. 53). It is not evident to me that Winch is so definite about this usage here, but even if he is, a belief can only be intelligible (rational) in what is alleged to be Winch's sense if it makes sense. I am raising questions about whether key concepts in religious discourse make sufficient sense such that we can be justified in claiming they are coherent. If they are not I am arguing that then we have good grounds for believing that the whole mode of discourse we call religious discourse is irrational because its key conceptions are incoherent. Winch tries to block such questions – to show that it makes no sense to raise them – but I have given grounds for doubting that and Kellenberger in his criticisms of me has given no good reasons for not doubting what I doubt. See James Kellenberger, *Religious Discovery, Faith and Knowledge* (Englewood Cliffs, New Jersey: Prentice-Hall, 1972) pp. 51–5.
42. Winch, 'Understanding a Primitive Society', 319.

43. Norman Malcolm, 'Is It a Religious Belief That "God Exists"?', in Hick, *Faith and The Philosophers*, pp. 105–6.

44. Ibid, p. 106.

45. Ibid, p. 107.

46. Ibid.

47. Crombie, 'The Possibility of Theological Statements', in Mitchell, *Faith and Logic*, p. 32.

48. Malcolm, 'Is It a Religious Belief', in Hick, *Faith and The Philosophers*, p. 107.

49. Ibid.

50. When I read an earlier version of this chapter to the New York University Colloquium William Barrett and Richard Martin took this line against me.

51. Malcolm, 'Is It a Religious Belief', in Hick, *Faith and The Philosophers*, p. 107.

52. Ibid, p. 106.

53. Malcolm, 'Anselm's Ontological Arguments', *The Philosophical Review*.

54. One might deny that this is so, using as evidence the proper English sentence 'I don't believe it's there, I *know* it's there.' But recall the rationale for such an utterance. It would be used to *stress* that one had no doubt at all about the claim one was making and that one had a right to make this very strong claim. But one could *not* say 'I don't believe p is true, still I know p' without some considerable explanation. That is, it is comparable to 'It's raining but I don't believe it'. If one knows p one believes p, but one doesn't *merely* believe p if one knows p.

55. Malcolm, 'Is It a Religious Belief', in Hick, *Faith and the Philosophers*, p. 108.

56. I admit this for the sake of the argument only. But surely such questions do arise as anyone knows who has ever told a child about God.

57. Malcolm, 'Is It a Religious Belief', in Hick, *Faith and the Philosophers*, p. 110.

58. Ibid.

59. Ibid.

60. Ibid, p. 109.

61. Ibid.

62. Ibid.

THE PHILOSOPHY OF RELIGION

THE PHILOSOPHY OF RELIGION

THE PHILOSOPHY OF RELIGION

THE PHILOSOPHY OF RELIGION

204 THE PHILOSOPHY OF RELIGION

5. Wittgensteinian Fideism II

1. See Ludwig Wittgenstein, *On Certainty* (Oxford, Blackwell, 1969). For a discussion of Wittgenstein's particular arguments in *On Certainty* and their bearing on religious discourse see James Kellenberger, 'The Language-game View of Religion and Religious Certainty', *Canadian Journal of Philosophy*, vol. 2, no. 2 (December 1972) 266–75.
2. Wittgenstein, *On Certainty*.
3. Stanley Cavell, 'Existentialism and Analytic Philosophy', *Daedalus*, vol. 93, no. 3 (Summer 1964) 963.
4. Ibid.
5. Ibid.
6. Ibid, 959.
7. Ibid.
8. Ibid, 958.
9. Ibid, 963.
10. Ibid, 961.
11. Ibid.
12. Ibid, 961.
13. Ibid, 963.
14. Ibid.
15. Ibid, 964.
16. Ibid, 963.
17. Ibid, 964, 969–71.
18. Ibid, 967.
19. Helmut Heiber, *Joseph Goebbels (München: Deutscher Taschenbuch Verlag*, 1965) p. 393. See also *Die Zeit* (25 June 1965) p. 33.
20. Rajendra Prosad, 'Religious Belief', *The Philosophical Quarterly*, vol. XXXVII, no. 4 (January 1965) 209–17.
21. Norman Malcolm, *Knowledge and Certainty* (Englewood Cliffs, New Jersey: Prentice-Hall, 1963) p. 120.
22. Jerry Gill makes much of this, but he likewise does nothing to elucidate it. Jerry H. Gill, 'Wittgenstein's Concept of Truth', *International Philosophical Quarterly*, vol. VI (March 1966) 872–3.
23. Ludwig Wittgenstein, *Philosophical Investigations* (Oxford: Blackwell, 1953) p. 8.
24. Ibid, p. 3.
25. Ibid, p. 11.

26. Ibid, pp. 226–7.

27. Gill, 'Wittgenstein's Concept of Truth', 872–3.

28. Wittgenstein, *Philosophical Investigations*, p. 8.

29. George Pitcher, *The Philosophy of Wittgenstein* (Englewood Cliffs, New Jersey: Prentice-Hall, 1964) pp. 242–3.

30. Stanley Cavell, 'The Availability of Wittgenstein's Later Philosophy', *The Philosophical Review*, vol. LXXI (1962) 74.

31. Wittgenstein, *Philosophical Investigations*, p. 226.

32. Malcolm, *Knowledge and Certainty*, p. 120.

33. Ibid, and see Wittgenstein, *Philosophical Investigations*, p. 49.

34. Geach, 'Nominalism', 12.

35. I am using the phrase 'relative term' in the way Stevenson does in his *Facts and Values* (New Haven, Connecticut: Yale University Press, 1963) Chapter V.

36. Martin Heidegger, *German Existentialism* (New York: Philosophical Library, 1965) pp. 26–8, 33, 42.

37. Geach, 'Nominalism', 12.

38. Ninian Smart, 'Social Anthropology and the Philosophy of Religion', *Inquiry*, vol. 6 (Winter 1963) pp. 287–99.

39. In addition to his book *Dialogues of Religion* (London: S.C.M. Press, 1960), Smart brings out considerations of this sort in his 'The Relation Between Christianity and The Other Religions', in A. R. Vidler (ed.), *Soundings* (Cambridge University Press, 1962) pp. 105–21.

40. William Alston has put this point well in his 'Religion and Philosophy of Religion', in William Alston (ed.), *Religious Belief and Philosophical Thought* (New York: Harcourt & Brace, 1963) pp. 1–15.

41. W. B. Gallie, *Philosophy and Historical Understanding* (London: Chatto & Windus, 1964) pp. 157–91.

42. Excellent examples of how contemporary analytic philosophers have engaged in this kind of argument are to be found in Kurt Baier, *The Meaning of Life* (Canberra, Australia: National University Press, 1957); and P. H. Nowell-Smith, 'Religion and Morality', in Paul Edwards (ed.), *Encyclopedia of Philosophy*, vol. 7 (New York: Macmillan, 1967) pp. 150–8. I have tried to do something of this myself in my 'An Examination of an Alleged Theological Basis of Morality', *The Iliff Review* (Autumn 1964), and in 'Ethics Without Religion', *The*

Ohio University Review, vol. VI (1964).

43. Patrick Sherry, 'Is Religion a "Form of Life"?', *American Philosophical Quarterly*, vol. 9, no. 2 (April 1972) 159–67. See also J. F. M. Hunter, '"Forms of Life" in Wittgenstein's Philosophical Investigations', *American Philosophical Quarterly*, vol. 5 (1968) 233–43.

44. Sherry, 'Is Religion a "Form of Life"?', 161.

45. Wittgenstein, *Philosophical Investigations*, p. 226.

46. Ibid, p. 226.

47. Sherry, 'Is Religion a "Form of Life"?', 160–1.

48. Ibid.

49. Ibid, 163.

50. Ibid.

51. Vernon Pratt, *Religion and Secularisation* (London: Macmillan, 1970) pp. 41–5.

52. Ibid, p. 42.

53. Ibid.

54. Ibid.

55. Ibid.

56. In a significant but neglected discussion on this topic Berlin, Murdoch and Hampshire have defended the view I have taken about philosophy and *Weltenschauung* and Quinton has opposed it. See A. Quinton, S. Hampshire, I. Murdoch and I. Berlin, 'Philosophy and Beliefs', *The Twentieth Century*, vol. CLVII (1955) 495–521. Sidney Hook has ably defended the inclusion of such *Weltanschauung* concerns in the opening sections of his 'Pragmatism and the Tragic Sense of Life', in Lionel Abel (ed.), *Moderns on Tragedy* (Greenwich, Connecticut: New Generation Press, 1967), and the application of such argumentation is carried off brilliantly by Alasdair MacIntyre in 'Breaking the Chains of Reason', in E. P. Thompson (ed.), *Out of Apathy* (London: Stevens, 1960).

57. For examples of analytic philosophers treating such problems, see the references given in note 42.

58. Justus Hartnack has put this point well in his *Wittgenstein and Modern Philosophy* (London: Methuen, 1965) p. 61.

59. Wittgenstein, *Philosophical Investigations*, p. 8.

60. Norman Malcolm, 'Ludwig Wittgenstein', in Edwards, *Encyclopedia of Philosophy*, vol. 8, p. 337.

61. Crucial things have been said about this matter by Steven

Lukes and Martin Hollis. See Martin Hollis, 'Witchcraft and Winchcraft', *Philosophy of Social Sciences*, vol. 2 (1972) pp. 89–103, and in the essays by Lukes and Hollis in Bryan R. Wilson (ed.), *Rationality* (Oxford: Blackwell, 1970) pp. 194–239.

62. 'Determinate thing', I would maintain, is a pleonasm. This has been powerfully argued by Hägerström, *Philosophy and Religion*. See also Einar Tegen, 'Axel Hägerström', *Theoria*, vol. v, Part III (1939) pp. 229–32.

63. See here Rajendra Prosad, 'Religious Belief', *The Philosophical Quarterly*, vol. XXXVII (January 1965) 212–13.

64. I argue for this in some detail in my chapter 'On Fixing the Reference Range of "God"'. See also here my 'On Speaking of God', *Theoria*, vol. XXVIII (1962, Part 2), and 'Religion and Commitment', in W. T. Blackstone and R. H. Ayers (eds), *Religious Language and Knowledge* (Athens, Georgia: University of Georgia Press, 1972).

65. Even Christian and specifically Catholic philosophers steeped in the tradition of natural theology recognise this. For one brilliant and neglected example of this reasoning, see C. J. F. Williams, 'Existence and the Meaning of the Word "God"', *Downside Review*, vol. 77 (1959) 53–71.

6. On Fixing the Reference Range of 'God'

1. Gareth B. Matthews, 'Theology and Natural Theology', *The Journal of Philosophy*, vol. LXI, no. 3 (30 January 1964) 101. For Flew's own statement of his challenge see his 'Theology and Falsification', in Flew and MacIntyre, *New Essays in Philosophical Theology*, pp. 96–9.

2. Emil L. Fackenheim, 'On the Eclipse of God', *Commentary*, vol. XXXVII, no. 6 (June 1964) 55.

3. I added the qualification 'certain of their very crucial putatively factual assertions' because, as Klemke and Blackstone have pointed out, there are historical autobiographical and psychological religious statements that are plainly factually intelligible, for example, 'Jesus was born in Nazareth', 'I believe Moses lived in Egypt' or 'People without religious convictions will fall into despair'. See E. D. Klemke, 'Are Religious Statements Meaningful?', *The Journal of Religion*, vol. XLIX (1960), and William Blackstone, *The Problem of Religious Knowledge* (New York: Prentice-Hall, 1963) pp. 36–46.

4. Matthews, 'Theology', 103.
5. Ibid, 105.
6. Kai Nielsen, 'Can Faith Validate God-Talk?', in Martin E. Marty and Dean G. Peerman (eds), (New York: Macmillan, 1964) pp. 131–49, and 'Religious Perplexity and Faith', *Crane Review*, vol. VIII, no. 1 (Autumn 1965) 1–17.
7. I. M. Crombie, 'Theology and Falsification', in Flew and MacIntyre, *New Essays in Philosophical Theology*, pp. 109–30; 'Theological Statements', in Mitchell, *Faith and Logic*, pp. 31–83.
8. Blackstone, *Religious Knowledge*, pp. 116–24.
9. I. M. Crombie, 'Theological Statements', in Mitchell, *Faith and Logic*, p. 34.
10. Ibid.
11. Ibid, p. 35.
12. Ibid, p. 37.
13. Ibid, p. 38.
14. Ibid.
15. Ibid, p. 40.
16. Ibid, p. 42.
17. Ibid, p. 43.
18. Ibid, p. 46.
19. Ibid, p. 49.
20. Ibid.
21. Ibid, p. 50.
22. Ibid.
23. Ibid. p. 56.
24. Ibid, p. 58.
25. Ibid.
26. Ibid.
27. Ibid.
28. Ibid. p. 59.
29. Ibid, p. 60.
30. Ibid, p. 61 [italics mine]. If we take Crombie literally here, we will have to say that his conception of what theological terms and utterances mean is unsatisfactory in much the same way Schleiermacher's claims are. If religious utterances merely express what we antecedently feel, then – given Crombie's remarks about this – 'There is a God' or 'God is our creator and redeemer' come to mean something to the effect that people

have feelings of contingency and finitude and come to feel a sense of absolute dependence and dissatisfaction with the world conceived in purely materialistic terms. But this fits ill with what Crombie says in the first few pages of 'The Possibility of Theological Statements' and, as Hägerström, MacIntyre and others have shown, such a claim is open to devastating objections, for, after all, this would mean that God's existence would be dependent on, because identical with, human beings having certain feelings. Hägerström, *Philosophy and Religion*, pp. 229–59, and A. MacIntyre, *Difficulties in Christian Belief* (London: S.C.M. Press, 1956). I am indebted to Lynn Boyer for the suggestion about Schleiermacher and Crombie.

31. Richard Taylor has argued this point ably in his *Metaphysics* (New York: Prentice-Hall, 1963) pp. 22–32.

32. Crombie, 'Theological Statements', in Mitchell, *Faith and Logic*, p. 62.

33. John Wisdom argues convincingly that an obscure concept is not for all that meaningless. See John Wisdom, 'The Modes of Thought and the Logic of God', in John Hick (ed.), *The Existence of God* (New York: Macmillan, 1964) pp. 275–98.

34. Crombie, 'Theological Statements', in Mitchell, *Faith and Logic*, p. 65.

35. Ibid.

36. Many of us, or at least many of us who become intellectuals, have had in our childhood a rather minimal or mild form of religious indoctrination. There is a sense in which we lack a real participant's understanding of these forms of life. To get a sense of such an indoctrination, read C. D. Broad's account of its effects on Axel Hägerström's life. (James Joyce, *The Portrait of an Artist as a Young Man*, is a rather more standard source here.) As I read of such forms of life, I feel a very considerable disinclination to think that all such forms of life are all right, are in good conceptual order, just as they are. See C. D. Broad, 'Memoir of Axel Hägerström', in Hägerström, *Philosophy and Religion*, pp. 15–29.

37. Blackstone, *Religious Knowledge*, pp. 116–24.

38. Crombie, 'Theology and Falsification', in Flew and MacIntyre, *New Essays in Philosophical Theology*, p. 118.

39. Ibid, p. 124.

40. Crombie, 'Theological Statements', in Mitchell, *Faith and*

Logic, p. 71.

41. Wittgenstein has well remarked, '. . . in ethical and religious language we seem constantly to be using similes. But a simile must be the simile for something. And if I can describe a fact by means of a simile I must also be able to drop the simile and to describe the facts without it.' See Wittgenstein, 'Lecture on Ethics', 10. In spite of Wittgenstein's emotional disquietude about this, his conclusion seems unassailable. If we have a putative non-literal or figurative mode of speech (as a simile or metaphor) and cannot possibly say *what* it is a simile or metaphor *of*, then what at first appears as a non-literal expression 'now seems mere nonsense'. If it is logically impossible to assert in some literal fashion what facts stand behind what appears to be a metaphor or a simile, then we are, in using such expressions, talking nonsense. That it is 'deep nonsense' expressive of powerful human drives does not make it any the less nonsense.

42. Bernard Williams, 'Tertullian's Paradox', in Flew and MacIntyre, *New Essays in Philosophical Theology*, pp. 187–211. Nielsen, 'Can Faith Validate God-Talk?', in Marty and Peerman, *New Theology*, no. 1, pp. 131–49.

43. Kai Nielsen, 'Eschatological Verification', *Canadian Journal of Theology*, vol. IX, no. 4 (1963) 271–81, and my *Contemporary Critiques of Religion*, pp. 71–93. See also William Bean, 'Eschatological Verification: Fortress or Fairyland', *Methodos*, vol. XVI, no. 62 (1964) 91–107.

44. Blackstone, *Religious Knowledge*, p. 123.

45. Crombie, 'Theology and Falsification', in Flew and MacIntyre, *News Essays in Philosophical Theology*, pp. 124–5.

46. Crombie, 'Theological Statements', in Mitchell, *Faith and Logic*, p. 72. There is a clash here between the two essays. In his later essay Crombie sets conditions that are open to disconfirmation while in 'Theology and Falsification' they are not. In 'Theology and Falsification' Crombie speaks of 'suffering which was utterly, *eternally* and irredeemably pointless' (p. 124, italics mine), while in 'Theological Statements' he speaks only of 'utterly and irremediably pointless suffering . . .' (p. 72).

47. Crombie, 'Theology and Falsification', in Flew and MacIntyre, *New Essays in Philosophical Theology*, p. 127.

48. Ibid, p. 130.

49. Ronald Hepburn, *Christianity and Paradox* (New York:

Humanities Press, 1958) pp. 50–90.

50. For all the changes in Carnap's point of view, he has stressed this point both in his early (1932) and in his latest work. See Rudolf Carnap, 'The Elimination of Metaphysics Through Logical Analysis of Language', in Ayer, *Logical Positivism*, pp. 66–7; P. A. Schilpp (ed.), *The Philosophy of Rudolf Carnap* (Lasalle, Illinois: Open Court Publishing, 1963) pp. 874–7. The first essay was written in 1932, though it was only translated into English in 1959. In connection with Carnap's point, see Otto Neurath, *Empirische Soziologie* (Vienna: Springer Verlag, 1931) Chapter 1.

7. *Empiricism, Theoretical Constructs and God*

1. Arthur Danto has forcefully pointed this out in his 'Faith, Language, and Religious Experience: A Dialogue', in Hook, *Religious Experience*, pp. 137–49.

2. During a discussion of my views on theology and falsification before the New York University graduate philosophy colloquim, Professors Sidney Morgenbesser and Raziel Abelson took this Quinean approach.

3. Willard Van Orman Quine, *From a Logical Point of View* (Cambridge, Massachusetts: Harvard Unversity Press, 1953) p. 41.

4. See here Father F. C. Copleston's remarks in his reviews of Richard Robinson's *An Atheist's Values* and Axel Hägerström's *Philosophy and Religion* in *The Heythrop Journal*, vol. 5 (1964) and vol. 7 (1966) respectively.

5. I have examined this problem in my 'Is God So Powerful that He Doesn't Even Have to Exist?', in Hook, *Religious Experience*, pp. 270–81.

6. I take the title from Albert Hofstadter's 'The Myth of the Whole: A Consideration of Quine's View of Knowledge', *The Journal of Philosophy*, vol. LI (July 1954) 397–417.

7. I have already given my reasons for rejecting Crombie's analysis. My criticisms of Hick and Wilson occur in: 'Eschatological Verification', and 'Christian Positivism and the Appeal to Religious Experience', *The Journal of Religion*, vol. XLII (October 1962).

8. See my 'Facts, Factual Statements and Theoretical Terms', and my 'Metaphysics and Verification Revisited'. See n. 39,

p. 196.

9. Basil Mitchell, 'Review of Religious Experience and Truth', Sidney Hook (ed.), *Philosophical Quarterly* (1963).

It could be and indeed has been objected that in criticising what I have called 'the interpretative move' in the way I have, I have, in so dismissing metaphysics, not taken the full measure of the opposition. An account of metaphysics such as W. H. Walsh's essentially treats metaphysics as an interpretative art and in arguing, as I do, I have ignored his elaborate defence of metaphysics. There are, it is pointed out, different ways of doing metaphysics and different conceptions of metaphysics. Not all metaphysics involves 'a project to penetrate beyond what can be known by empirical methods to its alleged supersensible substrate . . .' – W. H. Walsh, 'True and False in Metaphysics', in Elmer Sprague and Paul Taylor (eds), *Knowledge and Value* (New York: Harcourt, Brace & World, 1967) p. 199.

Such a criticism is, however, off the mark for I have not tried here to undermine metaphysics in general. Indeed, as I argue in some detail in my *Reason and Practice*, there are metaphysical accounts which are quite in order and are indeed important in any systematic perspicuous representation of our concepts. My arguments in the present context are directed at a certain kind of metaphysics. It is designed to show how viewing metaphysics as a discipline which gives a holistic interpretation of the facts, rather than providing new factual knowledge, does not enable us to solve or bypass vexing problems about the logical status of non-anthropomorphic God-talk. And Walsh, as distinct from Mitchell, in effect agrees with me, for he remarks, in commenting on the kind of illumination we receive from classical metaphysical works, that one:

cannot go through the processes of studying such writings and remain totally unaltered by the experience. And the alteration that occurs is not that one is, *per impossible*, put in touch with things supersensible, as if by some sort of intellectual spiritual-ism; it is rather that, after appreciating the author's point of view and grasping his system of ideas, one as it were sees familiar things with fresh eyes. Whatever the explanation, we have to admit that people find metaphysical works illuminating and revealing. To claim that they reveal what lies beyond experience would be to claim that they reveal the unrevealable. (Walsh, 'True and False', in Sprague and Taylor, *Knowledge and Value*, p. 200.)

Walsh more extensively develops his account of metaphysics in his *Metaphysics* (New York: Harcourt, Brace & World, 1963). I have extensively commented on the claims and varieties of metaphysics in my *Reason and Practice*, pp. 393–522.

10. Martin, *Religious Belief*, pp. 7–16.

11. John Passmore, 'Philosophy', in Edwards's *The Encyclopedia of Philosophy*, vol. 6, pp. 216–19.

12. That some poets and novelists have been of a different opinion, for example, that Coleridge and Wordsworth never supposed that their poetry came near Spinoza's *Ethics* in capacity to illuminate, does not affect my claim. Some poets and novelists have an exaggerated respect for metaphysical rubbish, for example, Shelley's admiration for Plotinus. Moreover, it may be true that Spinoza was a deeper man than Coleridge or Wordsworth. But we still learn more about the human condition from *War and Peace* than we do from *Being and Time*.

13. See his parody of Heidegger in *Dog Years*.

14. Nietzsche acutely raises such questions. For a powerful insistence on intrinsic value of truth see Richard Robinson, *An Atheist's Values* (Oxford: The Clarendon Press, 1964). For a discussion of the pros and cons here see my 'Hedonism and the Ends of Life', *The Philosophical Journal: Transactions of the Royal Philosophical Society of Glasgow*, vol. 10, no. 1 (January 1973) 14–26.

15. I have argued this in my *Ethics Without God*.

16. Some of the diverse considerations here are developed in my 'An Examination of an Alleged Theological Basis of Morality', *Iliff Review* (1964), and 'Linguistic Philosophy and "The Meaning of Life"', *Cross-Currents*, vol. xiv (Summer 1964).

INDEX